94.—Primer crimen en masa. 6 campesinos son detenidos cerca de Palma Mocha. En el guarda-costas 33 son lanzados al mar. Uno se salva.

...o Pérez se hace cargo ...e aterrizaje, por donde ...equipos para la gesta ...dora.

97.—Enero. 17, 1957. Herbert L. Matthews se entrevista con Fidel, en la Sierra. La Tele-visión en EE.UU. exhibe reportajes sobre la rebelión en Cuba.

...País. Millares de per-...lio que ha visto San-...ta las mujeres se sien-...atientes.

100.—Ante la vista del embajador americano, Mr. Smith, se atropella en la capital de Orien-te a una manifestación de damas que se sienten cubanas.

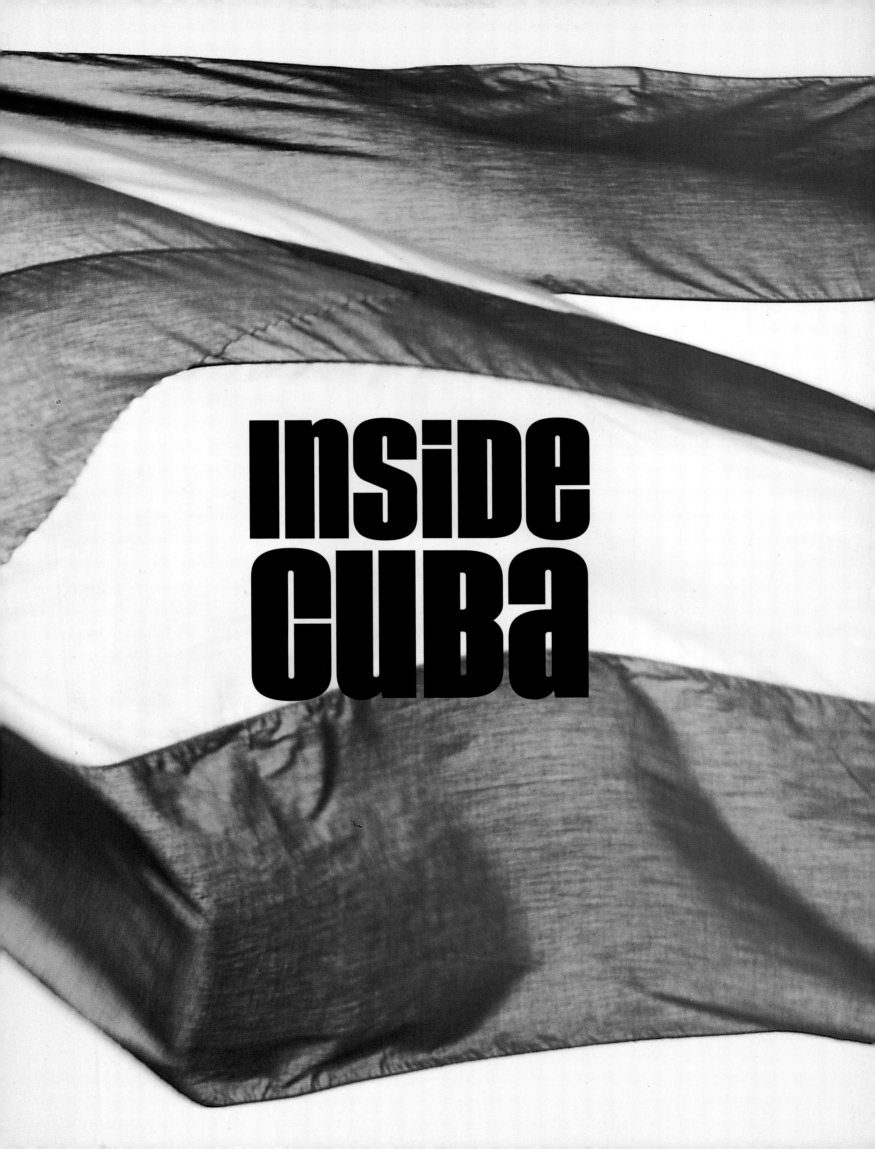

INSIDE CUBA

PHOTOS BY GIANNI BASSO / VEGA MG
TEXT BY JULIO CÉSAR PÉREZ HERNÁNDEZ
ED. ANGELIKA TASCHEN

INSIDE CUBA

TASCHEN

HONG KONG KÖLN LONDON LOS ANGELES MADRID PARIS TOKYO

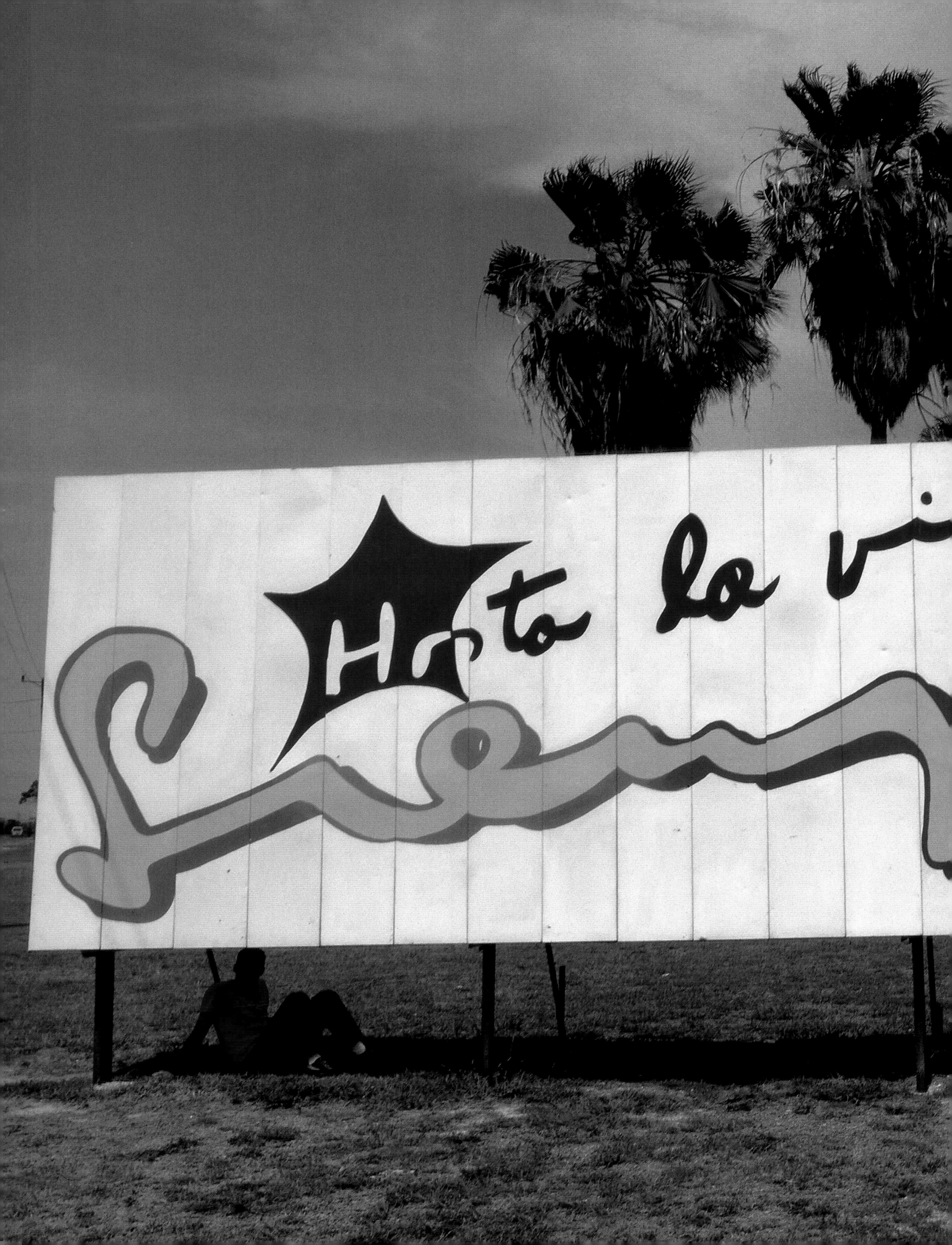
Hasta la vi

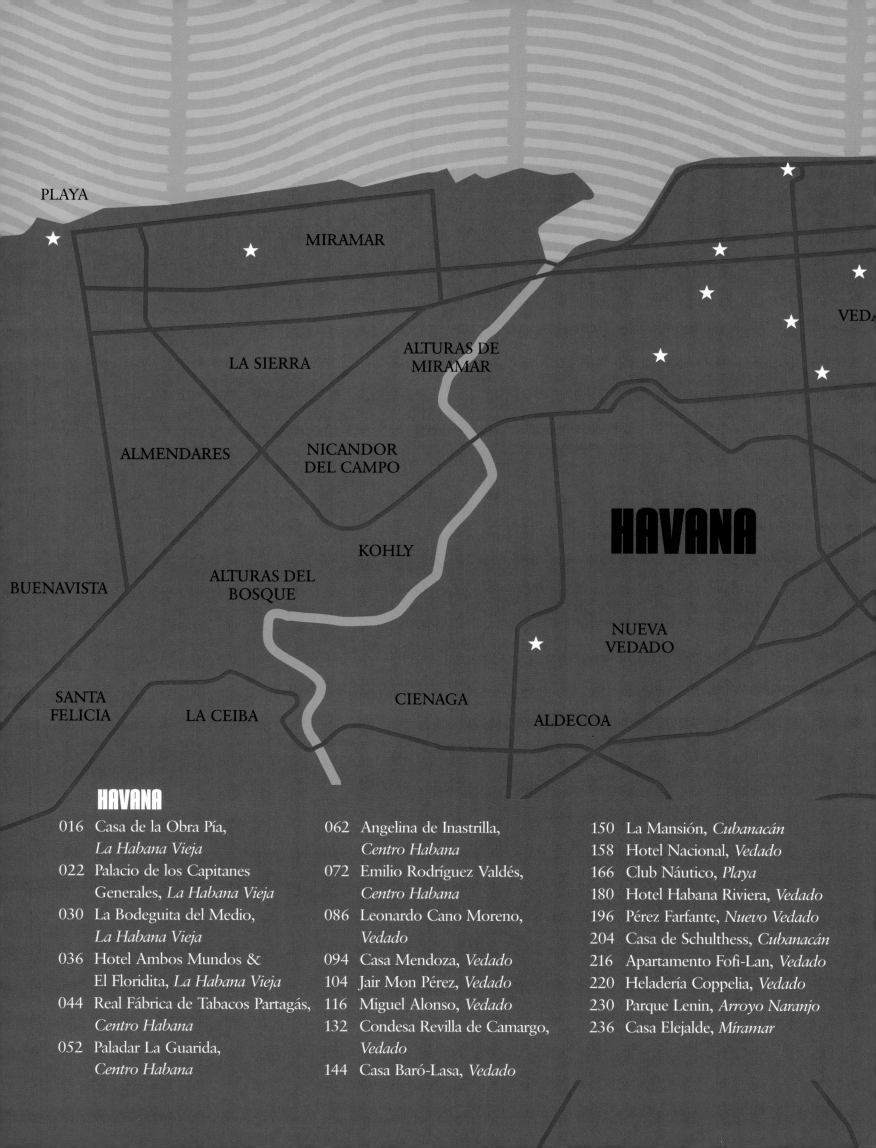

PLAYA

MIRAMAR

LA SIERRA

ALTURAS DE
MIRAMAR

ALMENDARES

NICANDOR
DEL CAMPO

HAVANA

KOHLY

BUENAVISTA

ALTURAS DEL
BOSQUE

NUEVA
VEDADO

SANTA
FELICIA

LA CEIBA

CIENAGA

ALDECOA

VEDA

HAVANA

016 Casa de la Obra Pía,
La Habana Vieja

022 Palacio de los Capitanes
Generales, *La Habana Vieja*

030 La Bodeguita del Medio,
La Habana Vieja

036 Hotel Ambos Mundos &
El Floridita, *La Habana Vieja*

044 Real Fábrica de Tabacos Partagás,
Centro Habana

052 Paladar La Guarida,
Centro Habana

062 Angelina de Inastrilla,
Centro Habana

072 Emilio Rodríguez Valdés,
Centro Habana

086 Leonardo Cano Moreno,
Vedado

094 Casa Mendoza, *Vedado*

104 Jair Mon Pérez, *Vedado*

116 Miguel Alonso, *Vedado*

132 Condesa Revilla de Camargo,
Vedado

144 Casa Baró-Lasa, *Vedado*

150 La Mansión, *Cubanacán*

158 Hotel Nacional, *Vedado*

166 Club Náutico, *Playa*

180 Hotel Habana Riviera, *Vedado*

196 Pérez Farfante, *Nuevo Vedado*

204 Casa de Schulthess, *Cubanacán*

216 Apartamento Fofi-Lan, *Vedado*

220 Heladería Coppelia, *Vedado*

230 Parque Lenin, *Arroyo Naranjo*

236 Casa Elejalde, *Miramar*

CENTRO
HABANA

CASABLANCA

LA
HABANA
VIEJA

CIUDAD DE
LA HABANA

Cojímar

LA HABANA

Viñales

PINAR DEL RIO

Varadero

MATANZAS

VILLA CLARA

CIENFUEGOS

ISLA DE LA
JUVENTUD

Trinidad

COJÍMAR ETC.

242 Finca Vigía,
    San Francisco de Paula
250 Casa Mederos, *Cojímar*
260 Casa Fúster, *Jaimanitas*

VARADERO

276 Hotel Internacional Varadero,
    Varadero

SANTIAGO DE CUBA & BAYAMO

290 Casa Diego Velázquez,
    Santiago de Cuba
296 Casa natal Heredia,
    Santiago de Cuba
300 Casa Quesada, *Santiago de Cuba*
308 Casa natal Céspedes, *Bayamo*

TRINIDAD

322 Palacio Brunet, *Trinidad*
334 Palacio Cantero, *Trinidad*
342 Casa Font, *Trinidad*
346 Casa del Cocodrilo, *Trinidad*

CIENFUEGOS

354 Palacio del Valle, *Cienfuegos*
364 Casa de la Teja, *Cienfuegos*

PINAR DEL RÍO

374 Casa Duporté & Hotel Moka,
    Communidad Las Terrazas

VIÑALES

384 Campensino Taller Raíces,
    Valle de Viñales
396 Yuseli Otaño, *Valle de Viñales*
400 Francisco Menéndez,
    Valle de Viñales

414 Addresses

Casa de la Obra Pía

Palacio de los Capitanes Generales

La Bodeguita del Medio

Hotel Ambos Mundos & El Floridita

Paladar La Guarida

Real Fábrica de Tabacos Partagás

HAVANA

016 Casa de la Obra Pía, *La Habana Vieja*

022 Palacio de los Capitanes Generales, *La Habana Vieja*

030 La Bodeguita del Medio, *La Habana Vieja*

036 Hotel Ambos Mundos & El Floridita, *La Habana Vieja*

044 Real Fábrica de Tabacos Partagás, *Centro Habana*

052 Paladar La Guarida, *Centro Habana*

062 Angelina de Inastrilla, *Centro Habana*

072 Emilio Rodríguez Valdés, *Centro Habana*

086 Leonardo Cano Moreno, *Vedado*

094 Casa Mendoza, *Vedado*

104 Jair Mon Pérez, *Vedado*

116 Miguel Alonso, *Vedado*

132 Condesa de Revilla de Camargo, *Vedado*

144 Casa Baró-Lasa, *Vedado*

150 La Mansión, *Cubanacán*

158 Hotel Nacional, *Vedado*

166 Club Náutico, *Playa*

180 Hotel Habana Riviera, *Vedado*

196 Pérez Farfante, *Nuevo Vedado*

204 Casa de Schulthess, *Cubanacán*

216 Apartamento Fofi-Lan, *Vedado*

220 Heladería Coppelia, *Vedado*

280 Parque Lenin, *Arroyo Naranjo*

286 Casa Elejalde, *Miramar*

Because of the geographical location of its harbor, Havana has been the capital of Cuba since 1607. In the 16th century, Spanish fleets carrying gold in convoys across the ocean gave the city great importance, which prompted Spain to build walls and fortresses as protection from attacks by pirates. The defensive structures helped delineate the urban landscape of the city on an irregular grid of narrow streets and a network of "piazzas" and "piazzetas," establishing its polycentric character. In 1982 UNESCO declared Old Havana's historic center a World Heritage Site. The abundance of civic space, the boulevards – such as Paseo del Prado and Alameda de Paula – and the

Havanna wurde 1607 dank der günstigen Lage des Hafens die Hauptstadt Kubas. Die Stadt gewann an Bedeutung, als die spanische Flotte im 16. Jahrhundert Gold in Konvois nach Havanna verschiffte. Bald ließen die Spanier Festungen und auch eine Mauer errichten, um sie von den Piraten zu schützen. Dadurch veränderte sich das Stadtbild nachhaltig. Aus dem losen Netzwerk aus schmalen Straßen, »Piazzas« und »Piazzetas« wurde eine Stadt mit verschiedenen Zentren. Bis in die 1930er entwickelte sich Havanna zur modernen Metropole mit großzügigen öffentlichen Plätzen, eleganten Boulevards wie dem »Paseo del Prado« und die »Alameda de Paula«, dem »Male-

Du fait de la position géographique de son port, La Havane est la capitale de Cuba depuis 1607. Au 16e siècle, les flottes espagnoles acheminant l'or à travers l'océan lui conférèrent une grande importance, incitant l'Espagne à construire des remparts et des forteresses pour la protéger des pirates. Ces structures défensives contribuèrent à façonner son plan irrégulier fait de ruelles étroites et d'un réseau de « piazzas » et de « piazzetas », d'où son caractère polycentrique. Dès les années 30, l'abondance d'espaces publics et de boulevards (Paseo del Prado, Alameda de Paula ainsi que le Malecón et ses beaux immeubles ont fait de la ville une métropole caribéenne moderne. En 1982,

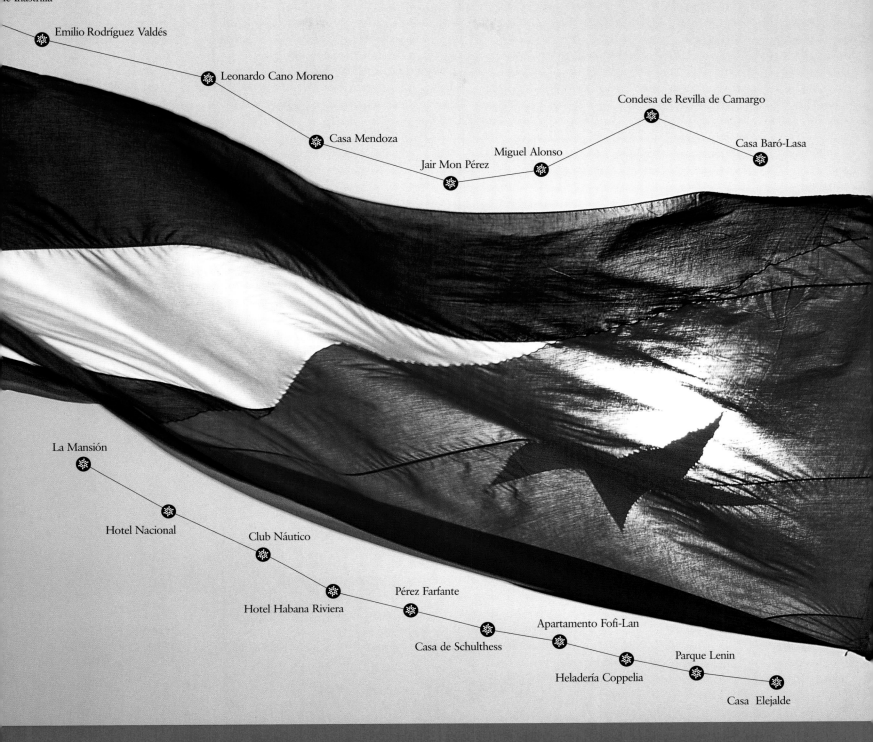

de Inastrilla

Emilio Rodríguez Valdés

Leonardo Cano Moreno

Condesa de Revilla de Camargo

Casa Mendoza

Miguel Alonso

Casa Baró-Lasa

Jair Mon Pérez

La Mansión

Hotel Nacional

Club Náutico

Pérez Farfante

Hotel Habana Riviera

Apartamento Fofi-Lan

Casa de Schulthess

Parque Lenin

Heladería Coppelia

Casa Elejalde

Malecón, along with a collection of fine buildings, had turned Havana into a modern Caribbean metropolis by the 1930s. Havana was spared the injurious urban renewal and overdevelopment seen around the world during the second half of the 20th century, but is now ready for a sensitive revival. A master plan aimed at preserving the city's historic and architectural legacy, while encouraging its future urban and economic development, is being established.

cón« und einer ganzen Reihe eleganter Häuser. 1982 erklärte die UNESCO die Altstadt zur Weltkultur-erbestätte. Während in der zweiten Hälfte des 20. Jahr-hunderts Städte überall auf der Welt eine rasante Ent-wicklung durchmachten, verfiel Havanna in einen Dornröschenschlaf. Nun ist die Stadt reif für eine sanf-te Renovation. Derzeit wird an einem Plan gearbeitet, der die zukünftige Stadt- und Wirtschaftsentwicklung fördern soll und gleichzeitig das historische und archi-tektonische Erbe der Stadt bewahrt.

l'UNESCO a déclaré le centre historique de la vieille Havane patrimoine universel. La Havane a échappé aux réaménagements hideux et au surdéveloppement qui a affecté les grandes villes dans la seconde moitié du 20e siècle, mais elle est désormais prête pour une restructuration intelligente. Un plan directeur visant à préserver l'héritage architectural et historique de la ville tout en encourageant son développement urbain et économique est à l'étude.

CASA DE LA OBRA PÍA

A Distinguished Example of Cuban Baroque.

José Martín Calvo de la Puerta, owner of Casa de la Obra Pía – "obrapía" meaning an act of charity – annually gave part of his fortune to five young orphans to help them create their own new family. Several features make this house not only one of the biggest but also one of the most distinguished examples of what is called Cuban baroque. In 1793, two adjacent properties that had been purchased around 1665 were merged, and renovation began. The impressive size of the house called for a massive sculptural stone doorway, exceptional and unique in colonial times its scale and design, it was crafted in Spain and shipped to Havana around 1686. Stone arcaded galleries surround the magnificent courtyard on three sides, and the dining room is located in the upstairs gallery between the main courtyard and the patio. There is an extraordinary variety of arches, ranging from the mixtilinear one of the entry hall, or "zaguán," to the three trefoil arches above the staircase that connects both floors. The upper gallery has friezes with floral motifs, which link the living spaces. They are all decorated with exquisite taste and fine furniture.

José Martín Calvo de la Puerta, der erste Besitzer der »Casa de la Obra Pía«, war ein großherziger Mann. Jedes Jahr spendete er einen Teil seines Vermögens fünf jungen Waisen, damit jeder seine eigene Familie gründen konnte. Das Haus mit dem Namen »Obra Pía«, was Wohltätigkeit bedeutet, ist ein typisches Beispiel für den kubanischen Barock. 1793 wurden die zwei aneinanderliegenden Anwesen, die de la Puerta 1665 erworben hatte, zu einem zusammengeschlossen, renoviert und ist nun von beachtlicher Größe. Das skulpturale Eingangstor ist dementprechend massiv. Seine Proportionen und das einzigartige Design sind für die Kolonialzeit außergewöhnlich. Es wurde in Spanien hergestellt und um 1686 nach Havanna transportiert. Galerien mit Arkaden aus Stein umsäumen den prächtigen Innenhof an drei Seiten. Die bestehen aus einer außergewöhnlichen Vielfalt an Torbögen – vom mixtilinearen »Zaguán« in der Eingangshalle bis zu den drei kleeblättrigen Torbögen über dem Treppenhaus, das beide Stockwerke miteinander verbindet. Die obere Galerie mit floralem Friesdekor verbindet die Wohnräume, die alle mit erlesenem Geschmack und elegantem Mobiliar eingerichtet sind.

José Martín Calvo de la Puerta, propriétaire de la Casa de la Obra Pía «l'œuvre pieuse», donnait chaque année une partie de sa fortune à cinq jeunes orphelins pour les aider à fonder une famille. Sa demeure est un exemples caractéristique du «baroque cubain». En 1973, les deux domaines adjacents achetés par la Puerta en 1665 fusionnèrent. La taille impressionnante de la maison rénovée appelait une porte sculpturale massive en pierre (exceptionnelle par son échelle et sa conception en ces temps coloniaux). Elle fut construite en Espagne et acheminée à la Havane vers 1686. Des arcades en pierre bordent trois côtés de la magnifique cour. La salle à manger est située sur la galerie supérieure entre la cour principale et le patio. La bâtisse abrite une extraordinaire variété d'arches, mixtilignes dans le «zaguán» ou hall d'entrée, ou en trèfle au-dessus de l'escalier qui mène à l'étage. La galerie supérieure ornée de frises aux motifs floraux relie les salles de séjour, toutes décorées avec un goût exquis et des meubles de qualité.

❋ **ABOVE** One of the most interesting architectural features is the courtyard, due to its exceptional size and its uniform arcaded stone galleries and columns on both floors. It is embellished with plants, following the tradition. **RIGHT** A trefoil arch marks the staircase landing on one of the galleries that wrap around the courtyard on the upper floor. The wooden ceiling is painted in a color known as Havana Blue, a reference to the city's proximity to the sea. **FACING PAGE** A lovely baroque-style porch embellished with pilasters decorates the semicircular arch leading to the staircase on one of the galleries in the courtyard.

❋ **OBEN** Der Innenhof ist eines der architektonisch interessantesten Elemente. Er besticht sowohl durch seine außergewöhnliche Größe als auch durch seine gleichförmigen Galerien mit Steinbögen und -säulen auf beiden Stockwerken und ist traditionsgemäß mit Pflanzen ausgeschmückt. **RECHTS** Ein Kleeblattbogen umrahmt den Treppenvorplatz in einer der Galerien des Obergeschosses, welche den Innenhof umgibt. Die Holzdecke ist in der als Havanna-Blau bekannten Farbe gehalten und spielt auf die Nähe zum Meer an. **RECHTE SEITE** Ein wunderschönes, mit Pilastern verziertes Portal barocken Ursprungs schmückt den Rundbogen am Treppenzugang in einer der Galerien des Innenhofs. ❋ **CI-DESSUS** Le patio, embelli de plantes comme le veut la tradition, est particulièrement intéressant d'un point de vue architectural de par ses dimensions exceptionnelles et ses galeries à arcades dont les deux niveaux sont soutenus par des colonnes en pierre. **A DROITE** L'escalier débouche sur un arc trilobé dans une des galeries de l'étage qui ceint le patio. Le plafond en bois est peint en « bleu havane », une référence à la proximité de la mer. **PAGE DE DROITE** Dans une des galeries du patio, un arc en plein cintre couronne la belle porte d'inspiration baroque flanquée de pilastres ouvragés donnant sur l'escalier.

※ **FACING PAGE** One of the beautiful bronze and crystal chandeliers hanging from the ceiling is reflected in the oval wall mirror at the back of the sumptuous living room. **RIGHT** Cuban Medallón-style chairs share space with a ceramic umbrella stand, a pink Sèvres vase and a copy of the anonymous portrait entitled "La Bella". In the background, the friezes with floral motifs retrieved during the restoration. **BELOW** The enormous living room, with 19th century Cuban furniture and objects of enormous artistic value — including French, Italian and German porcelain vases — is enhanced by its location near the street and the courtyard, providing proper ventilation and natural light. ※ **LINKE SEITE** Eine der wunderschönen Deckenlampen aus Kristall spiegelt sich in dem ovalen Wandspiegel am Ende des prächtigen Saals. **RECHTS** Kubanische Medaillonstühle teilen sich den Raum mit einem Schirmständer aus Steingut, einer Vase aus rosafarbenem Sèvres-Porzellan und einer Nachbildung des anonymen Portraits mit dem Titel »La Bella« (»Die Schöne«). Im Hintergrund sieht man die Zierleisten mit Blumenmotiven der bei der Renovierung freigelegten Wände. **UNTEN** Der gewaltige Saal, dekoriert mit kubanischem Mobiliar aus dem 19. Jahrhundert und mit künstlerisch wertvollen Werken – Vasen aus französischem, italienischem und deutschem Porzellan –, wird dank seiner Lage zwischen Straße und Innenhof von einer angemessenen Belüftung und natürlichem Tageslicht begünstigt. ※ **PAGE DE GAUCHE** Un des beaux lustres en bronze et cristal se reflète dans le miroir du somptueux salon. **CI-DESSOUS** Des chaises médaillons cubaines partagent l'espace avec un porte-cannes en faïence, une potiche rose de Sèvres et la copie d'un portrait anonyme intitulé « La Belle ». La plinthe peinte de motifs floraux a été récupérée lors de la restauration. **A DROITE** L'immense salon, décoré avec des meubles cubains du 19e siècle et de précieux objets d'art (potiches en porcelaine française, italienne et allemande) donne d'un côté sur la rue et de l'autre sur le patio. Il est donc bien aéré et inondé de lumière naturelle.

PALACIO DE LOS CAPITANES GENERALES

A Monumental but Not Imposing Palace.

The city's first square, the Plaza de Armas, was laid out near Havana's harbor early in the 16th century. In 1773, under the rule of Spanish governor Marquis de la Torre, it was transformed into a civic center, and the construction of the "Palacio de los Capitanes Generales" and the Palace of the Post Office, by Fernández Trevejos and Pedro de Medina, was finished by 1791. Unanimously acclaimed as the greatest building of the 18th century, and one of the most outstanding in all of Cuba, the Governor's palace has a monumental but not imposing presence thanks to its pleasing proportions, the sober, linear, baroque style, and the detailing of its coral-stone façades. A fine Carrara marble portal, executed by the Italian sculptor Giuseppe Gaggini in 1835, leads to the vestibule and magnificent arcaded central courtyard. In the middle, surrounded by lush tropical plants, is a statue of Christopher Columbus by J. Cucchiari from 1862. The White Hall upstairs and the Hall of Mirrors are decorated with emblems and portraits of Spanish kings and queens, and the flooring is made of marble from Genoa. While the White Hall was used for feasts and celebrations, the Hall of Mirrors was employed for official ceremonies such as the transfer of the island to the US government by the last Spanish governor in 1899.

Die Plaza de Armas in der Nähe des Hafens wurde im frühen 16. Jahrhundert als erster Platz Havannas angelegt. Der spanische Gouverneur Marquis de la Torre machte daraus 1773 ein Zentrum der öffentlichen Verwaltung, und bis 1791 wurden dort der Palast der Generalherrschaft und das palastartige Postgebäude von Fernández Trevejos und Pedro de Medina fertiggestellt. Der monumentale Gouverneurspalast ist ohne Zweifel das großartigste Gebäude des 18. Jahrhunderts in Kuba. Der nüchterne, lineare Barockstil und auch die Fassade aus Korallenstein verleihen seiner Monumentalität eine gewisse Leichtigkeit. Durch ein elegantes Portal aus Carrara-Marmor des italienischen Bildhauers Giuseppe Gaggini von 1835 gelangt man ins Vestibül und danach in den wunderbaren, mit Arkaden gesäumten Innenhof. Zwischen üppigen tropischen Pflanzen steht eine Christoph-Kolumbus-Statue von J. Cucchiari aus dem Jahr 1862. Im oberen Stockwerk befinden sich die Weiße Halle und der Spiegelsaal mit Wappen und Porträts der spanischen Könige und Königinnen. Die Böden sind mit Marmor aus Genua ausgelegt. Während die Weiße Halle für Feste und Feierlichkeiten benutzt wurde, diente der Spiegelsaal für offizielle Anlässe. Hier übertrug 1899 der letzte spanische Gouverneur die Herrschaft über Kuba der US-Regierung.

La première place de la Havane, la Plaza de Armas, fut créée près du port au début du 16e siècle. En 1773, le gouverneur espagnol, le marquis de la Torre, en fit un centre civique. La construction de la capitainerie générale et du palais de la poste par Fernández Trevejos et Pedro de Medina fut achevée en 1791. Unanimement salué comme le plus beau bâtiment du 18e siècle et l'un des fleurons de Cuba, le palais du gouverneur possède une présence monumentale sans être imposant grâce à ses proportions agréables, son style baroque sobre et linéaire, les détails de ses façades en pierre de corail. Un beau portail en marbre de Carrare, œuvre du sculpteur italien Giuseppe Gaggini (1835), mène au vestibule et à la magnifique cour centrale bordée d'arcades. Au milieu, une statue de Christophe Colomb par J. Cucchiari (1862) trône au milieu des plantes tropicales. À l'étage, la galerie blanche et la galerie des miroirs sont décorées d'écus et de portraits des rois et des reines d'Espagne. Leur sol est en marbre de Gênes. Le premier accueillait des banquets et des réceptions, tandis que le second servit à des cérémonies officielles telles que le transfert de l'île au gouvernement américain par le dernier gouverneur espagnol en 1899.

※ **PREVIOUS DOUBLEPAGE** The Hall of Mirrors is richly decorated with Baccarat crystal chandeliers, Sèvres porcelain and Venetian mirrors. **LEFT ABOVE** The White Hall, which served as an antechamber, is decorated with the emblems of the main fortresses in Havana and the Spanish kingdoms in Castilla y León. **LEFT** A mandolin, a French clock, several lovely candelabra and harpsichord in one of the corners of the White Hall. **ABOVE** The luxurious Hall of Mirrors was the most important room in the "Palacio de los Capitanes Generales," were official ceremonies held. **FOLLOWING PAGES** The French Baccarat crystal chandelier painstakingly reconstructed during the latest restoration of the "Palacio de los Capitanes Generales," now reflects the City Museum. In the background, the chapel with its baroque altar. ※ **VORHERGEHENDE DOPPELSEITE** Der Spiegelsaal ist reichlich dekoriert mit Lampen aus Baccarat-Kristall, Sèvres-Porzellan und venezianischen Spiegeln, deren Rahmen mit Gold überzogen sind. **OBEN LINKS** Der Weiße Saal diente einst als Vorzimmer und ist mit den Wappen der wichtigsten Festungen Havannas und der alten spanischen Königreiche von Kastilien und León dekoriert. **LINKS** Eine Mandoline, eine französische Uhr und prächtige Kandelaber auf einem Klavichord in einer Ecke des Weißen Saals. **OBEN** Im luxuriösen Spiegelsaal fanden die offiziellen Feierlichkeiten statt. **FOLGENDE DOPPELSEITE** Die französische Deckenlampe aus Baccarat-Kristall wurde rekonstruiert, als man den »Palacio de los Capitanes Generales« zuletzt für seine derzeitige Funktion als Stadtmuseum renovierte. Im Hintergrund sieht man die Kapelle mit ihrem Barockaltar. ※ **DOUBLE PAGE PRECEDENTE** Le salon des miroirs, richement décoré avec des lustres cristal de Baccarat, des porcelaines de Sèvres et des miroirs vénitiens dans des cadres dorés à la feuille. **PAGE DE GAUCHE, EN HAUT** Le salon blanc servait d'antichambre. Il est décoré des blasons des principales forteresses de la Havane et des anciens royaumes espagnols de Castilla y León. **A GAUCHE** Une mandoline, une horloge française et deux beaux candélabres sur un clavecin dans un coin du salon blanc. **CI-DESSUS** Le luxueux salon des miroirs accueillait les cérémonies officielles. **DOUBLE PAGE SUIVANTE** Lustre français en cristal de Baccarat minutieusement reconstitué lors de la dernière restauration du palais avant qu'il ne devienne le musée de la ville. Au fond, la chapelle avec son autel baroque.

LA B DEL M
UN BRINDIS LEJANO
LA BODEGUITA
LA BODEGUITA DE
A MAR
COHIBA

La Bodeguita del Medio

"My mojito in La Bodeguita."

You might not be able to make out the lyrics, but you can still enjoy the music and the mojito cocktails that Ernest Hemingway drank at this famous bar and restaurant: it was here, when asked about his favorite Cuban rum cocktails, that he answered, "My mojito in La Bodeguita, my daiquiri in El Floridita." No neon signs are needed – the bar and restaurant open onto a street near the cathedral square and it is always jammed with foreign tourists anxious to enjoy the "moros y cristianos" (black beans and white rice), the exquisite roasted pork, and the root vegetables and fried plantains. This unique place, once a grocery store and a printing office, became famous as a center of bohemian life; this is reflected by the graffiti its walls treasure. Robert de Niro, Jack Lemmon, Muhammad Ali, Paolo Rossi, and Claudia Cardinale are among the famous visitors who have left their autographs for posterity. If you want to make a mojito like Hemingway's, put sugar, limes and a sprig of mint into a tall glass. Add a jigger of Havana Club Silver Dry, fill with ice and club soda, then stir.

»My mojito in La Bodeguita, my daiquiri in El Floridita« pflegte Ernest Hemingway zu antworten, wenn man ihn nach seinen Lieblingscocktails fragte. Die Bar und das Restaurant »La Bodeguita« findet man auch ohne leuchtende Neonschilder. Die Stammbar Hemingways in der Nähe der Kathedrale ist immer vollbepackt mit Touristen, die zwischen Musik und Rumcocktails »Moros y Cristianos« (schwarze Bohnen mit weißem Reis), köstliches gebratenes Schwein, Wurzelgemüse und frittierte Kochbananen ausprobieren. »La Bodeguita«, früher ein Lebensmittelgeschäft und eine Buchdruckerei, hat sich einen Namen für ausgelassenes Vergnügen gemacht. Die Graffiti an den Wänden stammen aus den wilden Zeiten, in denen Robert de Niro, Jack Lemmon, Muhammad Ali, Paolo Rossi und Claudia Cardinale zu den prominenten Besuchern gehörten. Sie alle haben der Nachwelt ihre Autogramme hinterlassen. Wer einen Mojito genießen möchte, ohne nach Kuba zu reisen: Zucker, Limetten mit einem Zweig Pfefferminze in ein hohes Glas füllen und zerstampfen. Eis und ein Schnapsglas mit Havana Club Silver Dry dazugeben, mit Sodawasser auffüllen und umrühren.

Même sans comprendre les paroles, on peut apprécier la musique et le mojito qu'Hemingway buvait dans ce célèbre bar et restaurant : c'est ici que, interrogé sur le cocktail cubain à base de rhum qu'il préférait, il répondit : «Mon mojito à La Bodeguita, mon daiquiri à El Floridita.» Nul besoin d'une enseigne au néon : le bar/restaurant situé près de la place de la cathédrale est toujours bondé de touristes voulant goûter au «moros y cristianos » (« maures et chrétiens », haricots noirs et riz blanc), au délicieux porc rôti, aux racines végétales et aux plantains frits. Ce lieu unique, autrefois épicerie et imprimerie, devint un célèbre centre de la vie bohème, ce dont témoignent les graffitis qui recouvrent ses murs. Robert de Niro, Jack Lemmon, Muhammad Ali, Paolo Rossi et Claudia Cardinale comptent parmi ceux qui y ont laissé leurs autographes pour la postérité. Pour préparer un mojito à la Hemingway : mettre du sucre, du citron vert et une branche de menthe dans un grand verre avec de la glace ; ajouter une mesure de Havana Club Silver Dry, remplir de soda, remuer.

※ **FACING PAGE** The wooden bar, which serves the Cuban cocktail "mojito". **ABOVE** The bohemian restaurant is regarded as the sanctuaray of Cuban cuisine. **FOLLOWING DOUBLEPAGE** Graffiti on the tiled walls bears witness to the countless guests. ※ **LINKE SEITE** An der Bar wird der kubanische Cocktail Mojito serviert. **OBEN** Das Restaurant gilt als Tempel der kubanischen Küche. **FOLGENDE DOPPELSEITE** Die Inschriften über dem Fliesensockel zeugen von unzähligen Besuchern. ※ **PAGE DE GAUCHE**. Le comptoir en bois où l'on sert des « mojito ». **CI-DESSUS** Le restaurant bohème, considéré comme le sanctuaire de la cuisine cubaine. **DOUBLE PAGE SUIVANTE** Les graffitis qui recouvrent le mur au-dessus du lambris en azulejos témoignent des innombrables visiteurs.

HOTEL
AMBOS MUNDOS &
EL FLORIDITA

Hemingway in Cuba.

One of the main attractions of the "Hotel Ambos Mundos" is undoubtedly the same one that fascinated Hemingway: its discreet rooftop bar that has excellent views of Old Havana with the harbor in the background. He confessed in an interview that Ambos Mundos was a good place to write, and he rented the northeast corner room on the fifth floor every time he returned to the city. It was here, in 1939, that he began "For Whom the Bell Tolls," before his third wife, Martha Gellhorn, persuaded him to move to Finca Vigía. Hemingway loved walking from the "Ambos Mundos" down Calle Obispo to El Floridita for a drink. Located at the corner of Mercaderes and Calle Obispo – two of the busiest thoroughfares in Old Havana – the hotel looks inviting from the outside with its, eclectic pink façade and permanently opened doors that allow for interaction with the active street life near the Plaza de Armas. The lobby bar takes up most of the ground floor area, where you have the choice of having coffee or something a little stronger and then taking the old elevator up to room 511. Today the room is kept like a museum, housing some of Hemingway's personal belongings, and from its window you can look out at the same Old Havana Hemingway enjoyed, although it is now undergoing major restoration.

Die Bar des »Hotels Ambos Mundos« ist ein bekannter Treffpunkt. Bereits Ernest Hemingway war von der Bar auf dem Dach des Hotels begeistert. Von hier hat man eine tolle Sicht auf die Altstadt von Havanna und auf den Hafen. In einem Interview sagte Hemingway, das »Ambos Mundos« sei ein idealer Ort zum Schreiben. Wann immer er sich in der Stadt aufhielt, mietete er ein Zimmer im Nordost-Flügel im fünften Stock. Hier begann er auch seinen Roman »Wem die Stunde schlägt«. Seine dritte Frau, Martha Gellhorn, überzeugte ihn dann, die »Finca Vigía« zu seinem Wohnsitz zu machen. Hemingway liebte es, vom »Ambos Mundos« ins »El Floridita« an der Obispo Calle hinüberzulaufen. Das Hotel liegt an der Kreuzung der Mercaderes und Obispo Calle, zwei belebte Durchgangsstraßen in der Altstadt. Das rosa Hotel sieht einladend aus, die Türen sind stets offen, das Straßenleben auf der Plaza de Armas spielt sich so auch im Hotel ab. Die Bar in der Lobby nimmt fast das gesamte Erdgeschoss ein. Hier trinkt man Kaffee, aber auch Hochprozentiges. Gestärkt fährt man dann im Fahrstuhl hoch ins Zimmer 511, das ehemalige Zimmer Hemingways, heute ein kleines Museum. Von hier kann man sich an der Aussicht auf die Altstadt Havanas erfreuen, die allerdings gerade aufwändig renoviert wird.

Comme tout le monde, Hemingway n'a pas résisté à l'un des attraits principaux de l'«Hôtel Ambos Mundos»: son bar discret sur le toit qui jouit de vues imprena-bles sur la vieille Havane avec son port en toile de fond. Il a confié dans un entretien que l'hôtel était un bon endroit pour écrire. Il louait la chambre d'angle du cinquième étage donnant sur le nord-ouest chaque fois qu'il descendait en ville. C'est là, en 1939, qu'il a commencé «Pour qui sonne le glas» avant que sa troisième femme, Martha Gellhorn, ne le convainque de s'installer à la Finca Vigía. Il adorait descendre la rue Obispo pour aller prendre un verre au El Floridita. Situé au carrefour des Calle Obispo et Mercaderes, deux des artères les plus passantes de la vieille ville, l'hôtel possède une accueillante façade rose, ses portes ouvertes en permanence laissant filtrer l'animation de la Plaza de Armas voisine. Un bar occupe la quasi-totalité du rez-de-chaussée. Vous pouvez y prendre un café ou un verre de bon rhum avant de monter dans le vieil ascenseur jusqu'à la chambre 511. Devenue musée, elle abrite des effets personnels de l'écrivain. De la fenêtre, vous pourrez voir la même vieille Havane qu'aimait Hemingway, quoi qu'aujourd'hui en pleine restauration.

❋ **ABOVE LEFT** The corner of the reception hall at the "Hotel Ambos Mundos" with a white marble staircase and an old lift leading to the upper floors. **LEFT** The entrance to "Hotel Ambos Mundos" via Calle Obispo. Above the tile wainscot hang historical photos of the American writer Ernest Hemingway, which bear witness to his stints at the hotel during the 1930s. **ABOVE** The cozy Piano Bar in the main hall of the "Hotel Ambos Mundos" seen from the hotel's entrance via Calle Obispo. ❋ **OBEN LINKS** Die Ecke der Empfangshalle des »Hotel Ambos Mundos«, in der sich eine Treppe aus weißem Marmor und der alte Aufzug für die Obergeschosse befinden. **LINKS** Der Eingang des »Hotel Ambos Mundos« in der Calle Obispo. Über einem Fliesensockel hängen historische Aufnahmen des nordamerikanischen Schriftstellers Ernest Hemingway und zeugen von seinem Aufenthalt im Hotel in den 1930er-Jahren. **OBEN** Blick auf die einladende Piano-Bar in der Empfangshalle des »Hotel Ambos Mundos« vom Hoteleingang in der Calle Obispo. ❋ **PAGE DE GAUCHE, EN HAUT** Un coin du hall de réception de l'hôtel, avec son escalier en marbre blanc et son vieil ascenseur. **A GAUCHE** L'entrée de l'hôtel donnant sur la rue Obispo. Au-dessus des lambris en azulejos, des photos anciennes d'Ernest Hemingway témoignent de ses séjours au cours des années 30. **CI-DESSUS** L'accueillant piano-bar du vestibule, vu depuis la porte donnant sur la rue Obispo.

✻ **ABOVE AND FACING PAGE** Room number 511, where Ernest Hemingway began the final draft of "For Whom the Bell Tolls", conserved as a museum is decorated with some of his belongings. **FOLLOWING PAGES** The refined, cosmopolitan atmosphere of the Bar "El Floridita" with its statue of Ernest Hemingway in the background, at the spot at the bar where he used to drink daiquiris, the famous cocktail that the writer would help to immortalize. ✻ **OBEN UND RECHTE SEITE** Das Zimmer mit der Nummer 511, wo Ernest Hemingway seinen letzten Entwurf für den Roman »Wem die Stunde schlägt« begann, wird als Museum erhalten. Es ist mit einigen seiner Besitztümer dekoriert. **FOLGENDE DOPPELSEITE** Die Bar »El Floridita«, im Hintergrund die Bronzestatue von Hemingway an dem Thekenplatz, wo er sich für gewöhnlich einige Daiquiris genehmigte. ✻ **CI-DESSUS ET PAGE DE DROITE** La chambre 511, où Ernest Hemingway, entama le dernier jet de son roman « Pour qui sonne le glas ». Transformée en un musée, elle abrite quelques-uns de ses biens personnels. **DOUBLE PAGE SUIVANTE** Le bar « El Floridita », avec le buste d'Hemingway au fond, près du comptoir.

REAL FÁBRICA DE TABACOS

Partagás

The Ongoing Splendor of Cigar Manufacturing.

By the second half of the 19th century, tobacco manufacturing had become Havana's main industry. It is a non-polluting one, as cigar-making is an essentially manual activity. The cigar factory fits well in the existing urban fabric: its layout and decoration are the same as those of traditional mansions, with a central courtyard surrounded by arcades, a sign of refinement. There a person can read poetry out loud, tells stories, and read novels and newspapers for the men and women who sit on their wooden benches, day after day, rolling cigars. Cuban cigars, handmade "puros habanos," are considered the best in the world, and the Partagás factory, founded in 1845 and located behind the Capitol building in Havana, is among the finest and the oldest – a fact corroborated by the large, bold inscription carved into the elaborate parapet that crowns its eclectic brown and cream façade. Some of the greatest cigars in Cuba are produced here, from the "Partagás Lusitania" to the "Cohiba Robusto", to name just two. Partagás represents the ongoing splendor and tradition of cigar manufacturing, which is still one of the mainstays of the Cuban economy.

In der zweiten Hälfte des 19. Jahrhunderts wurde die Verarbeitung von Tabak zum wichtigsten Industriezweig Havannas. Da die Zigarren hauptsächlich in Handarbeit hergestellt werden, belasten sie ihre Umwelt in keinster Weise. Auch die Zigarrenmanufakturen fügen sich unauffällig in die bestehende Stadtstruktur ein. Sie haben den traditionellen Grundriss eines Wohnhauses, rund um einen Innenhof mit Arkaden, die damals als elegant galten. Dort sitzen Frauen und Männer Tag für Tag auf ihren Holzbänken und rollen Zigarren. Währenddessen werden Gedichte rezitiert, Geschichten erzählt, aus Romanen und aus der Zeitung vorgelesen. Zigarren aus Kuba, handgemachte »Puros Habanos«, gelten als die besten der Welt. Eine der renommiertesten und ältesten Manufakturen ist »Partagás«. Sie wurde 1845 gegründet und liegt hinter dem Kapitol. An der kunstvollen Attika über der braunen und cremefarbenen Fassade prangt der Name der stolzen Manufaktur in großen engravierten Lettern. »Partagás« steht für die glanzvolle Tradition der Zigarrenherstellung und produziert einige der besten Zigarren der Welt wie die »Partagás Lusitania« oder die »Cohiba Robusto«. Bis heute ist die Herstellung von Zigarren einer wichtigsten Wirtschaftszweige Kubas geblieben.

Dès la seconde moitié du 19e siècle, la production de cigares devint l'industrie principale de la Havane. Non polluante (étant une activité essentiellement manuelle), la manufacture s'intégrait bien dans le tissu urbain et suivait le même plan et la même décoration que les grandes demeures traditionnelles avec une cour centrale entourée d'arcades, signe de raffinement. Là, quelqu'un lisait à voix haute de la poésie, des contes, un roman ou le journal pour les cigariers et cigarières assis sur des bancs en bois, jour après jour. Les « Puras Habanos » sont considérés comme les meilleurs cigares du monde et la fabrique Partagás, fondée en 1845 et située derrière le capitole, est l'une des plus anciennes et plus réputées, ce que corrobore l'inscription gravée dans le parapet sophistiqué qui couronne sa façade brune et crème. On roule ici certains des meilleurs cigares de Cuba, tels que le « Partagás Lusitania » ou le « Cohiba Robusto », pour ne citer qu'eux. Partagás incarne la tradition et le prestige de la production de cigares, aujourd'hui encore un des piliers de l'économie cubaine.

※ **ABOVE LEFT** The staff is mixed in the area where the cigars are rolled. Men and women work eight-hour shifts. The apprentices of future rollers are also trained here. **LEFT** A skylight crowns the building's original inner courtyard to ensure that natural light reaches the different working areas. **ABOVE** The traditional job of tobacco factory reader consists of sharing news and reading aloud for the factory workers while they work, thus contributing to their entertainment and cultural education. **FOLLOWING DOUBLEPAGE** The area where the seals or labels are placed on the cigars before placing them in the beautiful cedar boxes. ※ **OBEN LINKS** Die Belegschaft der Abteilung, in der die Zigarren gedreht werden, ist gemischt. Männer und Frauen haben einen achtstündigen Arbeitstag. In diesem Bereich werden auch die Lehrlinge zu Zigarrendrehern ausgebildet. **LINKS** Ein Glasdach bedeckt den ursprünglichen Innenhof des Gebäudes, um die unterschiedlichen Arbeitsbereiche mit Tageslicht zu versorgen. **OBEN** Die traditionelle Tätigkeit des Vorlesers in der Tabakfabrik besteht darin, den Angestellten des Werks Informationen zu vermitteln und vorzulesen, während diese ihre Arbeit verrichten. Auf diese Weise trägt er zu ihrer Unterhaltung und kulturellen Bildung bei. **FOLGENDE DOP-PELSEITE** Die gesamte Arbeit wird von Hand verrichtet. Hier sieht man den Bereich, in dem die Zigarren mit den Siegeln bzw. Zigarrenbinden versehen werden, bevor man sie in die wunderschönen Kisten aus Zedernholz legt. ※ **PAGE DE GAUCHE, EN HAUT** Dans les ateliers où l'on roule les cigares, la main d'œuvre est mixte. Les ouvriers travaillent huit heures par jour. C'est aussi ici que l'on forme les futurs cigariers. **À GAUCHE** Une grande verrière couvre le patio original du bâtiment pour assurer l'entrée de la lumière naturelle dans toutes les aires de travail. **CI-DESSUS** Le rôle traditionnel du lecteur consiste à informer les employés et à leur lire des textes à voix haute, les distrayant tout en contribuant à leur éducation culturelle. **DOUBLE PAGE SUIVANTE** Le travail est entièrement manuel. La salle où l'on pose les bagues et les sceaux sur les cigares avant de les ranger dans leurs belles boîtes en cèdre.

SOLIDARIDAD CON LOS 5

REAL FABRICA DE TABACOS

Partagás

FUNDADA EN T

※ **ABOVE LEFT** The instrument used to adjust the sizes of the cigars is the so-called "chaveta", a flat steel plate with a large curved blade. **LEFT** The original illuminated factory sign being restored after having sustained hurricane damage. **ABOVE** The final sorting area where all the tobacco quality parameters are meticulously checked. ※ **OBEN LINKS** Das Werkzeug zur Angleichung der Zigarrengröße ist das so genannte »chaveta«, ein flaches Edelstahlmesser mit großer halbmondförmiger Klinge. **LINKS** Das originale Leuchtschild der Fabrik musste repariert werden, nachdem es kürzlich von einem Hurrikan beschädigt worden war. **OBEN** Der Bereich der Endauslese, in dem alle für Tabakwaren geltenden Qualitätsparameter gründlich geprüft werden. ※ **PAGE DE GAUCHE, EN HAUT** La « chaveta », longue lame d'acier incurvée, sert à uniformiser la taille des havanes. **A GAUCHE** L'enseigne lumineuse originale de la manufacture lors de sa restauration après qu'un ouragan l'avait endommagée. **CI-DESSUS** La salle de sélection finale où l'on vérifie méticuleusement tous les paramètres intervenant dans la qualité du tabac.

PALADAR
La Guarida

A Location of an Oscar-Nominated Movie.

One of the most controversial Cuban films ever, "Fresa y chocolate," was partly filmed in this apartment, located in the heart of Centro Habana, the most decaying district of the city. The movie was nominated for an Oscar in 1995, and the otherwise ordinary home became a very successful "paladar" – a privately owned restaurant. Today it is one of the most visited tourist venues in Havana. One enters from Concordia Calle into a vast, dilapidated, dark hall of an eclectic early 20th century building; an old marble staircase with an iron railing leads you up three floors to an apartment that has been turned into one of the most famous restaurants in Havana. Thoughtfully prepared food is served in an unassuming, informal ambience by owners Enrique Núñez and his wife Odeysis, whose delicious menu includes succulent red snapper, gazpacho soup, and other tasty Cuban and international dishes. All this can be enjoyed with a fine bottle of imported Spanish wine. Whether you are in the film business or not, you are always welcome at "La Guarida".

Der viel diskutierte kubanische Film »Erdbeer und Schokolade« wurde 1995 für den Oscar nominiert. Diese Wohnung im Herzen von Centro Habana, ein heruntergekommenes Viertel, diente als Drehort für einige der Filmszenen. Aus der ganz normalen Wohnung wurde dann ein erfolgreiches Privatrestaurant, ein »Paladar«, und einer der beliebtesten Treffpunkte der Stadt. Ins eklektische Haus aus dem 20. Jahrhundert an der Calle Concordia gelangt man über eine dunkle, große, abbruchreife Eingangshalle. Ein altes Treppenhaus aus Marmor und mit einem Eisengeländer führt drei Stockwerke hoch in die Wohnung, die heute das bekannteste Restaurant der Stadt beherbergt. Das Besitzerpaar Enrique und Odeysis Núñez bringt in einfacher, entspannter Umgebung liebevoll zubereitete Speisen auf den Tisch. Darunter einen saftigen Red Snapper, Gazpacho und andere leckere kubanische und internationale Gerichte. Dazu gibt es importierte Weine aus Spanien. Jeder ist im »La Guarida« willkommen, nicht nur Filmemacher.

«Fresa y chocolate», un des films cubains les plus controversés à ce jour, fut en partie tourné dans cet appartement situé au cœur de Centro Habana, le quartier le plus détérioré de la ville. Depuis que le film a été nominé aux Oscars en 1995, cette demeure ordinaire est devenue un «paladar» (restaurant privé) branché, halte incontournable des touristes. On entre par la rue Concordia dans le vaste hall délabré et sombre d'un immeuble hétéroclite du début du 20e siècle. Un vieil escalier en marbre avec une rampe en fer forgé vous mène, trois étages plus haut, dans un appartement converti en un des plus célèbres restaurants de la Havane. Dans une ambiance bon enfant, les propriétaires Enrique Núñez et sa femme Odeysis vous mitonnent avec soin de succulentes spécialités telles que la dorade locale, le gazpacho ou d'autres plats cubains et internationaux, à savourer arrosés d'un vin espagnol. Que vous travailliez dans le cinéma ou pas, vous serez toujours bienvenu à «La Guarida».

❋ **PREVIOUS DOUBLEPAGE** The height of the ornate staircase even allows vehicles to pass underneath into the building's courtyard. * On one of its walls, painted with a Cuban flag with the face of one of the martyrs of the Cuban Revolution, Camilo Cienfuegos, marks a site where the patriots of the revolution were venerated. **ABOVE LEFT** Varying sized carved wooden chairs with wickerwork form part of the original furnishings. **LEFT** The rooms surrounding the courtyard have windows with French louvered doors and small colored glass. **ABOVE** The lovely white marble staircase with its beautiful wrought-iron banister joins together the different floors of the building where "Paladar La Guarida" is located. ❋ **VORHERGEHENDE DOPPELSEITE** Die Treppe erreicht eine Höhe, die sogar die Einfahrt von Fahrzeugen in den Innenhof erlaubt. * An einer der Wände des Innenhofs weist eine gemalte kubanische Flagge mit dem Gesicht eines Märtyrers der Kubanischen Revolution, Camilo Cienfuegos, darauf hin, dass es sich um eine Kultstätte für Patrioten handelt. **LINKE SEITE OBEN** Stühle und Sessel mit Holzschnitzerei und Korbgeflecht sind Teil des originellen Mobiliars. **LINKS** Die an den Innenhof grenzenden Zimmer besitzen Fenster mit Lamellenläden und Oberlichtern aus farbigem Glas. **OBEN** Die Treppe aus weißem Marmor mit ihrem prächtigen schmiedeeisernen Geländer verbindet die verschiedenen Stockwerke des Gebäudes, in dem sich das »Paladar La Guarida« befindet. ❋ **DOUBLE PAGE PRECEDENTE** La hauteur du plafond sculpté sous l'escalier de l'immeuble où se trouve « Paladar La Guarida » permet même aux véhicules d'entrer dans le patio devenu parking. Sur un des murs, un drapeau cubain avec le portrait d'un des martyrs de la révolution, Camilo Cienfuegos, vénéré par les patriotes. **PAGE DE GAUCHE, EN HAUT** Le mobilier d'origine du restaurant. **A GAUCHE** Les fenêtres des pièces qui entourent le patio sont protégées par des persiennes et surmontées de lucarnes en verre coloré. **CI-DESSUS** Le grand escalier en marbre blanc agrémenté d'une belle rampe en fer forgé relie les différents étages de l'immeuble.

✳ **PREVIOUS DOUBLEPAGE** One of the graceful sculptures presiding over each flight in the staircase of the building. * A shared vestibule is used as a living room, resting place and as a place for drying clothes. A succession of semicircular arches over slender marble columns frames the views of the courtyard. **ABOVE LEFT** Photographs of Ernesto "Che" Guevara and the meeting between Fidel Castro and Ernest Hemingway are just a few of the pictures hanging on the walls at "Paladar La Guarida". **LEFT** A religious sculpture rendered by a friend of the main character one of the figures in the film "Fresa y Chocolate" is part of the current decoration at the "Paladar La Guarida". **ABOVE** The dining room, one of the settings in the Oscar-nominated Cuban film "Fresa y Chocolate", gains atmosphere through photographs from several scenes in the film. ✳ **VORHERGEHENDE DOPPELSEITE** Grazile Statuen befinden sich an jedem Treppenabschnitt des Gebäudes, welches das »Paladar La Guarida« im Viertel Centro Habana beherbergt. * Ein gemeinschaftlicher Eingangsbereich dient sowohl als Aufenthaltsraum als auch zum Trocknen der Wäsche. Eine Reihe von Rundbögen auf schlanken Marmorsäulen geleitet die Besucher in den Innenhof. **OBEN LINKS** Historische Aufnahmen von Ernesto »Che« Guevara und dem Treffen zwischen Fidel Castro und Ernest Hemingway im Jahr 1960 und weiteren Motiven an einer Wand des »Paladar La Guarida«. **LINKS** Eine religiöse Skulptur, die ein Freund des Hauptdarstellers im Film »Erdbeer und Schokolade« anfertigte, ist Teil der Einrichtung des »Paladar La Guarida«. **OBEN** Der Speiseraum war einer der Drehorte des kubanischen Films »Erdbeer und Schokolade«, der eine Oscar-Nominierung in Hollywood erhielt. Der Raum ist mit Aufnahmen einiger Filmszenen dekoriert. ✳ **DOUBLE PAGE PRECEDENTE** Une des élégantes statues qui domine chaque palier de l'escalier de l'immeuble. * Un vaste palier pour se détendre ou sécher le linge. Une série d'arcs en plein cintre sur de fines colonnes encadrent les vues sur le patio. **PAGE DE GAUCHE, EN HAUT** Sur des murs de « Paladar La Guarida », des photos historiques du Che Guevara et de la rencontre entre Fidel Castro et Ernest Hemingway. **A GAUCHE** La décoration actuelle du restaurant inclut une sculpture religieuse réalisée par un ami du héros de « Fresa y Chocolate », qui, dans le film, lui organise une exposition personnelle. **CI-DESSUS** Dans la salle à manger, un des décors de « Fresa y Chocolate », quelques photos montrent des scènes du film, nominé aux Oscars à Hollywood.

ANGELINA
DE INASTRILLA

A Typical Row House in Havana of the 19th Century.

Havana's first organized expansion beyond its original boundary walls was propagated by the engineer Antonio María de la Torre around 1819. Old country roads would later become main thoroughfares, or "calzadas," built with neoclassical porticoes that helped define the city. Havana was later called "the City of Columns" by the Cuban writer Alejo Carpentier. The sheltered streets were suitable for merchants to sell their wares, and so they became commercial in character, and structured linear centers across the city reflecting an aspiration for modernity that would be echoed in other notable urban development projects during the government of Miguel Tacón. He promoted avenues and walkways decorated with fountains and statues, such as that of Paseo de Tacón, also called Carlos III to honor the king of Spain. This completed the appearance of the oldest of these roads, Calzada de la Reina. Angelina de Inastrilla's home is typical for this street. The façade, with its wrought-iron railing and rounded arches crowned by a cornice, echoes the decaying but still decorative richness of the interior. The entry hall has beautiful grills, and tile wainscots with floral motifs, but the most distinctive feature of the house is undoubtedly the living room's stained-glass windows, which vividly depict a galleon in front of "Castillo del Morro".

Die Ideen des Ingenieurs Antonio María de la Torre prägten um 1819 das Bild Havannas. Die Stadt wuchs über die Grenzen der ursprünglichen Stadtmauern hinaus, und aus alten Landstraßen wurden »Calzadas«, Hauptstraßen mit neoklassizistischen Säulenbögen, die das Stadtbild prägten. Deshalb nannte der kubanische Schriftsteller Alejo Carpentier Havanna »die Stadt der Säulen«. Unter den Arkaden konnten Händler ihre Ware geschützt vor Sonne und Regen feilbieten und so entstand eine Art Marktplatz. Miguel Tacón und seine Regierung planten damals eine bemerkenswert moderne Stadtentwicklung. Die Linienführung der Straßen war gerade, und es wurden Alleen und Spazierwege mit Brunnen und Statuen gebaut. Der Paseo de Tacón, auch Paseo Carlos III. nach dem damaligen König von Spanien, ergänzten das Erscheinungsbild der Stadt, das von der Calzada de la Reina, einer der ältesten Straßen, geprägt war. Das Haus von Angelina de Inastrilla ist ein für diese Straße typisches Gebäude. Die Fassade mit dem schmiedeeisernen Geländer, den runden Torbögen und ihrem Sims weist auf das opulente Dekor im Inneren hin – auch wenn heute der Zerfall daran nagt. In der Eingangshalle befinden sich wunderschöne schmiedeeiserne Gitterwerke und Wandverkleidungen aus Kacheln mit floralen Motiven. Es sind jedoch die Buntglas-Fenster, die eine Galeone vor dem »Castillo del Morro« darstellen, die als Erstes auffallen.

Vers 1819, l'ingénieur Antonio María de la Torre fut chargé de la première expansion planifiée de la Havane hors de ses remparts. Les anciennes routes de campagne devinrent de grandes rues, ou «calzadas», dont les portiques néoclassiques donnaient à la ville une allure nouvelle. L'auteur cubain Alejo Carpentier baptisa plus tard la Havane «la cité des colonnes». Les artères ainsi protégées pouvaient abriter des échoppes et devinrent commerçantes, tandis que les lignes droites qui quadrillaient la ville témoignaient d'un désir de modernité confirmé par d'autres grands travaux d'urbanisme sous le gouvernement de Miguel Tacón. Ce dernier fit tracer des avenues et des allées ornées de fontaines et de statues, telles que le Paseo de Tacón appelé aussi Paseo Carlos III en hommage au roi d'Espagne, qui parachevaient l'aspect de la plus ancienne d'entre elles, la Calzada de la Reina. La maison d'Angelina de Inastrilla en est représentative. Sa façade, avec ses balustrades en fer forgé et ses arcs surmontés d'une corniche, reflète la richesse délabrée de l'intérieur. Le hall possède de belles grilles et des lambris carrelés aux motifs floraux, mais ce sont surtout les vitraux du salon, représentant un galion devant le «Castillo del Moro», qui frappent les esprits.

❋ **FACING PAGE** The living room of Angelina de Inastrilla's home is located between the courtyard and the "zaguán". The bays of the courtyard are crowned by semicircular arches, enclosed by stained glass windows worthy of restoration due to their enormous artistic value. **RIGHT** A portrait of Angelina in her youth hanging above a mahogany table with several porcelain knick-knacks is highly symbolic. The polychrome of the tile wainscots contrasts with the oppressive atmosphere of the flaking walls. **BELOW** The house's beautiful grills and the tiles on the wainscots are a testimony to the past splendor of Angelina de Inastrilla's home. ❋ **LINKE SEITE** Das Wohnzimmer im Haus von Angelina de Inastrilla befindet sich zwischen dem Innenhof und dem Hausflur. Die Fenster zum Innenhof enden in Rundbögen und sind mit Buntglasfenstern verschlossen, die angesichts ihres künstlerischen Werts restauriert werden müssten. **RECHTS** Das Porträt der jungen Angelina, das über einem Mahagonitisch mit verschiedenen Dekorationsgegenständen aus chinesischem Porzellan hängt, ist sehr symbolträchtig. Die glanzvolle Farbenpracht der Fliesensockel steht im Gegensatz zu den abbröckelnden Wänden. **UNTEN** Das prächtige schmiedeeiserne Gitterwerk und die Fliesensockel zeugen vom vergangenen Glanz des Hauses von Angelina de Inastrilla. ❋ **PAGE DE GAUCHE** Le séjour se trouve entre le vestibule et la cour intérieure. Les arcs en plein cintre donnant sur le patio sont fermés par de très beaux vitraux qui mériteraient d'être restaurés. **A DROITE** Tout un symbole: le portrait de jeunesse d'Angelina suspendu au-dessus d'une console en acajou sur laquelle sont posés divers bibelots en porcelaine chinoise. Les azulejos polychromes contrastent avec l'atmosphère oppressante des murs délabrés. **CI-DESSOUS** Les belles grilles et les azulejos des lambris témoignent de la splendeur passée de la maison d'Angelina de Inastrilla.

※ **FACING PAGE AND ABOVE** The spacious dining room has a wainscot made of Spanish tiles. **FOLLOWING DOUBLEPAGES** The bedrooms, run parallel to the longest side of the inner courtyard.* The mosaic floors in the bedrooms create a certain visual unity. ※ **LINKE SEITE UND OBEN** Das geräumige Esszimmer besitzt einen Sockel aus spanischen Fliesen. **FOLGENDE DOPPELSEITEN** Die hohen Schlafzimmer grenzen an die Längsseite des Innenhofs. * Die Mosaikböden der Schlafzimmer sind gut erhalten. ※ **PAGE DE GAUCHE ET CI-DESSUS** La spacieuse salle à manger, est également tapissée d'azulejos espagnols. **DOUBLES PAGES SUIVANTES** Les chambres, spacieuses avec de hautes portes, sont parallèles au grand côté du patio. * Les sols en mosaïque des chambres à coucher ont été préservés.

EMILIO RODRÍGUEZ VALDÉS

A Home Where You Seek Spiritual Guidance.

Myths help man justify his existence and explain the world. African mythology is integral to Cuban culture: It is poetic and mysterious, attractive and artistic, full of light, rhythm and color. Afro-Cuban deities, or "orishas," from the Yoruba religion – introduced to Cuba by slaves brought from Africa to work on the sugar and tobacco plantations – are sometimes amalgamated with the saints from Catholicism, the country's dominant religion. This practice mirrors Cuba itself, whose people are a mix of European and African. The resulting religious system, "santería" or "Regla de Ocha," derives from the slaves' beliefs and ritual practices, which have survived several centuries. Emilio Rodríguez Valdés' home, on Concordia street in Centro Habana, is a Yoruba temple where people from different backgrounds come from all over seeking spiritual guidance and relief from health problems or from existential conflicts. A priest, or "babalao," with 35 years experience, consults and leads "Santería" and "Yoruba" ceremonies. The house's façade has an arrangement of vertical gaps with a continuous balcony over the heavy wooden double-leaf door that leads to the upper floor via a marble staircase.

Die afrikanische Mythologie ist ein wichtiger Teil der kubanischen Kultur. »Orishas«, afro-kubanische Gottheiten, sind Teil des Yoruba-Glaubens, den die afrikanischen Sklaven, die für Arbeit auf den Zucker- und Tabakplantagen hergeholt wurden, mit nach Kuba brachten. Ihr Glaube hat sich zusammen mit dem in Kuba vorherrschenden Katholizismus zu einer neuen Religion entwickelt, genau wie in jedem anderen Land, dessen Bewohner eine Mischung aus Europäern und Afrikanern darstellen. Die »Santería« oder »Regla de Ocha« ist stark von den Ritualen der Sklaven geprägt und hat die Jahrhunderte überlebt. Einer der Yoruba-Tempel ist das Haus von Emilio Rodríguez Valdés an der Calle Concordia im Zentrum Havannas. Menschen verschiedenster Herkunft suchen hier spirituelle Führung bei der Suche nach dem Sinn des Lebens und Hilfe bei gesundheitlichen Problemen. Rodríguez Valdés ist seit 35 Jahren ein »Babalao«-Priester und führt durch »Santería«- und »Yoruba«-Zeremonien. Die Fassade des Hauses besteht aus vertikalen Fugen und einem durchgängigen Balkon über einer schweren Doppeltüre. Von hier gelangt man in ein Treppenhaus aus Marmor, das ins obere Stockwerk führt.

Les mythes aident l'homme à justifier son existence et à expliquer le monde. La mythologie africaine fait partie intégrante de la culture cubaine, reflet d'un peuple dont les racines africaines et européennes se mêlent. Poétique, mystérieuse, séduisante et artistique, elle est pleine de lumière, de rythmes et de couleurs. Les divinités afro-cubaines ou «orishas» introduites par les esclaves yoruba amenés d'Afrique pour travailler sur les plantations de cannes à sucre et de tabac sont parfois amalgamées avec les saints catholiques, culte dominant sur l'île. Le système religieux qui en résulte, la «Santería» ou «Regla de Ocha», est imprégné des croyances et des rites des esclaves qui ont survécu au fil des siècles. La demeure d'Emilio Rodríguez Valdés, sur la rue Concordia dans Centro Habana, est un temple yoruba où toutes sortes de gens viennent chercher un soutien spirituel pour des problèmes de santé ou existentiels. Le «babalao», fort de ses 35 ans d'expérience, les reçoit et dirige des cérémonies «santería» et «yoruba». La façade de la maison, percée d'ouvertures verticales, possède un balcon panoramique qui surmonte la lourde double porte en bois s'ouvrant sur un escalier en marbre menant à l'étage.

❊ **ABOVE LEFT** An old car from the United States parked in front of the building located in the Centro Habana neighborhood awaits a customer who is undergoing a check-up by the "babalao" Emilio Rodríguez Valdés. **LEFT** On one of the walls in the sitting room of Emilio Rodríguez Valdés's house, there is a small glass cabinet with religious icons above a photograph of Ernesto "Che" Guevara. **ABOVE** The wide doors of the living room lead to the balcony and illuminate the living room and the hall, which are solely divided by unique Moorish arches painted blue. The staircase lands in the sitting room, watched over by a dog. **FOLLOWING DOUBLEPAGE** On one of the walls in the living room, an image of "Changó", the "Santería" name of the Catholic Saint Barbara of Bitinia, on a small altar. ❊ **OBEN LINKS** Ein altes nordamerikanisches Auto parkt vor dem Gebäude im Viertel Centro Habana und wartet auf einen Kunden, während sich dieser vom »Babalao«-Priester Emilio Rodríguez Valdés beraten lässt. **LINKS** An einer Wand des kleinen Vorzimmers im Haus von Emilio Rodríguez Valdés hängt eine kleine Vitrine mit religiösen Ikonen über einem Foto von Ernesto »Che« Guevara. **OBEN** Die großen Balkontüren des Wohnzimmers durchfluten diesen Raum und das Vorzimmer mit Licht. Beide Zimmer werden nur durch außergewöhnliche, blau gestrichene, maurisch anmutende Bögen getrennt. Die Treppe endet im Vorzimmer, wo ein Hund wacht. **FOLGENDE DOPPELSEITE** An einer Wand im Wohnzimmer hängt ein kleiner Altar mit dem Bildnis von »Changó«, wie der »Santería«-Kult die im Katholizismus als Heilige Barbara von Bithynien bekannte Figur kennt. ❊ **PAGE DE GAUCHE, EN HAUT** Une vieille voiture américaine, garée devant l'immeuble dans le quartier de Centro Habana, attend un client en consultation avec le « babalao » Emilio Rodríguez Valdés. **A GAUCHE** Sur un mur de la petite salle, une vitrine accueille des statuetts de saints au-dessus d'une photo d'Ernesto « Che » Guevara. **CI-DESSUS** Les grandes portes-fenêtres qui donnent sur le balcon laissent pénétrer la lumière dans les deux salles, divisées uniquement par des arcs en fer à cheval peints en bleu. L'escalier débouche sur la petite salle, gardée par un chien. **DOUBLE PAGE SUIVANTE** Sur un mur de la grande salle, un petit autel accueille une représentation de « Changó », l'équivalent dans la « santería » de sainte Barbe de Bithynie.

※ **FACING PAGE** The laundry area has a wooden staircase for drying clothes on the roof. **RIGHT** An altar with images and offerings to the Afro-Cuban deities. **BELOW** The room where Emilio Rodríguez Valdés consults is decorated with an altar featuring diverse attributes of the syncretic religious cults of worship. The colored robes correspond to the different deities in the Yoruba religion called "Santería". **FOLLOWING DOUBLEPAGES** The spacious and well-lit kitchen with its tile veneer in white, one of the symbolic colors in Santería that corresponds to "Obatalá", a syncretism of "Our Lady of Mercy". * The bright, spacious dining room is also used as a classroom for teaching initiates the rituals and meaning of the objects of worship. ※ **LINKE SEITE** Vom Waschraum führt eine Holztreppe zur Dachterrasse hinauf, wo die Wäsche zum Trocknen aufgehängt wird. **RECHTS** Ein Altar mit Abbildungen und Opfergaben für die Gottheiten der afro-ku-banischen Religion. **UNTEN** Das Beratungszimmer von Emilio Rodríguez Valdés ist mit einem Altar eingerichtet, der diverse Merkmale der synkretischen Religionskulte auf-weist. Die bunten Kleidungsstücke entsprechen den verschiedenen Gottheiten der als »Santería« bezeichneten Yoruba-Religion. **FOLGENDE DOPPELSEITEN** Die geräumige, helle Küche ist mit weißen Kacheln verkleidet, denn Weiß ist eine der symbolträchtigen Farben des »Santería«-Kults und wird »Obatalá« zugeschrieben, die der Jungfrau »Nuestra Señora de las Mercedes« entspricht.* Das große, helle Esszimmer des Hauses wird auch genutzt, um den Eingeweihten Unterricht in den Ritualen und der Bedeutung der Kultobjekte zu erteilen. Religiöse Figuren sind Teil der Dekoration. ※ **PAGE DE GAUCHE** Dans la buan-derie, un escalier en bois mène à la terrasse où l'on fait sécher le linge. **A DROITE** Un autel avec des offrandes et des représentations de divinités afro-cubaines. **CI-DESSOUS** Dans la salle de consultation d'Emilio Rodríguez Valdés, un autel avec divers attributs des cultes syncrétiques. Les habits colorés correspondent aux différentes divinités de la « santería », dérivant de la religion yoruba. **DOUBLE PAGE SUIVANTE** La cuisine, spacieuse et claire, avec son carrelage blanc, la couleur symbole d'« Obatalá », syncrétisme de « Notre-Dame des Grâce » dans la « santería », * Dans la grande salle à manger bien éclairée, on enseigne aussi les rituels et la signification des objets de culte aux initiés.

LEONARDO

Cano Moreno

A Painter's Home.

Because of Leonardo Cano Moreno's extraordinary taste and imagination his otherwise ordinary two-storey house has been used in films such as "Mascaró: el cazador Americano," and more recently the striking "Siete días, siete noches." He is a painter and cartoon illustrator whose award-winning drawings for the 1990s Cuban cartoon "Vampiros en La Habana" have been exhibited at the Museum of Modern Art in New York. His house, located in the Vedado neighborhood of Havana, was built in the early 20th century and currently seems to have been invaded by nature: a climbing orange tree has weaved its way around the cement balusters and Corinthian columns of the façade's front terrace. The hedonistic and almost surreal interior combines beautiful 18th century furniture, a reproduction of "The Three Graces," old lamps, and clocks with contemporary erotic painting and stained glass. Friezes have been painted by the artist in an art nouveau style. The bedrooms and the dining room are arranged along an open corridor, filled with ferns, birds, and plants, that supplies natural light and ventilation to the rooms.

Eigentlich ist dies ein ganz gewöhnliches Haus. Doch der Maler und Illustrator Leonardo Cano Moreno hat es äußerst fantasievoll eingerichtet und damit einige Filmemacher angelockt. So wurde der Film »Mascaró: el cazador Americano« dort gedreht und kürzlich »Siete días, siete noches«. Cano Morenos preisgekrönte Zeichnungen für den kubanischen Comic aus den 1990ern, »Vampiros en La Habana«, wurden bereits im »Museum of Modern Art« in New York ausgestellt. Sein Haus liegt in Vedado, einem Viertel in Havanna, und stammt aus dem frühen 20. Jahrhundert. Heute wirkt es verwildert, rund um die Balustraden aus Beton und die korinthischen Säulen der vorderen Terrasse wächst ein Orangenbaum. Das hedonistische, leicht sukurrile Interieur besteht aus wunderschönen Möbeln aus dem 18. Jahrhundert, einer Reproduktion der »Drei Grazien«, alten Lampen und Uhren, zeitgenössischen erotischen Malereien und Buntglas. Dazu hat der Künstler ein Art-Nouveau-Friesdekor an die Wände gemalt. Ein offener Korridor, voller Farn, Vögel, Pflanzen, frischer Luft und Sonnenlicht, führt ins Schlafzimmer und ins Wohnzimmer.

Décorée avec goût et imagination, cette maison du début du 20e siècle, au départ ordinaire, a servi de décor à des films tels que «Mascaró : el cazador Americano» et, plus récemment, «Siete días, siete noches». Elle appartient au peintre et dessinateur Leonardo Cano Moreno, dont la bande dessinée créée dans les années 90, «Vampiros en La Habana», a été exposée au Musée d'Art Moderne de New York. Située dans le quartier de Vedado, elle est envahie par la nature. Un oranger grimpant s'est enroulé autour de la balustrade en ciment et des colonnes corinthiennes de la terrasse qui domine la façade. La décoration intérieure hédoniste et presque surréaliste associe de beaux meubles du 18e siècle, une reproduction des «Trois Grâces», des lampes et des pendules anciennes, avec des peintures érotiques contemporaines et des vitraux. Cano Moreno y a peint des frises dans un style Art nouveau. Les chambres et la salle à manger donnent sur un couloir aéré rempli de fougères, d'oiseaux et de plantes vertes, qui les inonde de lumière naturelle.

✳ **ABOVE** The nude is one of the recurring themes in the oeuvre of painter Leonardo Cano Moreno. One of his paintings hangs over a lovely piece of wood furniture with relief decorations. **FACING PAGE** The studio of painter and illustrator Leonardo Cano Moreno in one of the rooms in his house displays several of his works illuminated by a lovely chandelier hanging from the ceiling. ✳ **OBEN** Der Akt ist eines der immer wiederkehrenden Motive im Werk des Malers Leonardo Cano Moreno. Eines seiner Gemälde hängt über einem reizenden, mit Reliefschnitzereien verzierten Holzschränkchen. **RECHTE SEITE** Das Atelier des Malers und Illustrators Leonardo Cano Moreno wird von einer prächtigen Deckenlampe ins rechte Licht gerückt. ✳ **CI-DESSUS** Le nu est un des thèmes récurrents de l'œuvre de Leonardo Cano Moreno. Une de ses peintures au-dessus d'un beau meuble en bois sculpté. **PAGE DE DROITE** Dans l'atelier du peintre et illustrateur, quelques-unes de ses œuvres, éclairées par un beau lustre en cristal.

Casa Mendoza

Styles of Choice.

Vedado was a forbidden forest until José Yboleón laid out a plan for a new district in 1860, based on modern planning principles and a grid defined by wide, tree-lined avenues. As the Cuban War of Independence lasted from 1868 until 1898, this plan could only be realized in the first decades of the 20th century. In 1916, Cuban architect Leonardo Morales built a residence for banker and landowner Pablo González de Mendoza on Paseo Avenue. Influenced by classicism as it was practiced in the US, his architectural style is prevalent in this neighborhood as it was popular at that time among the wealthy who were building stately new residences. Set back from the street, the house was approached via a driveway leading first to a fountain, then to a circular iron-and-glass-canopied porch and entry hall. A lovely marble staircase lit by a stained-glass window makes a strong impression. The living room, reception room and dining hall all have views to the rear garden. In 1918, Morales and US architect John H. Duncan added a pavilion for a Roman-style pool: A statue of Aphrodite is surrounded by classical columns and wooden screens, and the highly refined wooden trusses and skylight above her make this space reminiscent of a Pompeian impluvium.

Das Viertel Vedado war früher ein unberührter Wald. José Yboleón entwarf 1860 auf diesem Gebiet einen neuen Bezirk nach modernen Planungsprinzipien. Er bestand aus einem Netzwerk weiter Alleen. Allerdings wurde er wegen des kubanischen Unabhängigkeitskrieges zwischen 1868 bis 1898 erst in den ersten Jahrzehnten des 20. Jahrhunderts umgesetzt. Für den Banker und Landbesitzer Pablo González de Mendoza baute der kubanische Architekt Leonardo Morales 1916 am Paseo in Vedado ein Haus. Die auffällige Architektur orientierte sich am amerikanischen Klassizismus, und schnell wurde das Haus für die damaligen Reichen zum Vorbild für ihre aristokratischen Residenzen. Ein Anfahrtsweg mit einem Brunnen führt zum von der Straße zurückversetzten Haus. Hinter einer runden, gedeckten Veranda aus Eisen und Glas befindet sich die Eingangshalle mit herrlichem Marmortreppenhaus, in das farbiges Licht durch Buntglasfenster fällt. Wohnzimmer, Empfangsraum und Esszimmer haben alle Sicht auf den Garten hinter dem Haus. Morales baute 1918 zusammen mit dem amerikanischen Architekten John H. Duncan einen Pavillon als römisches Bad mit einer Statue von Aphrodite, klassischen Säulen und Holzgittern, edlem Fachwerk aus Holz und einem Oberlicht. Dies war an ein pompejanisches Impluvium angelehnt.

Vedado était autrefois une forêt interdite, jusqu'à ce que, en 1860, José Yboleón n'établisse le plan d'un nouveau quartier basé sur des principes modernes d'urbanisme avec de grandes avenues bordées d'arbres. La guerre d'indépendance ayant duré de 1868 à 1898, son projet ne put être réalisé qu'au cours des premières décennies du 20e siècle. En 1916, l'architecte cubain Leonardo Morales bâtit une résidence pour le banquier et propriétaire terrien Pablo González de Mendoza sur l'avenue Paseo. Influencé par le classicisme nord-américain, son style fit école dans le quartier, devenant très prisé des riches qui, à l'époque, se faisaient construire de nouvelles grandes demeures. On accède à la maison, en retrait de la rue, par une allée menant à une fontaine, puis à un perron couronné d'une marquise ronde et vitrée en fer forgé. Dans le hall, un escalier en marbre éclairé par un vitrail est du plus bel effet. Le salon, la réception et la salle à manger donnent sur le jardin arrière. En 1918, Morales et l'architecte américain John H. Duncan ajoutèrent un pavillon pour abriter une piscine à la romaine. La statue d'Aphrodite entourée de colonnes classiques et d'écrans en bois, la charpente richement ouvragée et l'ouverture dans le toit rappellent un impluvium pompéien.

※ **ABOVE LEFT** The main façade of the house is preceded by a fountain in the middle of the entryway via Calle 15 in the neighborhood of Vedado. The house is currently the residence of the British ambassador to Cuba. **LEFT** A circular iron and glass marquee hangs from a semicircular arch at the house's main entrance. **ABOVE** The terrace that serves as an antechamber to the swimming pool. The large bay dividing both spaces is closed off by a door made of wooden strips, flanked by two mirrors with latticework frames. **FOLLOWING DOUBLEPAGE** The fabulous Roman swimming pool, an exquisite and extremely beautiful space due to its unique, refined atmosphere. ※ **OBEN LINKS** Der Hauptfassade des Hauses geht ein Brunnen voraus, der sich in der Mitte der Zufahrt von der Calle 15 im Stadtviertel Vedado befindet. Derzeit hat hier der britische Botschafter in Kuba seinen Wohnsitz. **LINKS** Ein rundes Sonnendach aus Eisen und Glas hängt am Haupteingang des Hauses von einem Rundbogen herab. **OBEN** Die Terrasse dient als Vorraum des Swimmingpools. Die große Lichtöffnung zwischen beiden Räumlichkeiten ist mit einer aus Holzlatten gestalteten Tür verschlossen. Auf beiden Seiten der Tür befinden sich Spiegel, die von einem zarten Holzgeflecht gerahmt werden. **FOLGENDE DOPPELSEITE** Der großartige, römisch gestaltete Swimmingpool befindet sich in einem erlesenen, prächtigen Raum, der durch sein einzigartiges und elegantes Ambiente besticht. ※ **PAGE DE GAUCHE, EN HAUT** La façade principale, précédée d'une fontaine. On y accède par une allée depuis la Calle 15, dans le quartier de Vedado. C'est aujourd'hui la résidence de l'ambassadeur du Royaume-Uni. **A GAUCHE** Une marquise ronde et vitrée en fer forgé suspendue à une arche en plein cintre dans l'entrée principale. **CI-DESSUS** La terrasse servant d'antichambre à la piscine. La grande baie qui divise les espaces est fermée par une porte en lattes de bois, flanquée de deux miroirs bordés de treillis en osier. **DOUBLE PAGE SUIVANTE** La somptueuse piscine romaine, lieu de détente exquis et raffiné.

❋ **FACING PAGE** The dining room in the Pablo González de Mendoza home, next to the entrance hall, has views of the gardens. A lovely chandelier is suspended over the table. **RIGHT** The piano takes up a corner in the house's living room which features a beautiful lamp hanging from the ceiling. **BELOW** The cozy, intimate atmosphere in the sitting room, with its high ceilings and its eclectic yet exquisite decoration based on gypsum friezes.
❋ **LINKE SEITE** Der Speiseraum der Casa Pablo González de Mendoza grenzt an das Vestibül und bietet eine Aussicht auf die Grünanlagen. Über dem Tisch hängt eine prunkvolle Lampe. **RECHTS** Das Klavier steht in einer Ecke des Wohnzimmers, an dessen Decke eine schöne Lampe hängt. **UNTEN** Das gemütliche und einladende Ambiente des Wohnraums mit seiner hohen Decke und der eklektischen, jedoch erlesenen Einrichtung mit einem Fries aus Stuckleisten aus Gips. ❋ **PAGE DE GAUCHE** La salle à manger, contiguë au vestibule, donne sur les deux jardins. Au-dessus de la table, un beau lustre. **A DROITE** Le piano occupe un coin du salon, sous une belle suspension. **CI-DESSOUS** Le petit salon, intime et accueillant, avec son haut plafond, sa décoration éclectique mais raffinée, ses belles frises en plâtre.

✻ **ABOVE** The entrance gallery to the upper storey is protected by a white marble balustrade. In the background are the stained glass windows that illuminate the elegant staircase joining the two stories. **RIGHT** A beautifully designed wrought-iron grill delimits the private bedroom area on the upper floor of the house. **FACING PAGE** The sumptuous marble staircase connecting the two stories, bathed by the colorful light penetrating through the stained glass windows. ✻ **OBEN** Diese Galerie im Obergeschoss ist mit einer Balustrade aus weißem Marmor geschützt. Die Buntglasfenster im Hintergrund beleuchten die Treppe, welche die beiden Stockwerke des Hauses vereint. **RECHTS** Ein herrliches schmiedeeisernes Gitter begrenzt den Privatbereich der Schlafzimmer im Obergeschoss. **RECHTE SEITE** Die üppige Marmortreppe zwischen beiden Stockwerken erstrahlt im farbigen Licht, das durch die Buntglasfenster fällt. ✻ **CI-DESSUS** Le grand palier à l'étage est protégé par une balustrade en marbre blanc. Au fond, les vitraux qui éclairent l'élégant escalier. **A DROITE** À l'étage, une belle grille en fer forgé isole les chambres à coucher du reste de la maison. **PAGE DE DROITE** Le somptueux escalier en marbre est baigné par la lumière colorée qui filtre par les vitraux.

Jair Mon Pérez

A Feast of Spanish Tiles

Reproductions of several works by the famous Spanish painter Francisco de Goya and some passages from Spanish writer Miguel de Cervantes' masterpiece "Don Quixote" are found among the thousands of tiles that decorate the walls of the Casa Mon. These colorful tiles from Seville, depicting bullfighting scenes and heraldic motifs, are repeated almost ad infinitum inside the house, which was originally built in Havana's Vedado district in 1928 for a Jewish jeweler, today it is owned by Jair Mon Pérez, inherited from his father. From the street one can see a riot of tiles on the planters in the front garden and on the steps leading to the porch. They continue along the façade where the main entrance and two windows are surrounded by tiles, which form a wainscot recalling the magnificent Alhambra palaces in Granada, the so-called "palacios nazaries". The entry vestibule leads to the spacious dining room which is also decorated with grand wainscoting around the windows. But the star of the show is another hallway, where a marble staircase with elaborate wrought-iron railings is lit by an arched stained-glass window – a fantastic display of many jewel-like colors!

An den Wänden der »Casa Mon« stellen tausende von farbigen Kacheln aus Sevilla Werke des spanischen Malers Francisco de Goya dar und auch Szenen aus »Don Quixote«, dem Meisterwerk des spanischen Schriftstellers Miguel de Cervantes. Im Haus, das ursprünglich im Viertel von Havanna Vedado für einen jüdischen Juwelier gebaut wurde, begegnet man unzähligen Stierkampfszenen und heraldischen Motiven. Heute wohnt hier Jair Mon Pérez, der das Haus von seinem Vater geerbt hat. Die Kacheln sind bereits von der Straße aus zu sehen: an Pflanzentöpfen, die auf den Stufen der Treppe stehen, die zur Veranda hinaufführt, rund um den Haupteingang und die beiden Fenster. Die Kachelverkleidung erinnert an die großartigen Alhambra-Paläste in Granada, den so genannten »palacios nazaries«. Das Vestibül führt in das Esszimmer, in einen großen Raum, dessen Fenster auch nochmals mit Kacheln verziert sind. Am schönsten ist allerdings der Flur mit einem Marmortreppenhaus mit einem kunstvollen schmiedeeisernen Geländer. Das Licht, das durch ein Buntglasfenster fällt, funkelt dabei wie Juwelen.

Parmi les milliers de carreaux qui ornent les murs de la Casa Mon, on trouve des reproductions de tableaux de Goya ou l'illustration de certains passages de « Don Quichotte », le chef-d'œuvre de Miguel de Cervantès. Ces compositions colorées provenant de Séville dépeignent également des scènes de corrida ou des motifs héraldiques et se répètent à l'infini à l'intérieur de la maison, construite à Vedado en 1928 pour un joaillier juif. Aujourd'hui Jair Mon Pérez, qui a hérité la demeure de son père, habite ici. Dès la rue, on aperçoit une profusion de carreaux sur les jardinières et les marches qui mènent au porche. Ils se poursuivent le long de la façade, encadrent l'entrée principale et les deux fenêtres, évoquant le magnifique palais de l'Alhambra à Grenade. Le vestibule et la salle à manger donnent sur un grand salon dont les lambris grandioses bordent les fenêtres. Mais le clou de la visite se trouve dans un autre couloir, où un escalier en marbre avec une belle rampe en fer forgé est éclairé par un vitrail en demi-lune, véritable joyau projetant mille feux colorés !

✳ **PREVIOUS DOUBLEPAGES** Entrance to the house of Jair Mon Pérez. The main façade is decorated with magnificent wainscots made of tiles from Seville. **ABOVE LEFT** The lovely stained glass window illuminating the landing on the staircase is a point of light amidst a riot of bright colors. **LEFT** The wainscot on the main façade of the Jair Mon Pérez house with tiles depicting works by Goya. **ABOVE** Even the soffit of the staircase is decorated. **FOLLOWING DOUBLEPAGE** Detail of the portal wainscot with tiles depicting parts of Goya's 1776 painting "Baile a Orillas del Río Manzanares", now in the Prado. ✱ Inside, the tile wainscots also include mosaics with chivalric scenes and vignettes from works by Goya. Partial view of his work "La Vendimia/El Otoño" rendered in 1786. ✳ **VORHERGEHENDE DOPPELSEITE** Der Eingang des Hauses von Jair Mon Pérez. Die Hauptfassade besticht durch prachtvolle Sockel und eine Umrahmung der Haustüre mit Fliesen aus Sevilla. **OBEN LINKS** Das wunderschöne Buntglasfenster lässt den Treppenabsatz wie in einem Meer von Farben erstrahlen. **LINKS** Auf dem Fliesensockel bilden die Keramikkacheln die Werke des spanischen Malers Francisco de Goya nach. **OBEN** Die dekorativen Keramikfliesen sind sogar an der Treppenuntersicht angebracht. **FOLGENDE DOPPELSEITE** Nahansicht des Portalsockels, auf dem die Fliesen Ausschnitte von Goyas Werk »Picknick am Ufer des Manzanares« von 1776 nachbilden. Das Original befindet sich im Prado-Museum in Madrid. ✱ Im Inneren zeigen die Fliesensockel auch Mosaike mit Reitszenen und Ausschnitte aus den Werken des spanischen Malers Goya. Teilansicht des 1786 von Francisco de Goya geschaffenen Werks »Die Weinlese/Der Herbst«. ✳ **DOUBLE PAGE PRECEDENTE** L'entrée de la maison. La façade est tapissée de magnifiques frises et scènes en azulejos sévillans. **PAGE DE GAUCHE, EN HAUT** Le beau vitrail est un point lumineux dans un océan de couleurs vives. **À GAUCHE** Les carreaux en céramique reprennent des scènes empruntées. **CI-DESSOUS** Les carreaux en céramique couvrent même le dessous de l'escalier. **DOUBLE PAGE SUIVANTE** Détail des lambris du vestibule avec les carreaux représentant partiellement la « Danse de majos au bord du Manzanares » de Goya (1776), dont l'original est conservé au Musée du Prado à Madrid. ✱ À l'intérieur, les lambris en azulejos incluent également des scènes de chevaleries et des œuvres de Goya. Vue partielle de « L'Automne ou la vendange », d'après un carton réalisé par Goya en 1786.

❋ **ABOVE** Bottles filled with Havana Club, the best rum in the world, and ceramic vessels. **FACING PAGE** The sober tiled walls of the kitchen contrast with the colourful mosaic of Goya's 1792 work "Muchachos trepando a un árbol", visible in the background. **FOLLOWING DOUBLEPAGE** An antique piece of furniture for storing glassware. ❋ **OBEN** Flaschen der weltbesten kubanischen Rummarke Havana Club und Keramikgeschirr. **RECHTE SEITE** Der Kontrast zwischen der schlichten Verkachelung der Küche und dem farbenprächtigen Mosaik an der Wand im Hintergrund, welches Goyas Werk »Jungen beim Klettern auf einen Baum« aus dem Jahr 1792 zeigt. **FOLGENDE DOPPELSEITE** Ein altes Vitrinenschränkchen für Gläser. ❋ **CI-DESSUS** Des bouteilles de rhum cubain Havana Club, le meilleur du monde, et des petits vases en céramique. **PAGE DE DROITE** Le sobre carrelage blanc contraste avec les azulejos aux couleurs vives reproduisant les « Enfants grimpant à un arbre », de Goya (1792), sur le mur du fond. **DOUBLE PAGE SUIVANTE** Un vieux meuble en bois sculpté.

Miguel ALONSO

Splendor of the Past.

Miguel Alonso's home was used for several scenes in the Cuban film "Las Noches de Constantinopla." The mysterious house is barely visible from the street because of the lush trees that have grown up around it. Built in 1926, the house has a cylindrical volume with an elaborate balcony and a curved pediment. This feature anchors the two wings containing the living rooms on the ground floor and the bedrooms on the upper floor – their side porches and terraces catch delightful breezes and allow one to gaze out and watch the world go by. The unassuming entrance has terrazzo floors and is protected by a shaded porch with Corinthian columns. It leads to an elongated entrance hall with marble floors that links the spacious living room and the library on one side to the dining room and kitchen on the other. The dining room itself is decorated with gypsum moldings and friezes, and has high ceilings with an antique chandelier. But it is the magnificent marble staircase with a wrought-iron railing and dark mahogany handrail that dominates this house.

Das Haus von Miguel Alonso ist im kubanischen Film »Nächte in Konstantinopel« in mehreren Szenen zu sehen. Von der Straße hat man wegen der üppigen Bäume beschränkte Sicht auf das mysteriös aussehende Haus. Der mittlere Teil des 1926 gebauten Hauses wurde in zylindrischer Form und mit einem kunstvollem Balkon gebaut. Der gewölbte Dachgiebel hält zwei Flügel zusammen; im Erdgeschoss befinden sich die Wohnräume und im oberen Stockwerk die Schlafzimmer. Durch die seitlichen Veranden und Terrassen wehen angenehme Brisen, und man kann von hier die Welt rundherum beobachten. Der unspektakuläre Eingang mit Terrazzoböden liegt unter einer schattigen Terrasse mit korinthischen Säulen. Von da gelangt man in eine in die Länge gezogene Eingangshalle mit Marmorböden. Sie verbindet die verschieden großen Wohnräume und die Bibliothek auf der einen, das Esszimmer und die Küche auf der anderen Seite. Das Esszimmer mit hohen Decken und einem antiken Kronleuchter ist mit Gipsformen und Friesdekor verziert. Doch es ist das wunderschöne Marmortreppenhaus mit schmiedeeisernem Geländer und einem Handlauf aus dunklem Mahagoni, das sofort ins Auge sticht.

La demeure de Miguel Alonso a servi de décor à plusieurs scènes du film cubain «Les Nuits de Constantinople». Mystérieuse, on la devine à peine depuis la rue entre les arbres au feuillage dense qui l'entourent. Bâtie en 1926, elle est cylindrique avec un beau balcon et un fronton incurvé. Les deux ailes abritent des salles de séjour au rez-de-chaussée et des chambres à l'étage, leurs porches latéraux et leurs terrasses, balayées par une douce brise, permettant de contempler la vie suivre son cours au dehors. L'entrée sobre, avec son sol en mosaïque, est protégée d'un porche soutenu par des colonnes corinthiennes. Elle donne sur un long hall au sol en marbre qui relie le spacieux salon et la bibliothèque d'un côté, la cuisine et la salle à manger de l'autre. Cette dernière, ornée de moulures en stuc et de frises, possède un haut plafond auquel est suspendu un lustre ancien. Mais c'est le magnifique escalier en marbre avec sa balustrade en fer forgé et sa rampe en acajou qui domine la maison.

※ **ABOVE** The curved volume that joins the terraces in front of each façade of the house has an elegant balcony, highlighting its corner location. **RIGHT** The imperial marble staircase, on the same axis as the entrance, is the most striking element on the ground floor. Its lovely wrought-iron banister has a handrail made of Cuban mahogany. **FACING PAGE** The eclectic house of Miguel Alonso with its equally eclectic furnishings. The spacious sitting room reflects the home's overall state of deterioration, with its peeling ceilings where the rusted iron can be seen. ※ **OBEN** Der gebogene Gebäudevorsprung, der die Terrassen an allen Fassaden des Hauses mit einem eleganten Balkon verbindet, unterstreicht dessen Ecklage. **RECHTS** Die prächtige Marmortreppe bildet eine Linie mit dem Eingang und ist das herausragende Element des Erdgeschosses. Das schöne Eisengeländer ist mit einem Handlauf aus kubanischem Mahagoni versehen. **RECHTE SEITE** Miguel Alonsos eklektisches Haus mit seinem eklektischen Mobiliar. Das geräumige Vorzimmer mit der abgebröckelten Decke und den zerfressenen Stahlstreben spiegelt den allgemeinen Verfall des Hauses. ※ **CI-DESSUS** Les terrasses donnant sur chaque façade sont reliées par des pavillons d'angle arrondis. **A DROITE** L'escalier impérial en marbre blanc, en face de l'entrée, domine le rez-de-chaussée. Sa belle balustrade en fer forgé est surmontée d'une rampe en acajou cubain. **PAGE DE DROITE** La décoration éclectique de la maison de Miguel Alonso avec son mobilier dépareillé. Le grand séjour reflète le délabrement général de la maison avec ses plafonds crevés qui laissent apparaître les poutres métalliques rouillées.

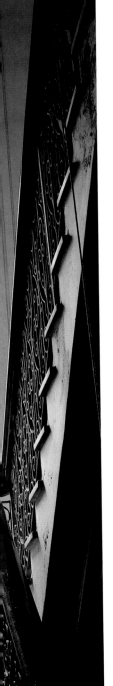

※ **ABOVE AND FACING PAGE** The living room of the Miguel Alonso house, with its lovely wood and cut glass doorways and elegant English Chippendale-style furniture. **FOLLOWING DOUBLEPAGE** Large windows illuminate the dining room, one of the best-preserved spaces in the house. ※ **OBEN UND RECHTE SEITE** Das Wohnzimmer des Hauses von Miguel Alonso betritt man durch Holztüren mit geschliffenen Glaseinsatz, und man sitzt im eleganten englischen Mobiliar im Chippendale-Stil. **FOLGENDE DOPPELSEITE** Große Fenster erhellen das Esszimmer, einen der am besten erhaltenen Räume des Hauses. ※ **CI-DESSUS ET PAGE DE DROITE** Le séjour, avec ses belles portes en bois et verre taillé, et son mobilier Chippendale. **DOUBLE PAGE SUIVANTE** La salle à manger, l'espace le mieux conservé de la maison, est éclairée par de grandes fenêtres.

ABOVE The well-lit library, used in the Cuban film "Las Noches de Constantinopla". **FACING PAGE** An image of the Virgen del Rosario on top of an English console. **FOLLOWING DOUBLEPAGES**
A traditional image from Cuban Catholic religious iconography. "The Sacred Heart", over a kitchen cabinet. * A spiral staircase leads from the kitchen, with its lovely mosaic floors,
to the upper floor. ❊ **OBEN** Die lichtdurchflutete Bibliothek diente als Kulisse für den kubanischen Film »Nächte in Konstantinopel«. **RECHTE SEITE** Eine »Jungfrau des Rosenkranzes«
auf einer englischen Konsole. **FOLGENDE DOPPELSEITE** Das in der katholischen Ikonographie Kubas traditionelle Bild »Herz Jesu« über einem Küchenschrank. ❊ **CI-DESSUS** La bibliothèque
est une des pièces utilisées lors du tournage du film « Les Nuits de Constantinople ». **PAGE DE DROITE** Une Vierge du Rosaire posée sur une console anglaise. **DOUBLES PAGES SUIVANTES** Dans la
cuisine, au-dessus d'un buffet, une image traditionnelle de l'iconographie catholique cubaine, appelée « Le cœur de Jésus ». * L'escalier métallique en colimaçon monte à l'étage.

※ **FACING PAGE** The cube-shaped cabinet in one of the corners of the kitchen becomes an artistic object due to its bright red color, which marks a clear contrast with the yellow walls. **ABOVE** A lovely oval-shaped stained glass window illuminates the spectacular master bathroom in the Miguel Alonso house, located on the upper floor. ※ **LINKE SEITE** Der quadratische rote Schrank in einer Ecke der Küche wirkt aufgrund seiner leuchtenden Farbe, die einen starken Kontrast zu den gelben Wänden herstellt, wie ein Kunstobjekt. **OBEN** Ein prächtiges, oval geformtes Buntglasfenster wirft Licht in das riesige Hauptbad im Obergeschoss des Hauses von Miguel Alonso. ※ **PAGE DE GAUCHE** Avec sa couleur rouge intense qui contraste avec le reste de la cuisine aux murs jaunes, ce placard cubique devient un objet d'art. **CI-DESSUS** Un beau vitrail ovale illumine la spectaculaire salle de bains principale, située à l'étage.

CONDESA REVILLA
DE CAMARGO

A French Mansion for a Cuban Countess.

The early 20th century saw a carnival of styles, and in the 1920s ornament was *not* a crime for the enlightened Cuban bourgeoisie, flush with money from the high war price of sugar. These tycoons were inspired by European extravagance, and in 1927 the very wealthy José Gómez Mena commissioned French architects P. Viard and M. Destugue to design a mansion for him in Vedado. The gardens surrounding it are named "The Four Seasons and The Night." The main entrance to the residence is framed by four Ionic columns, and a small vestibule opens directly onto a stunning grand hall which contains a sumptuous staircase of monumental proportions. It is aligned along an axis with the ornate glass and metall ceiling which is said to have been influenced by the Paris Opera. The house is composed around this grand hall, somehow echoing traditional Cuban architecture, which is designed around a central place. This luxurious mansion was decorated by "Maison Jansen" of Paris with Carrara marble floors and walls in the dining room, bronze and gold iron work, oriental pieces, and porcelains from Sèvres, Limoges and Meißen.

Im frühen 20. Jahrhundert tauchten in Kuba die verschiedensten Stilrichtungen auf. Die aufgeklärten kubanischen Bürger der 1920er, die nach dem Krieg mit viel Geld aus den hohen Zuckerpreisen gesegnet waren, hatten eine besondere Vorliebe für Dekoratives und ließen sich von der europäischen Extravaganz inspirierten. 1927 beauftragte der superreiche José Gómez Mena die französischen Architekten P. Viard und M. Destugue mit dem Bau einer Villa in Vedado. Die Gartenanlagen der Villa nannte er »Die vier Jahreszeiten und die Nacht«. Der Haupteingang der Residenz wird von vier ionischen Säulen flankiert und führt in ein schmales Vestibül, das sich zu einer großen Halle mit einem prächtigen, monumentalen Treppenhaus öffnet. Die Treppe liegt in der Achse mit dem Eingang und ist von einer Glas-Eisen-Konstruktion bekrönt, die den Bau der Pariser Oper beeinflusst haben soll. Das Haus ist um die große Halle herum angelegt und erinnert damit an traditionelle kubanische Architektur rund um einen Innenhof. Die luxuriöse Villa wurde vom der Pariser »Maison Jansen« eingerichtet. Für die Böden wählten sie Carrara-Marmor, aber auch die Wände im Esszimmer sind aus Marmor, dazu gesellen sich Arbeiten aus Bronze und vergoldetem Eisen, Objekte aus dem Orient und Porzellan aus Sèvres, Limoges und Meißen.

Le début du 20ᵉ siècle vit défiler une ribambelle de styles et l'excentricité des années folles n'avait rien de honteux pour la bourgeoisie cubaine cultivée qui avait fait fortune grâce à la hausse des prix du sucre dans l'après-guerre. En 1927, le richissime José Gómez Mena demanda aux architectes français P. Viard et M. Destugue de lui construire un manoir à Vedado dans le style de la renaissance française. Les jardins qui l'entourent sont baptisés «Les quatre saisons et la nuit». L'entrée principale est flanquée de quatre colonnes ioniques et le petit vestibule s'ouvre sur un hall grandiose abritant un somptueux escalier monumental placé dans l'axe de l'entrée qui est coiffée d'une structure de verre ouvragé et de métal, dont on a dit qu'elle aurait influencé l'Opéra de Paris. La maison respecte toutefois l'architecture traditionnelle cubaine avec une grande cour centrale entourée de galeries qui donnent sur les nombreuses chambres. Cette luxueuse demeure fut décorée par la «maison Jansen» de Paris, avec des sols en marbre de Carrare tout comme les murs de la salle à manger, des grilles ouvragées en bronze et fer doré, des antiquités orientales, des porcelaines de Sèvres, de Limoges et de Meißen.

✳ **FACING PAGE AND ABOVE** "The Four Seasons and The Night" garden at the house of Countess Revilla de Camargo with its beautiful marble statues watched over by the slim Cuban royal palm trees. **FOLLOWING DOUBLEPAGE** The elegant and sumptuous double-storey space of the grand hall, with its Carrara marble floors, is decorated with great refinement. The Guéridon table with its inlaid Italian marble top and the Venetian torch holders with figures of Moors date from the 19th century. ✳ **LINKE SEITE UND OBEN** Der Garten des Hauses der Gräfin Revilla de Camargo mit wunderschönen Marmorstatuen zwischen hoch gewachsenen kubanischen Königspalmen. **FOLGENDE DOPPELSEITE** Die elegante, prächtige Eingangshalle erstreckt sich über zwei Geschosshöhen und besitzt einen aufwändig verzierten Boden aus Carrara-Marmor. Der Guéridon-Tisch mit einer Platte mit Intarsien aus italienischem Marmor stammt ebenso aus dem 19. Jahrhundert wie die venezianischen Leuchter mit maurischen Figuren. ✳ **PAGE DE GAUCHE ET CI-DESSUS** Le jardin « Les quatre saisons et la nuit » avec ses belles statues en marbres protégées par de sveltes palmiers royaux de Cuba. **DOUBLE PAGE SUIVANTE** Le somptueux grand hall, avec sa double hauteur sous plafond et ses sols en marbre de Carrare, est décoré avec un grand raffinement. Le guéridon en marqueterie de marbre et les torchères vénitiennes représentant des maures sont du 19e siècle.

❊ **PREVIOUS PAGES** The luxurious imperial staircase made of Carrara marble and surrounded by columns. Its ceiling boasts an iron and glass structure resembling a skylight. **FACING PAGE** The antechamber of the staircase with the Venetian lamps crafted out of kiln-dried wood and polychromed. **RIGHT** "The Hunter's Rest", is one of the four Sèvres biscuit porcelain figures crafted by the Frenchman Bachelier in the 18th century. **BELOW** The walls of the dining room, decorated in 19th century Regency style, are paneled with Italian marble, at the centre is an Aubusson tapestry. **FOLLOWING PAGES** One of the Girándola bronze and rock crystal candelabra in the main salon, which is decorated in rococo style. * One of the Baccarat crystal candelabras alongside the rich Limoges dinnerware on the dining room table. ❊ **VORHERGEHENDE DOPPELSEITE** Die prächtig und aufwändig gestaltete Treppe aus Carrara-Marmor ist von Säulen gesäumt. Über ihr befindet sich ein aus Eisen und Glas gefertigtes Oberlicht. **LINKE SEITE** Blick durch eine der reich dekorierten Türen des Hauptsalons auf den Treppenaufgang und die venezianischen Lampen aus mehrfarbigem Holz mit Sgraffitotechnik. **RECHTS** »Die Ruhe des Jägers« ist eine der vier Figurengruppen, die der Franzose Bachelier im 18. Jahrhundert aus Biskuitporzellan von Sèvres fertigte. **UNTEN** Das Esszimmer ist im Regency-Stil des 19. Jahrhunderts gehalten und an den Wänden mit italienischem Marmor verkleidet; in der Mitte hängt ein Aubusson-Teppich. **FOLGENDE DOPPELSEITE** Ein Kandelaber aus Bronze und Bergkristall aus dem 18. Jahrhundert steht im Hauptsalon, der im Rokokostil eingerichtet ist. * Außerdem ein Kandelaber aus Baccarat-Kristall, umringt vom prachtvollen Limoges-Geschirr auf dem Esszimmertisch. ❊ **DOUBLE PAGE PRECEDENTE** Les colonnes rendent le luxueux escalier impérial en marbre de Carrare plus impressionnant encore. Il est éclairé par une verrière à armature en fer forgé. **PAGE DE GAUCHE** Le grand hall avec ses torchères vénitiennes en bois polychrome stuqué vu à travers une des portes richement décorées du salon principal. **A DROITE** Dans le grand salon, une pièce d'une beauté extraordinaire, « Le Repos du chasseur », faisant partie d'un ensemble de quatre biscuits réalisés pour la manufacture de Sèvres par le Français Bachelier au 18e siècle. **CI-DESSOUS** Dans la salle à manger, décorée dans le style Regency 19e siècle les murs sont tapissés de marbres italiens ; au centre, une tapisserie d'Aubusson. **DOUBLE PAGE SUIVANTE** Un des candélabres en bronze et cristal de roche du 18e siècle faisant partie de la décoration rococo du grand salon. * Sur la table de la salle à manger, un des deux candélabres en cristal de Baccarat entouré d'une belle vaisselle en porcelaine de Limoges.

Casa Baró-Lasa

Love at First Sight.

Catalina Lasa and Juan Pedro Baró fell in love at first sight when they met at a ball; but their love caused a big scandal as they were both married, and divorce did not exist in Cuba. Catalina was the most beautiful woman in Havana – she had won beauty contests in 1902 and 1904 – and Juan Pedro was a rich landowner. Rejected by society, they left for Europe where Juan Pedro arranged for the Pope to annul their previous marriages and the Cuban president to approve a divorce law. They were married in Paris, returned to Havana with presents for those they defied, and invited them to the grand opening of the home Juan Pedro had secretly built as a gift for his new wife. The Italian Renaissance-style villa was designed by Cuban architects Govantes and Cabarrocas, with interiors by the fashionable French designer René Lalique in art deco style with Egyptian details, and gardens by French landscape designer J. C. N. Forestier. The 1927 mansion is noted not only for its elegant proportions, but also for the beauty and luxury of the materials used: French and Italian marbles, Parisian wrought-iron grills, special stucco made with sand from the Nile, and glasswork by Lalique.

Catalina Lasa und Juan Pedro Baró lernten sich auf einem Ball kennen und verliebten sich auf der Stelle. Da beide verheiratet waren, provozierten sie einen Skandal, zumal Scheidung in Kuba undenkbar war. Catalina war die schönste Frau in Havanna – 1902 und 1904 gewann sie Schönheitswettbewerbe – und Juan Pedro war ein reicher Landbesitzer. Das Liebespaar reiste, von der kubanischen Gesellschaft ausgeschlossen, nach Europa. Dort brachte Juan Pedro den Papst dazu, seine erste Ehe und auch die seiner Geliebten zu annulieren, und der kubanische Präsident stimmte einem Scheidungsgesetz zu. Das Paar heiratete in Paris, kehrte vollbepackt mit Geschenken für die, die sie verachtet hatten, nach Havanna zurück und lud zur Einweihungsparty in das Haus, das Juan Pedro heimlich als Geschenk für seine neue Frau hatte bauen lassen. Die Villa im italienischen Renaissance-Stil wurde 1927 von den kubanischen Architekten Govantes und Cabarrocas gebaut, und der französische Designer René Lalique entwarf eine Inneneinrichtung im Art-Déco-Stil mit ägyptischen Anklängen. Den Garten gestaltete der französische Landschaftsarchitekt J. C. N. Forestier. Mit luxuriösen Materialen wie französischem und italienischem Marmor, schmiedeeisernen Gittern aus Paris, Stuck und Wänden aus Nilsand und Glasarbeiten von Lalique hat sich die elegante Villa einen Namen gemacht.

Catalina Lasa et Juan Pedro Baró tombèrent éperdument amoureux dès leur première rencontre dans un bal. Leur liaison fit scandale car ils étaient tous deux mariés et le divorce n'existait pas à Cuba. Catalina était la plus belle femme de la Havane (élue deux fois reine de beauté en 1902 et 1904) et Juan Pedro un riche propriétaire terrien. Rejetés par la société, ils s'enfuirent en Europe où Juan Pedro convainquit le pape d'annuler leurs premières unions et le président cubain d'approuver une loi autorisant le divorce. Ils se marièrent à Paris, rentrèrent à la Havane chargés de présents pour ceux qu'ils défiaient et les invitèrent à la pendaison de crémaillère de la demeure que Juan Pedro avait fait construire en secret pour sa nouvelle épouse. La villa de style renaissance conçue en 1927 par les architectes cubains Govantes et Cabarrocas, décorée par René Lalique dans le style Art Déco avec des détails égyptiens, entourée d'un parc dessiné par le paysagiste français J. C. N. Forestier, est célèbre non seulement pour ses proportions élégantes mais aussi pour la beauté et le luxe des matériaux utilisés : marbres français et italiens, grilles en fer forgé importées de Paris, stuc fabriqué avec du sable du Nil, verreries de Lalique.

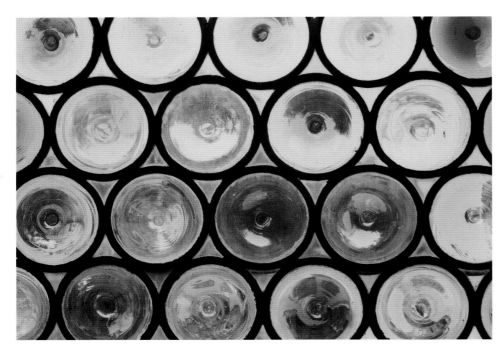

❋ **PREVIOUS DOUBLEPAGE** The beautifully proportioned entrance hall of the Baró-Lasa house evokes the majesty of hypostyle halls, with their Egyptian references. The walls were covered with sand brought over from the River Nile, and the floors with different types of Italian marble. **ABOVE** The stained glass windows that illuminate the staircase were built using the bases of French wine glasses. **BELOW** A colorful canvas protects the space from the afternoon sun and imitates the initials "BL" of the couple that was incorporated in the original grills. The original chandelier hangs from the ceiling. **FACING PAGE** The Palm Room, with its modern iron and glass lamp designed by the famous French designer René Lalique and the trelace structure attached to the walls and vaulted ceiling for climbing plants. ❋ **VORHERGEHENDE DOPPELSEITE** Das wohl proportionierte Vestibül der »Casa Baró-Lasa« erinnert mit seinen ägyptischen Anklängen an die Erhabenheit eines Hypostylons. Seine Wände wurden mit importiertem Nilsand verputzt; der Boden besteht aus verschiedenen italienischen Marmorarten. **OBEN** Das Buntglasfenster an der Treppe wurde aus den Füßen französischer Weingläser gefertigt. **UNTEN** Eine bunte Markise schützt vor der Nachmittagssonne. Darauf prangen die Buchstaben »BL« – es sind die Initialen des Paares, das ursprünglich einen Teil des Original-Eisengeflechts* darstellte. An der Decke hängt der Originalleuchter. **RECHTE SEITE** Das so genannte »Palmenzimmer« besticht durch eine moderne Lampe aus Eisen und Glas nach einem Entwurf des berühmten französischen Designers René Lalique sowie durch das feine Holzlattengerüst, das für Kletterpflanzen an den Wänden und an der Bogendecke befestigt wurde. ❋ **DOUBLE PAGE PRECEDENTE** Le vestibule, avec ses belles proportions et ses références égyptiennes, a la majesté des salles hypostyles. Ses murs sont revêtus d'un enduit réalisé avec du sable du Nil et ses sols sont en différents types de marbre italien. **CI-DESSUS** Le vitrail qui illumine l'escalier a été réalisé avec des pieds de verres à vin français. **CI-DESSOUS** Une toile aux couleurs vives protège l'espace du soleil de l'après-midi et reproduit les initiales « BL » du couple que l'on retrouve également dans les grilles. Au plafond, le lustre d'origine. **PAGE DE DROITE** Le « salon aux palmiers », avec sa suspension moderne en métal et verre dessinée par René Lalique et son treillis en fines baguettes de bois qui recouvre les murs et le plafond voûté.

La Mansión

A Florentine Palace in Havana.

The house, built for the rich businessman Mark A. Pollack, was the swansong both of eclecticism and of its most important practitioner, architect Leonardo Morales. No more would the traditional Cuban courtyard, here majestic and opulent, suggest a Florentine "cortile." Water gushes in the fountain of the extraordinary central patio, surrounded by galleries of imported columns, vaulted ceilings, marble floors and decorated with Catalonian tiles. In the morning the sun strikes the fountain; it becomes a blinding flash of light that changes in intensity throughout the day, and casts different light and shadows on the beautiful arcade. Located in the middle of a huge corner lot in the exclusive old Country Club area, the building, finished in 1930, is surrounded by large gardens. Morales masterfully balances airy terraces and huge windows against the spacious rooms. The double-height main room by the entrance loggia, with its coffered ceilings, is especially beautiful, as is the upstairs studio. The lavish decoration employs the widest choice of rich materials, ranging from precious woods to stained glass. In the end, art conspires with magic to lift the spirits in this refined atmosphere where the muses seem to dwell.

Das Haus, ein Schwanengesang auf den Architekten Leonardo Morales, ein Experte des eklektischen Stils, wurde für den reichen Geschäftsmann Mark A. Pollack gebaut. Der traditionelle kubanische Innenhof, hier majestätisch und opulent, könnte auch ein florentinischer »Cortile« sein. Aus dem Brunnen plätschert das Wasser, rundherum stehen Galerien mit gewölbten Decken und importierten Säulen, die Böden sind aus Marmor, an den Wänden katalanische Kacheln. Am Morgen fällt Sonnenlicht auf den Brunnen und wirft ein Licht- und Schattenspiel auf die Arkaden, das sich je nach Tageszeit verändert. Das Gebäude mitten in einem großen Garten liegt auf einem Eckgelände in der Nähe des exklusiven alten Country Clubs von Havanna und wurde 1930 fertiggestellt. Morales hatte ein außerordentliches Gespür für Proportionen und wusste die luftigen Terrassen mit den großen Fenstern und den großzügigen Räumen untereinander auszubalancieren. Das doppelt hohe Hauptzimmer mit Kassettendecke neben der Eingangshalle ist besonders schön, genau wie das Studio im oberen Stockwerk. Aufwändige Dekorationen aus Edelhölzern, Buntglas und anderen schweren Materialien bringen Kunst und Magie zusammen.

Achevée en 1930 pour le riche homme d'affaires Mark A. Pollack, cette demeure fut le chant du cygne de l'éclectisme et de son principal contributeur, l'architecte Leonardo Morales. Le patio traditionnel cubain, ici majestueux et opulent, n'aurait plus jamais des allures de « cortile » florentin. L'eau gargouille dans la fontaine de cette superbe cour intérieure bordée de galeries soutenues par une colonnade, avec des plafonds voûtés, des sols en marbre et des lambris en carreaux catalans. Le matin, le soleil fait briller le bassin, lançant des éclats aveuglants qui changent d'intensité au fil des heures, projetant des ombres changeantes sur les arcades. Située au milieu d'un immense terrain d'angle dans le quartier chic du Country Club, la maison est entourée de vastes jardins. Morales a su créer un bel équilibre entre les terrasses, les grandes fenêtres et les intérieurs spacieux. La grande salle qui donne sur la loggia de l'entrée, avec ses hauts plafonds à caissons, est particulièrement belle, tout comme l'atelier d'artiste à l'étage. La décoration luxueuse recourt à un large éventail de matériaux, des bois précieux aux vitraux. L'art s'unit à la magie pour engendrer une atmosphère raffinée et exaltante qui semble habitée par les muses.

※ **ABOVE** A lovely wrought-iron grill frames the view of the extraordinary inner courtyard with its columns made of different types of marble imported from several countries. The vast proportions of the courtyard and its painstaking design make it enormously attractive. **RIGHT** The monumental entrance portal with its lovely vaulted ceiling evokes memories of Florentine "palazzos". The columns, which recall the Palladian motif so often employed in the works of Cuban architect Leonardo Morales, frame the views toward the gardens. **FACING PAGE** The terrace that serves as an antechamber to the entrance portal acts as a transition between the gardens and the "loggia" and initiates a spatial sequence traversing the spacious main salon in the house and culminating in the courtyard. **FOLLOWING DOUBLE PAGE** The house's main salon with its high ceilings is exceptional due to its size, its pleasant proportions based on two perfect cubes, and its decoration. The primary and secondary concrete ceiling beams are clad in cedar wood.

※ **OBEN** Ein wunderschönes schmiedeeisernes Gitter rahmt den Blick auf den außergewöhnlichen zentralen Innenhof und seine Säulen aus unterschiedlichen Marmorarten, die aus verschiedenen Ländern importiert wurden. Die riesigen Ausmaße des Innenhofs und seine besondere Gestaltung machen ihn besonders reizvoll. **RECHTS** Das monumentale Eingangsportal mit seiner prächtigen Bogendecke erinnert an einen florentinischen Palast. Der Säulengang erinnert an den häufig von dem kubanischen Architekten Leonardo Morales zitierten Andrea Palladio und lenkt den Blick auf die Gartenanlagen. **RECHTE SEITE** Die Terrasse dient als Vorhalle des Zugangsportals sowie als Übergang zwischen Garten und Loggia. Sie leitet eine Raumfolge ein, die durch den großen Hauptsalon des Hauses führt und in den Innenhof mündet. **FOLGENDE DOPPELSEITE** Der Hauptsalon erstreckt sich über eine doppelte Geschosshöhe und beeindruckt mit seinen Ausmaßen und den harmonischen Proportionen, die auf zwei perfekten Würfeln basieren. Die aus Beton bestehenden Haupt- und Nebenträger der Decke sind mit Zedernholz verkleidet.

※ **CI-DESSUS** Une belle grille en fer forgé s'ouvre sur l'extraordinaire patio central, avec ses différentes colonnes en marbre importées de plusieurs pays. Les vastes proportions du patio et son plan soigné en font un lieu unique. **A DROITE** Le porche monumental avec son beau plafond voûté évoque les palais florentins. La colonnade, un motif d'Andrea Palladio fréquemment utilisé par l'architecte cubain Leonardo Morales, encadre la vue sur les jardins. **PAGE DE DROITE** La terrasse devant le porche de l'entrée assure la transition entre les jardins et la loggia, amorçant une perspective qui culmine avec le patio en passant par le grand salon de la maison. **DOUBLE PAGE SUIVANTE** Le salon principal, avec sa double hauteur sous plafond, est exceptionnel de par ses dimensions, ses proportions agréables basées sur deux cubes parfaits et sa décoration. Les poutres et solives en béton sont revêtues d'un placage en cèdre.

❋ **FACING PAGE** An exquisite vase located in the dining room is visible from the vestibule of the house's carriage entrance. **ABOVE** The master bathroom of the house is clad in Mexican marble. ❋ **LINKE SEITE** Eine prachtvolle Vase steht im Esszimmer, von dem man in die Kutscheneinfahrt des Hauses blickt. **OBEN** Das Hauptbadezimmer des Hauses ist mit mexikanischem Marmor verkleidet. ❋ **PAGE DE GAUCHE** Derrière la belle potiche de la salle à manger, on aperçoit le vestibule donnant sur la porte cochère. **CI-DESSUS** La salle de bains principale avec ses marbres provenant du Mexique.

Hotel Nacional

Where the Rich and Famous –
and the Gangsters – Liked to Stay.

Sunsets are spectacular and unforgettable in Havana, especially if you enjoy them from the luxurious Hotel Nacional. From the moment it opened its doors on the evening of December 30, 1930, it became the place for the international rich and famous: gangsters Meyer Lansky and Charles "Lucky" Luciano, Hollywood stars like Errol Flynn, Frank Sinatra, Ava Gardner and Marlon Brando, and other public figures such as Sir Alexander Fleming, Sir Winston Churchill, and the Duke of Windsor have all stayed here. More recent visitors include Pierre Cardin, Naomi Campbell, and winner of the Nobel Prize for Literature Gabriel García Márquez. The hotel was built on a hill that housed the Santa Clara gun battery; this position allows for superb views of both the Florida Straits and the city. The building was designed by the acclaimed New York firm McKim, Mead & White in an eclectic style that combined details from art deco, neoclassicism, and the architecture of the Spanish revival. It is set back from the street by a palm-tree-lined "alley," which leads to an elegant foyer decorated with Sevillean tiled wainscoting and a coffered ceiling. Doors open onto the large verandah by the gardens. The foyer also connects the various indoor and outdoor restaurants as well as the popular cabaret, where several members of the legendary Buena Vista Social Club perform Cuban music on weekends.

Sonnenuntergänge in Havanna sind ein unvergessliches Erlebnis, besonders wenn man sie vom Luxushotel »Nacional« aus betrachtet. Es wurde am Abend des 30. Dezember 1930 eröffnet und zog gleich eine illustre Klientel an: Errol Flynn, Frank Sinatra, Ava Gardner und Marlon Brando reisten aus Hollywood an. Persönlichkeiten wie Sir Alexander Fleming, Sir Winston Churchill und der Duke of Windsor stiegen hier ab, und sogar Meyer Lansky und Charles »Lucky« Luciano, zwei schwergewichtige amerikanische Mafiosi packten im »Nacional« ihre Koffer aus. Heute heißen die berühmten Gäste Pierre Cardin und Naomi Campbell, auch der Nobelpreisträger für Literatur Gabriel García Márquez gehört dazu. Das Hotel wurde auf dem Hügel gebaut, wo sich früher die Unterkunft der Geschütztruppe von Santa Clara befand. Von hier hat man einen tolle Sicht auf Havanna und die Meeresenge von Florida. Das Gebäude, eine Mischung aus Art Déco, Neoklassizismus und spanischem Revival, wurde von den renommierten New Yorker Architekten McKim, Mead & White entworfen. Über eine Palmenallee wird man ins elegante Foyer mit Kassettendecke und Kacheln aus Sevilla geführt. Das Foyer verbindet die Restaurants innen und im Garten mit dem Kabarett des Hotels, wo an den Wochenenden Mitglieder des legendären Buena Vista Social Clubs auf der Bühne stehen.

Les couchers de soleil de la Havane sont spectaculaires et inoubliables, surtout contemplés depuis le luxueux Hotel Nacional. Dès son inauguration le soir du 30 décembre 1930, il fut adopté par les riches et célèbres : les gangsters Lucky Luciano et Meyer Lansky y côtoyaient les stars de Hollywood – Errol Flynn, Frank Sinatra, Ava Gardner, Marlon Brando – et d'autres personnalités telles que sir Alexander Fleming, sir Winston Churchill ou le duc de Windsor. Plus récemment, ses hôtes illustres ont inclus Pierre Cardin, Naomi Campbell et le lauréat du prix Nobel de littérature Gabriel García Márquez. Construit sur la colline qui abritait la batterie de canons de Santa Clara, l'hôtel jouit de vues imprenables sur le détroit de Floride et la ville. Il fut conçu par le célèbre cabinet d'architectes new-yorkais McKim, Mead & White dans un style éclectique qui conjugue des détails Art Déco, néoclassiques et méditerranéens. Depuis la rue, une allée bordée de palmiers mène à l'élégant hall d'entrée décoré de lambris en carreaux sévillans et d'un plafond à caissons. La large véranda qui donne sur les jardins relie les restaurants intérieur et extérieur ainsi que le fameux cabaret. Plusieurs membres du légendaire Buena Vista Social Club y jouent de la musique cubaine les week-ends.

※ **ABOVE LEFT** The Historical Gallery in the "Hotel Nacional de Cuba" displays a jumble of photographs of many Cuban and foreign celebrities who have visited the hotel since 1930. **LEFT** One of the "classic" automobiles that forms part of the hotel's rental vehicle fleet. **ABOVE** The privileged location of the "Hotel Nacional de Cuba", in a central area of the capital city, provides outstanding views of both the sea and the city. **FOLLOWING PAGES** The main entrance to the hotel's vestibule is framed by colorful wainscoting made of tiles from Seville. * The giant poster behind a scale model of the hotel, features Raúl Capablanca, Fred Astaire, Gary Cooper, Rita Hayworth, Errol Flynn, Robert De Niro, Sara Montiel, Ava Gardner, Nat "King" Cole and Geraldine Chaplin. ※ **OBEN LINKS** Die »Galería Histórica« im »Hotel Nacional de Cuba« vereint Fotos von kubanischen und ausländischen Berühmtheiten, die diese Einrichtung seit ihrer Eröffnung, 1930 besucht haben. **LINKS** Einer der »klassischen« Wagen, die zum Mietfuhrpark des Hotels gehören. **OBEN** Der privilegierte Standort des »Hotel Nacional de Cuba« im Zentrum der Hauptstadt bietet ausgezeichnete Aussichten auf das Meer und die Stadt. **FOLGENDE DOPPELSEITE** Der Haupteingang des Hotels wird von einem großen Sockel aus sevillanischen Fliesen umrahmt. * Hinter einer Nachbildung des Hotels hängt ein großes Plakat, auf dem Raúl Capablanca, Fred Astaire, Gary Cooper, Rita Hayworth, Errol Flynn, Robert De Niro, Sara Montiel, Ava Gardner, Nat »King« Cole und Geraldine Chaplin zu sehen sind. ※ **PAGE DE GAUCHE, EN HAUT** La galerie historique est décorée de nombreuses photographies des célébrités cubaines et étrangères qui ont séjourné dans l'hôtel depuis son inauguration, 1930. **À GAUCHE** Une des automobiles « classiques » faisant partie du parc de véhicules de location de l'hôtel. **CI-DESSUS** Le site privilégié de « l'Hotel Nacional de Cuba », au cœur de la capitale, offre d'excellentes vues sur la mer et la ville. **DOUBLE PAGE SUIVANTE** L'entrée principale est bordée d'une grande frise en azulejos sévillans. * Sur l'affiche géante derrière une maquette de l'hôtel, on reconnaît Raúl Capablanca, Fred Astaire, Gary Cooper, Rita Hayworth, Errol Flynn, Robert de Niro, Sara Montiel, Ava Gardner, Nat « King » Cole et Géraldine Chaplin.

※ **ABOVE LEFT** In the vestibule near the entrance, the reception desk of the "Hotel Nacional de Cuba" with its wood counter clad in tiles from Seville. **LEFT** Another huge poster in the hotel's Historical Gallery displays yet another group of famous personalities: Buster Keaton, Tom Mix, Rita Montaner, Johnny Weissmuller, Ernesto Lecuona, Jack Dempsey, the Dukes of Windsor, and the mobsters Meyer Lansky and Charles "Lucky" Luciano. **ABOVE** The lovely, welcoming vestibule of the "Hotel Nacional de Cuba" with its beautiful wainscoting made of ceramic tiles from Seville and its ceiling with decorative wooden beams. In the background, the Cabaret Parisién, where some members of the Buena Vista Social Club perform. ※ **OBEN LINKS** Im Vestibül befindet sich in der Nähe des Eingangs die Rezeption des »Hotel Nacional de Cuba« mit einem Tresen aus Holz und sevillanischen Fliesen. **LINKS** Ein anderes großes Plakat der »Galería Histórica« zeigt eine weitere Gruppe von Berühmtheiten: Buster Keaton, Tom Mix, Rita Montaner, Johnny Weissmuller, Ernesto Lecuona, Jack Dempsey, die Herzoge von Windsor sowie die Mafiosi Meyer Lansky und Charles »Lucky« Luciano. **OBEN** Der prachtvolle, einladende Eingangsbereich des »Hotel Nacional de Cuba« mit seinen wunderschönen Sockeln aus sevillanischen Fliesen und der mit Holzbalken dekorierten Decke. Im Hintergrund sieht man das »Cabaret Parisién«, in dem Mitglieder des Buena Vista Social Club auftreten. ※ **PAGE DE GAUCHE, EN HAUT** Dans le hall, près de la porte d'entrée, la réception avec son comptoir en bois tapissé d'azulejos sévillans. **A GAUCHE** Un seconde grande affiche dans la galerie historique présente un autre groupe de célébrités : Buster Keaton, Tom Mix, Rita Montaner, Johnny Weissmuller, Ernesto Lecuona, Jack Dempsey, le duc et la duchesse de Windsor, les gangsters Meyer Lansky et Charles « Lucky » Luciano. **CI-DESSUS** Beau et chaleureux, le grand hall avec ses hautes frises en azulejos sévillans et son toit en poutres décorées. Au fond, le Cabaret parisien, où se produisent quelques-uns des musiciens du Buena Vista Social Club.

CLUB Náutico

An Oversized, Manmade Crustacean.

Both the shady interior and the bright exterior of the "Club Náutico" merge in this unusual organic form. Inside, you have the impression of being in a large, manmade crustacean; when looking at the colorful structure from the sea, the huge, undulating vaults make an explicit reference to the ocean waves as well as to underwater creatures. The seductive atmosphere achieved inside the building – the sense of openness and airiness, the interesting play of light, shadows, and reflections, and the telescopic effect of forced perspective towards both the sea and the entrance – was produced by tilting the central section of the thin vaulted shells upwards, which also allows natural light in from the skylights above. This intriguing and unique space was designed in 1953 by Cuban architect Max Borges Recio, who used the same idea in his successful project for the award-winning cabaret "Tropicana" two years earlier. In both of his masterpieces he accomplished great formal clarity by integrating simple natural forms with natural light. This original use of reinforced concrete vaults made it feasible to shelter large crowds of people dancing and relaxing in the tropical ambience.

Schatten und Licht verbinden sich im »Club Náutico« zu einem ungewöhnlichen, organischen Gebilde. Im Innern fühlt man sich wie in einem riesigen Schalentier. Das Gebäude erinnert in seiner Form an die Wellen des Ozeans und an irgendwelche Unterwasserwesen. Die dünnen, gewölbten Schalen des Daches wurden so ausgerichtet, dass der mittlere Teil nach oben ragt. Damit wird ein großzügiger und luftiger Effekt erzielt, der das interessante Spiel von Licht, Schatten und Reflexionen sowie die Perspektive zum Meer und zum Eingang hin verstärkt. Gleichzeitig kann das Sonnenlicht durch die Oberlichter ins Innere dringen. Dieses einzigartige, faszinierende Gebäude wurde vom kubanischen Architekten Max Borges Recio. 1953 entworfen, der bereits zwei Jahre zuvor die gleiche Idee bei dem preisgekrönten Kabarett »Tropicana« umgesetzt hatte. Die beiden Meisterwerke bestechen durch die formale Klarheit, die durch das Zusammenspiel von einfachen, organischen Formen und Sonnenlicht entsteht. Unter den verstärkten Betongewölben kann man in tropischem Ambiente tanzen und entspannen.

La forme organique originale du «Club Náutico» fait fusionner la fraîcheur des intérieurs et le soleil des terrasses. Dedans, on se croirait dans un grand crustacé modelé par la main de l'homme. Quand on regarde l'étrange bâtiment depuis la mer, ses immenses voûtes ondoyantes renvoient explicitement aux vagues de l'océan et à ses créatures sous-marines. La belle atmosphère qui règne à l'intérieur – l'impression d'ouverture et d'air, les intéressants jeux de lumière, d'ombres et de reflets, l'effet télescopique de la perspective vers la mer et l'entrée – est renforcée par la surélévation de la coque centrale, laissant la lumière s'engouffrer par de grandes verrières. Cet espace intrigant et unique a été conçu en 1953 par l'architecte cubain Max Borges Recio., qui a réutilisé l'idée de son projet pour le cabaret «Tropicana», primé deux ans plus tôt. Ses deux chefs-d'œuvre sont d'une grande clarté formelle, leurs lignes simples et fluides épousant la lumière naturelle. Le recours original aux voûtes en béton armé permet de créer des espaces capables d'accueillir de grandes foules venues danser ou se détendre dans une ambiance tropicale.

✳ **ABOVE LEFT** The enlargement of the "Club Náutico" building, designed in 1953 by the Cuban architect Max Borges Recio who took care to create covered areas near the little beach that would hold a maximum number of people with a minimum number of architectural supports. **LEFT** Fiberglass chairs in one of the salons at the Club Náutico. The background mural depicts several colonial architectural monuments in Old Havana. **ABOVE** The sensual curves of the vast roof allude to the movement of the waves in the sea. **FOLLOWING DOUBLEPAGE** The interior space is open and transparent, with an interesting play of light, shadow and reflection. ✳ **OBEN LINKS** Der Anbau des Gebäudes, in dem sich der »Club Náutico« befindet, wurde 1953 von dem kubanischen Architekten Max Borges Recio entworfen und beinhaltete große überdachte Bereiche in der Nähe des kleinen Strands, um mit wenigen Mitteln eine große Personenzahl aufnehmen zu können. **LINKS** Glasfaserstühle in einem der Aufenthaltsräume des »Club Náutico«. Das Wandbild im Hintergrund zeigt verschiedene Kolonialbauten des Viertels »Habana Vieja«. **OBEN** Die sinnlichen Kurven des großen Dachs sind eine Anspielung auf die Wellen des Meers. **FOLGENDE DOPPELSEITE** Der Innenraum ist offen und transparent und bietet ein interessantes Spiel von Lichtern, Schatten und Spiegelungen. ✳ **PAGE DE GAUCHE, EN HAUT** L'extension du club nautique, construite en 1953 par l'architecte cubain Max Borges Recio inclut des zones couvertes proches de la petite plage et capables d'accueillir un grand nombre de personnes avec le minimum de moyens. **À GAUCHE** Des sièges en fibres de verre dans un des salons du club. La fresque du fond représente divers monuments coloniaux de la Vieille Havane. **CI-DESSUS** Les courbes sensuelles du grand toit évoquent le mouvement des vagues. **DOUBLE PAGE SUIVANTE** L'espace intérieur est ouvert et transparent, avec un intéressant jeu de lumières, d'ombres et de reflets.

✳ **TOP** The overhang of the undulating roof serves as an entrance marquee to the "Club Náutico" from both the street and the beach, where the building resembles a large crustacean.
BELOW The reinforced concrete vaults are characteristic of the enlargement undertaken by the architect Borges, in contrast to the rectilinear lines of the pre-existing building, although attempts were made to integrate both parts through the use of color. **FOLLOWING DOUBLEPAGE** The attractive marine landscape invades the premises of the "Club Náutico": a symphony of blues begins with the immensity of the sea and extends throughout the building. ✳ **OBEN** Die Auskragung des Wellendachs dient als Vordach des Eingang zum »Club Náutico« – sowohl an der Straße als auch am Sandstrand, von wo das Gebäude wie ein großes Krustentier wirkt. **UNTEN** Die Gewölbe aus Stahlbeton kennzeichnen den Ausbau durch den Architekten Borges. Dieser bildet einen Kontrast zur geradlinigen Gestaltung des bestehenden ursprünglichen Gebäudes, wenngleich mit der Farbgebung eine harmonische Verbindung beider

Elemente angestrebt wurde. **FOLGENDE DOPPELSEITE** Die reizvolle Wasserlandschaft verschmilzt mit der Architektur des »Club Náutico«: Eine Symphonie von Blautönen beginnt in der Weite des Meeres und wird mit dem Gebäude fortgesetzt. ❋ **EN HAUT** La corniche ondoyante du toit forme un auvent au-dessus de l'entrée, tant côté rue que côté plage, donnant à la structure l'allure d'un grand crustacé. **EN BAS** Les voûtes en béton armé de l'extension réalisée par Borges contrastent avec les lignes droites du bâtiment initial, même si, dans les deux cas, on a tenté d'harmoniser l'ensemble à l'aide des couleurs. **DOUBLE PAGE SUIVANTE** Le beau paysage marin s'immisce jusque dans le club nautique. La symphonie de bleus commence avec l'immensité de la mer et se prolonge dans l'édifice.

※ **TOP AND BOTTOM** The wooden beach chairs are lined up along the narrow wharf and in two rows at the game areas in order to enjoy the views of the sea. ※ **OBEN UND UNTEN** Die bunten hölzernen Strandstühle stehen aufgereiht entlang einer schmalen Mole und der Flure in den Spielbereichen, damit der Besucher den Meerblick genießen kann. ※ **EN HAUT ET EN BAS** Des fauteuils de plage en bois alignés le long d'un quai étroit et dans les allées de l'aire de jeux pour mieux profiter de la vue sur la mer.

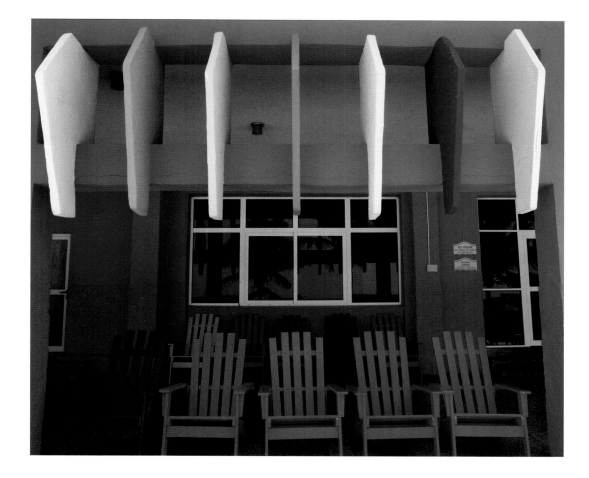

❈ **FOLLOWING DOUBLEPAGE** The fascinating interior atmosphere of the building benefits from the light and color of the natural setting which was assimilated by elevating the ceiling vaults.
❈ **FOLGENDE DOPPELSEITE** Das faszinierende Ambiente im Innern des Gebäudes nutzt das Licht und die Farben der umliegenden Naturlandschaft, die dank der Höhenverschiebung der Gewölbe eingefangen werden. ❈ **DOUBLE PAGE SUIANTE** La fascinante atmosphère à l'intérieur du bâtiment, où la lumière et les couleurs du milieu naturel se confondent avec l'exhausse-ment des voûtes du plafond.

HOTEL HABANA RIVIERA

The Empire of the Mafia in Cuba.

The history of the "Hotel Habana Riviera" is intertwined with the presence of the US mafia in Cuba. Mobster Meyer Lansky – sometimes seen driving his cream-color Chevrolet convertible along the Malecón – was in charge of a powerful empire in the glamorous Havana of the 1950s. The first plans for the hotel were drawn up by New York architect Philip Johnson, who traveled from the US to present his design to the developers; the meeting went well until Johnson felt offended by one of the gangster's suggestions to include an overhead mural depicting gambling dice. Johnson withdrew, saying, "Gentlemen, let's not be vulgar." This disagreement with the investors at their first meeting made them hire the Miami firm of Polevitzky, Johnson and Associates, who freely borrowed from Morris Lapidus's "too much is never enough" ideology and spread it throughout the building. They even included an iconic "staircase leading nowhere," which Lapidus used in his Fontainebleau Hotel in Miami Beach. From the time it was built in 1957, the Riviera became one of the symbols of modern architecture in Havana, a landmark in the city thanks to its prominent 20-storey tower, the colorful ceramic-clad dome covering the casino, and its prime corner site close to the ocean.

Die Geschichte des »Hotel Habana Riviera« ist eng mit der der amerikanischen Mafia in Kuba verbunden. Meyer Lansky war der Boss eines mächtigen Mafia-Imperiums, und im eleganten Havanna der 1950er pflegte er mit einem cremefarbenen Chevrolet am Malecón entlang zu fahren. Die ersten Pläne für das Hotel stammten vom New Yorker Architekten Philip Johnson, der aus den USA anreiste, um sie den Bauherrn zu präsentieren. Alles lief gut, bis einer der Gangster vorschlug, ein Wandbild mit einem Spielwürfelmotiv zu gestalten. Johnson zog sich mit den Worten »Gentlemen, seien wir nicht vulgär« aus dem Projekt zurück. Daraufhin wurden die Architekten Polevitzky, Johnson and Associates aus Miami für den Bau des Hotels engagiert, die hemmungslos den Leitspruch »auch zu viel ist nie genug« des exzentrischen Architekten Morris Lapidus, der in den 1950ern den Hotelstil in Miami Beach prägte, im ganzen Gebäude umsetzten. Sie bauten eine Kopie von Lapidus' »Treppenhaus, das nirgends hinführt«, das er für das »Fontainebleau Hotel« in Miami Beach plante. Das »Riviera« wurde seit der Erstellung 1957 zu einem Wahrzeichen der modernen Architektur in Havanna. Das Hotel mit einem zwanzigstöckigen Turm, einem mit Kacheln verkleideten Dom über dem Kasino und der Lage am Ozean ist eine Sehenswürdigkeit geworden.

L'histoire de l'« Hôtel Habana Riviera » est indissociable de celle de la pègre nord-américaine à Cuba. Dans les années 1950, le gangster Meyer Lansky, que l'on voyait parfois remonter le Malecón au volant de sa Chevrolet décapotable beige, était à la tête d'un puissant empire à la Havane. L'architecte new-yorkais Philip Johnson dessina les premiers plans de l'hôtel et vint sur place présenter son projet aux promoteurs. La réunion tourna court quand un des gangsters suggéra de peindre au plafond une fresque représentant des dés. Offensé, Johnson se retira en déclarant : « Messieurs, ne sombrons pas dans la vulgarité. » Les investisseurs firent ensuite appel au cabinet de Miami, Polevitsky, Johnson and Associates, qui adopta la devise de Morris Lapidus « trop n'est jamais assez » et l'appliqua dans tout le bâtiment. Il reprit même l'idée de « l'escalier menant nulle part » que Lapidus, qui a marqué de son empreinte l'architecture hôtelière à Miami au cours des années 1950, avait conçu pour l'hôtel Fontainebleau de Miami. Depuis sa construction en 1957, le Riviera est devenu un des symboles de l'architecture moderne de la Havane, un véritable monument avec sa tour de vingt étages, le dôme en céramiques de son casino et son site privilégié au bord de l'océan.

❋ **PREVIOUS DOUBLE PAGE** All 368 rooms at the "Hotel Habana Riviera" have views of the sea thanks to its exceptional city location next to Havana's Malecón. **ABOVE** A great deal of the Cuban capital can be glimpsed from the hotel. **RIGHT** The entrance to the hotel is accentuated by clusters of sculptures and fountains by the Cuban sculptor Florencio Gelabert. The wall's cement slabs are reminiscent of the façades of some of the California houses designed by the U.S. architect Frank Lloyd Wright. **FACING PAGE** The orientation of the hotel's west façade provides views of both the sea and the swimming pool.

❋ **VORHERGEHENDE DOPPELSEITE** Alle 368 Zimmer des »Hotel Habana Riviera« bieten dank des einzigartigen Standorts an Havannas Kai eine Aussicht aufs Meer. **OBEN** Vom Hotel aus überblickt man einen Großteil der kubanischen Hauptstadt. **RECHTS** Der Hoteleingang ist mit Skulpturgruppen und Brunnen des kubanischen Bildhauers Florencio Gelabert versehen. Die Betontfliesen der Mauer erinnern an die der Fassaden einiger kalifornische Bauten des Architekten Frank Lloyd Wright. **RECHTE SEITE** Die Westfassade des Hotels ist so ausgerichtet, dass man von dort einen Blick aufs Meer und auf den Swimmingpool hat.

❋ **DOUBLE PAGE PRECEDENTE** Grâce à l'emplacement exceptionnel de l'hôtel sur le boulevard qui longe la côte, ses 368 chambres ont une vue sur la mer. **CI-DESSUS** L'entrée de l'hôtel, avec un groupe de sculptures et de fontaines du sculpteur cubain Florencio Gelabert. **A DROITE** Les dalles en ciment du mur rappellent celles de certaines façades de maisons californiennes dessinées par l'architecte Frank Lloyd Wright. **PAGE DE DROITE** La façade ouest de l'hôtel est orientée de sorte à avoir une vue sur la mer et la piscine.

※ **PREVIOUS DOUBLE PAGE** A curious chime called "La Religión del Palo", the work of artist Rolando López Dirube, re-creates features of Cuban religious syncretism and is integrated into the lovely staircase made of solid terrazzo that closes the visual perspective of the elongated lobby. **BELOW** Circulation from both the hotel's entrances converges at the cut-off staircase which only leads to the basement. The design of the lovely marble floor in the vestibule resembles a rug. ※ **VORHERGEHENDE DOPPELSEITE** Eine sonderbares Mobile mit dem Titel »La Religión del Palo«, Werk des Künstlers Rolando López Dirube, zeigt Aspekte des kubanischen religiösen Synkretismus. Sie ist in die schöne Terrazzotreppe integriert, welche die Perspektive des länglichen Vestibüls abrundet. **UNTEN** Die Wege beider Hoteleingänge laufen an einer Stelle zusammen, an der sich die spiralförmige Treppe befindet, über die man aber lediglich in den Keller gelangt. Das Muster des wunderschönen Marmorbodens im Vestibül ähnelt einem Teppich. ※ **DOUBLE PAGE PRÉCÉDENTE** Un étrange mobile baptisé « La Religion du Palo », œuvre de l'artiste cubain Rolando López Dirube qui reprend des aspects du syncrétisme cubain, orne le bel escalier en granit qui ferme la perspective du grand hall. **CI-DESSOUS** Les deux entrées de l'hôtel convergent vers ce hall où se trouve l'escalier spiralé qui ne mène qu'au sous-sol. Les motifs du beau dallage de marbre rappellent un tapis.

❋ **BELOW** The reception area of the "Hotel Habana Rivier" a has lower ceilings than the rest of the vestibule and is decorated with geometrical motifs. On the back wall, three different clocks display the time in different time zones. **FOLLOWING DOUBLE PAGES** The work entitled "Ritmo Cubano" by Cuban sculptor Florencio Gelabert, wrought in bronze, occupies a pre-eminent place in the decoration of the vestibule of the "Hotel Habana Riviera". * The staircase leading nowhere becomes a sculpture in the vestibule and is part of the spread of kitsch forms derived from the influence of works by U.S. architect Morris Lapidus. * The mural relief at the entrance to the former casino, created by the Cuban artist Rolando López Dirube, portrays mythical religious symbols of the secret society, "Abakuá", founded in Cuba in 1836 by the Black African Carabalis. ❋ **UNTEN** Der Rezeptionsbereich des »Hotel Habana Riviera« besitzt eine niedrigere Decke als das übrige Vestibül und ist mit geometrischen Motiven dekoriert. An der Rückwand zeigen drei verschiedene Uhren die Zeiten unterschiedlicher Längengrade an. **FOLGENDE DOPPELSEITEN** Das aus Bronze gefertigte Werk »Ritmo Cubano« des kubanischen Bildhauers Florencio Gelabert besitzt einen Ehrenplatz in der Lobby des »Hotel Habana Riviera«. * Das »Treppenhaus, das nirgends hinführt«, wirkt wie eine Skulptur im Vestibül und ist Teil der weitverbreiteten Kitsch-Sprache, die dem Einfluss der Architekten Morris Lapidus zuzuschreiben sind. * Das Wandrelief im Eingangsbereich des alten Kasinos stammt von dem kubanischen Künstler Rolando López Dirube und zeigt Symbole der religiösen Riten der Geheimgesellschaft »Abakuá«, die Schwarzafrikaner aus Carabalis 1836 in Kuba gründeten. ❋ **CI-DESSOUS** Le comptoir de réception de l'hôtel se distingue par son plafond plus bas et sa moquette. Cette partie est décorée de motifs géométriques. Sur le mur du fond, trois horloges donnent l'heure sous différentes latitudes. **DOUBLES PAGES SUIVANTES** Rythme cubain, une œuvre en bronze du sculpteur Florencio Gelabert, occupe une place de choix dans le hall de l'hôtel * Dans le hall, l'escalier qui ne mène nulle part devient une sculpture, s'intégrant dans l'ensemble de formes kitsch inspirées de l'œuvre de l'architecte américain Morris Lapidus. * La peinture murale qui orne l'entrée de l'ancien casino, réalisée par l'artiste cubain Rolando López Dirube, représente des symboles propres aux mythes religieux de la société secrète « Abakuá », fondée par les Africains des Caraïbes à Cuba en 1836.

❈ **ABOVE** The walls of the swimming pool's café are decorated with marine motifs. **FACING PAGE** The "L'Aiglon" restaurant conserves the original design of its lamps, furnishings and mural decorations. The Spanish artist Hipólito Hidalgo de Caviedes blends scenes from Spanish theater with others from Cuban Mardi Gras in the mural on the back wall.
❈ **OBEN** Die Wanddekoration im Schwimmbadcafé besteht aus bunten Meeresmotiven. **RECHTS** Im Restaurant »L'Aiglon« sind die ursprünglichen Lampen, Möbel und Wanddekoration erhalten geblieben. In dem Wandgemälde kombinierte der spanische Künstler Hipólito Hidalgo de Caviedes Szenen des spanischen Theaters mit anderen des kubanischen Karnevals. ❈ **CI-DESSUS** Les peintures murales de la cafétéria de la piscine sont basées sur des thèmes marins. **PAGE DE DROITE** Le restaurant « L'Aiglon » conserve ses lampes, son mobilier et ses décorations murales d'origine. Sur la fresque du fond, l'artiste espagnol Hipólito Hidalgo de Caviedes a marié le théâtre espagnol et le carnaval cubain.

Pérez Farfante

The Three Ps.

Patios, porticoes and "persiennes" are the three major features of Cuba's architectural legacy, and the most suitable means of dealing with its tropical climate and idiosyncratic, extroverted way of life. In the 1950s these elements were creatively reinterpreted by Cuban architects. Frank Martínez achieved a synthesis between the international avant garde and Cuban tradition in creating an original, contemporary architectural language: his design for the Pérez Farfante family in Nuevo Vedado in 1955 successfully combined Corbusian syntax with traditional Cuban architecture. The clever layout separates the prismatic structure on stilts into two separate housing blocks by means of a central soaring space. The open ground floor becomes an extended porch set upon a clifftop. The floor-to-ceiling carpentry, which includes both louvers and panes of glass, reasserts the lines of the windows, which provide cross-ventilation as well as natural light. The two apartments are identical, with terrazzo floors, exposed concrete blocks and wood paneling to display works of art by contemporary Cuban artists such as Amelia Peláez. Martínez's approach to segregating the living spaces from the bedrooms by using traditional features shows that form *can* follow function, and it can also reaffirm cultural identity.

Die wichtigsten Merkmale der tradtionellen kubanischen Architektur sind die Innenhöfe, Säulengänge und Jalousien. Sie passen zum tropischen Klima und extrovertierten Lebenstil der Kubaner. In den 1950ern interpretieren Architekten diese Elemente neu. Frank Martínez' Synthese zwischen internationaler Avantgarde und kubanischer Tradition brachte eine originelle, zeitgemäße Architektursprache hervor. Sein Entwurf für das Haus der Familie Pérez Farfante in Nuevo Vedado von 1955 ist eine gelungene Synthese zwischen der Formensprache Le Corbusiers und traditioneller kubanischer Architektur. Das prismatische Gebäude steht auf Stelzen und wird von einem hohen Raum in der Mitte in zwei verschiedene Wohnblöcke getrennt. Das offene Erdgeschoss erweitert sich zu einer Veranda, die auf einem Felsen liegt. Deckenhohe Holzverkleidungen, Fensterwände mit integrierten Lamellenjalousien verleihen den Räumen Struktur. Beide Wohnblöcke sind identisch: Böden aus Terrazzo, Wände aus unbehandelten Betonblöcken und Holzpaneelen mit Kunstwerken zeitgenössischer kubanischer Künstler wie Amelia Peláez. Martínez' Werk zeigt, dass Form der Funktion folgen kann, ohne damit die kulturelle Identität zu verleugnen.

Patios, portiques et persiennes sont les trois grandes caractéristiques des vieilles maisons cubaines, étant parfaitement adaptées à son climat tropical et à son style de vie extraverti. Dans les années 50, ces éléments ont été réinterprétés par des architectes cubains. Frank Martínez a synthétisé l'avant-garde internationale et la tradition cubaine en créant un langage original et contemporain : la demeure qu'il a conçue pour les Pérez Farfante à Nuevo Vedado en 1955 marie avec succès la syntaxe le-corbusienne et l'architecture cubaine traditionnelle. Son plan ingénieux divise la structure sur pilotis en deux corps de bâtiments à l'aide d'un puits central. La charpenterie s'étend du sol au plafond, les persiennes et les baies vitrées soulignant la ligne de fenêtres tout en laissant passer l'air et la lumière naturelle. Les deux appartements jumeaux ont des sols en mosaïque, des murs de béton brut et des boiseries où sont accrochées des œuvres d'artistes cubain contemporains tels qu'Amelia Peláez. La séparation des espaces de séjour des chambres à coucher à l'aide d'éléments traditionnels prouve que la forme peut épouser la fonction tout en réaffirmant l'identité culturelle.

※ **ABOVE** A central space, which evokes the courtyard found in traditional architecture, functionally, spatially and volumetrically separates the bedroom block from the other one containing the living and dining rooms. The building is supported on stilts, following Corbusian postulates. **RIGHT AND FACING PAGE** The simple, minimalist conception of the tubular steel staircase with wooden steps, suspended from the mezzanine level, reinforces the building's transparency while leaving views of the landscape unhampered.

※ **OBEN** Ein zentraler Raum, der an den Innenhof der traditionellen Architektur erinnert, trennt den Schlafzimmerblock funktional, räumlich und volumetrisch von dem Bereich mit Wohn- und Esszimmer. Das Gebäude steht – den Postulaten des Architekten Le Corbusiers folgend – auf Stelzen. **RECHTS UND RECHTE SEITE** Das minimalistische Konzept der im Zwischengeschoss befestigten Treppe aus Stahlrohr und Holzstufen verstärkt die Transparenz des Gebäudes und gibt den Blick auf die Landschaft frei. ※ **CI-DESSUS** Un espace central évoquant le patio traditionnel sépare le bloc des chambres à coucher de celui du séjour et de la salle à manger. L'édifice repose sur des pilotis suivant les principes de Le Corbusier. **A DROITE ET PAGE DE DROITE** La conception simple et minimaliste de l'escalier tubulaire en acier avec des marches en bois, partant de l'entresol, renforce la transparence du bâtiment sans couper la vue sur le paysage.

❋ **LEFT AND ABOVE** The spatial fluidity and integration of the different spaces, which may be opened and closed at will, are some of the most outstanding features of the modern concept of what a building should be. ❋ **LINKE SEITE UND OBEN** Der Raumfluss und das Ineinanderübergehen unterschiedlicher Wohnbereiche, die ganz nach Belieben geöffnet oder abgetrennt werden können, sind einige der herausragenden Eigenschaften dieses modernen Gebäudekonzepts. ❋ **PAGE DE GAUCHE ET CI-DESSUS** La fluidité spatiale et l'intégration des différents espaces qui peuvent s'ouvrir et se fermer à volonté font partie des caractéristiques les plus frappantes de cette architecture moderne.

※ **FACING PAGE** The study is illuminated by the large floor-to-ceiling windows. **RIGHT** One of the terraces with a gallery-type ceiling over the central entrance space that divides the building's two functional blocks. **BELOW** The living room and dining room areas are integrated into a single space near the kitchen. ※ **LINKE SEITE** Das Arbeitszimmer der Appartements erhält sein Licht durch die großen Fenster, die sich vom Boden bis zur Decke erstrecken. **RECHTS** Eine der überdachten, galerieähnlichen Terrassen über dem zentralen Eingangsbereich, der die Funktionsblöcke des Gebäude unterteilt. **UNTEN** Wohn- und Esszimmer gehen ineinander über und befinden sich in der Nähe der Küche. ※ **PAGE DE GAUCHE** Le bureau, éclairé par de grandes fenêtres qui vont du sol au plafond. **A DROITE** Une des terrasses couvertes telle une galerie au-dessus de l'entrée centrale qui divise les blocs fonctionnels du bâtiment. **CI-DESSOUS** Le séjour et la salle à manger sont intégrés dans un même espace jouxtant la cuisine.

CASA DE SCHULTHESS

A Richard Neutra House in the Tropics.

When young architect Richard Neutra wrote in his diary in 1919 that he wished he could get to an idyllic tropical island, he hardly imagined that 35 years later he would design an award-winning house in Cuba for Swiss banker Alfred de Schulthess. Located on a huge site in the most exclusive suburb of the city, the house is today the residence of the Swiss Ambassador and is one of the best modern houses to have been built in Havana. It is a straight-edged, C-shaped house in a park-like setting, with steps down to a garden designed by Brazilian landscape designer Roberto Burle Marx. A pool mirrors the magical deep blue sky. The elongated two-storey block contains living spaces that open onto terraces sheltered by porches, which emphasize the horizontal aspect of the building and visually connect the interior with the exterior. The most spectacular feature is the home's interior, which confirms Neutra's mastery of light and space. The ground floor is a single spacious hall with extensive glass surfaces that convey a complete sense of openness and transparency. The varying ceiling heights, textures from different materials, and the hanging staircase that connects both levels give an extraordinary spatial richness to this great example of modern architecture.

Er war ein junger Architekt, als Richard Neutra 1919 in sein Tagebuch schrieb, er wünschte sich, auf eine tropische, idyllische Insel reisen zu können. Damals konnte er noch nicht ahnen, dass er 35 Jahre später in Kuba ein Haus für den Schweizer Bankier Alfred de Schulthess bauen würde. Die heutige Residenz des Schweizer Botschafters liegt auf einem riesigen Gelände im nobelsten Vorstadtviertel und ist eines der schönsten modernen Häuser, das in Havanna je gebaut wurden. Das Haus in der parkähnlichen Anlage hat die Form eines eckigen »C«, und ein paar Stufen führen hinunter in den Garten, der vom brasilianischen Landschaftsarchitekten Roberto Burle Marx entworfen wurde. Im Pool spiegelt sich das Dunkelblau des Himmels wider. Die Wohnräume des in die Länge gezogenen zweistöckigen Blocks öffnen sich auf Terrassen, die von kragenden Vordächern bedeckt sind. Dadurch verschmelzen Innen und Außen optisch zu einer Einheit. Die Inneneinrichtung zeugt von Neutras meisterhaftem Umgang mit Licht und Raum. Das Erdgeschoss besteht aus einem einzigen, offenen Raum mit großflächigen Fensterwänden. Verschieden hohe Decken, eine Vielfalt an Materialien und die hängende Treppe, die beide Stockwerke untereinander verbindet, verleihen diesem preisgekrönten modernen Haus räumliche Fülle.

Quand, en 1919, le jeune architecte Richard Neutra écrivit dans son journal qu'il rêvait d'une île tropicale idyllique il n'imaginait pas que, 35 ans plus tard, il serait primé pour sa villa construite à Cuba pour le banquier suisse Alfred de Schulthess. Située dans une banlieue sélecte de la ville, la résidence de l'ambassadeur suisse est l'une des plus belles maisons modernes de la Havane. Tout en lignes droites, la structure en U se dresse au milieu d'un parc et quelques marches mènent au jardin dessiné par le paysagiste brésilien Roberto Burle Marx. Une piscine reflète le ciel d'un bleu magique. Le corps de bâtiment d'un étage comporte des espaces de séjour s'ouvrant sur des terrasses protégées d'auvents en console, ce qui renforce l'horizontalité du bâtiment et relie visuellement l'intérieur et l'extérieur. L'intérieur est particulièrement spectaculaire, confirmant la maîtrise de la lumière et de l'espace de Neutra. Le rez-de-chaussée n'est qu'un grand espace dont les nombreuses surfaces en verre donnent une impression d'ouverture et de transparence. Les différentes hauteurs sous plafond, le mélange de matériaux et l'escalier suspendu confèrent une richesse spatiale extraordinaire à ce superbe exemple d'architecture moderne.

❊ **ABOVE LEFT** The well-tended garden at the entrance to the house, designed by the Brazilian landscape architect Roberto Burle Marx, encroaches into the guest area, protected by a curved stone wall. **LEFT** The curved lines of the metallic spiral staircase leading to the roof terrace contrasts with the building's straight lines. **ABOVE** View of the spacious terraces at the de Schulthess residence, Gold Medal winner from the National Architects' Association in 1958. **FOLLOWING DOUBLE PAGE** The main façade, made up of terraces with floor-to-ceiling glass walls, is oriented toward the house's gardens, the pond and the swimming pool. The geometrical flower beds contrast with the sinuousness of the general lines of the gardens.

❊ **OBEN LINKS** Der vom brasilianischen Landschaftsarchitekten Roberto Burle Marx entworfene Garten im Eingangsbereich dringt bis zum Gästebereich vor, der durch eine gekrümmte Steinmauer geschützt ist. **LINKS** Die metallene Wendeltreppe führt zur Sonnen- und Dachterrasse und bildet einen Kontrast zur Geradlinigkeit des Gebäudes. **OBEN** Die ausgedehnten Terrassen des Wohnhauses von de Schulthess, das im Jahr 1958 die Goldmedaille der Nationalen Architektenkammer erhielt, spiegeln sich im Swimmingpool des von erlesenen Grünanlagen umgebenen Gebäudes. **FOLGENDE DOPPELSEITE** Die Hauptfassade besteht aus Terrassen mit vom Boden bis zur Decke reichenden Glasfronten, mit Blick auf die Gärten, den Teich und den Swimmingpool. Die geometrischen Blumenbeete stehen im Kontrast zur allgemein bogenförmig gehaltenen Gartenanlage. ❊ **PAGE DE GAUCHE, EN HAUT** Le jardin soigné devant la maison, dessiné par l'architecte paysagiste brésilien Roberto Burle Marx, s'avance dans l'aile des invités, protégée par un mur arrondi. **A GAUCHE** Les courbes de l'escalier métallique en colimaçon qui mène au solarium et à la terrasse sur le toit contrastent avec les lignes droites du bâtiment. **CI-DESSUS** Les vastes terrasses de la résidence de Schulthess, médaille d'or du Collège National des Architectes en 1958, se reflètent dans la piscine entourée de jardins raffinés. **DOUBLE PAGE SUIVANTE** La façade principale, avec ses terrasses et ses baies vitrées du sol au plafond, est orientée vers les jardins, le bassin et la piscine. Les plates-bandes géométriques contrastent avec la sinuosité du tracé général des jardins.

❋ **ABOVE LEFT** The striking horizontal expression of the building is emphasized by the broad eaves with jutting supports. **LEFT** A series of slender, inverted U-shaped porticoes resting directly on the grass hold up the marquee at the entrance to the house. **ABOVE** From the house's rooftop, one has views of the entire property. A black tile pond with a jet in the middle is surrounded by the lush garden designed by the famous Brazilian landscaper, Roberto Burle Marx. **FOLLOWING DOUBLE PAGE** The continuous, fluid and transparent space in the main living room with views of the private garden can be subdivided using sliding wooden panels. The furniture includes "Barcelona" chairs by Mies van der Rohe and a "Wassily" chair by Marcel Breuer. ❋ **OBEN LINKS** Die stark horizontale Gestaltung des Baus wird durch die großen Vordächer, gestützt von auskragenden Trägern, noch verstärkt. **LINKS** Eine Reihe schlanker Portiken in umgekehrter U-Form sind im Rasen verankert und tragen den Sonnenschutz des Hauseingangs. **OBEN** Von der Dachterrasse des Gebäudes aus hat man einen guten Blick über das gesamte Grundstück. Ein mit schwarzen Fliesen ausgekleideter Teich mit zentraler Fontäne liegt umgeben von einem üppigen Garten, der auf den Entwurf des berühmten brasilianischen Landschaftsarchitekten Roberto Burle Marx zurückgeht. **FOLGENDE DOPPELSEITE** Das offen, fließend und transparent gestaltete große Wohnzimmer mit Gartenblick lässt sich anhand von verschiebbaren Holzpaneelen unterteilen. Die Einrichtung beinhaltet Stühle der Modelle »Barcelona« von Mies van der Rohe und »Wassily« von Marcel Breuer. ❋ **PAGE DE GAUCHE, EN HAUT** L'horizontalité de l'édifice est encore accentuée par les vastes balcons soutenus par des solives en saillie. **A GAUCHE** Une série de portiques élancés en U inversé et plantés dans la pelouse soutiennent la marquise de l'entrée. **CI-DESSUS** Depuis le toit, on peut contempler l'ensemble de la propriété. Un bassin en carrelages noirs, avec un jet d'eau au centre, est bordé de l'exubérant jardin dessiné par le célèbre paysagiste brésilien Roberto Burle Marx. **DOUBLE PAGE SUIVANTE** L'espace continu, fluide et transparent du grand salon avec vue sur le jardin privé, peut se subdiviser grâce à des panneaux coulissants en bois. Le mobilier inclut des fauteuils « Barcelona » de Mies van der Rohe et « Wassily » de Marcel Breuer.

※ **ABOVE** The airy semi-transparent staircase suspended from a beam in the entrance hall of the de Schulthess house, a mature avant-garde work designed by the Austrian-born, U.S. architect Richard Neutra in conjunction with the Cuban architects Álvarez and Gutiérrez. **BELOW** The different atmospheres in the residence are skillfully separated through changes in floor and ceiling levels and by the use of different materials and textures. ※ **OBEN** Die grazile und transparente Treppe ist an einem Träger im Eingangsbereich der »Casa de Schulthess« befestigt. Sie ist ein spätavantgardistisches Werk des nordamerikanischen Architekten Richard Neutra, österreichichen Ursprungs, in Zusammenarbeit mit den kubanischen Architekten Álvarez und Gutiérrez. **UNTEN** Die verschiedenartigen Räumlichkeiten der Wohnung sind gekonnt anhand unterschiedlicher Boden- und Deckenhöhen sowie der Verwendung unterschiedlicher Materialien und Texturen getrennt. ※ **CI-DESSUS** Dans le vestibule, un escalier léger et transparent suspendu à une poutre, une œuvre avant-gardiste d'une belle maturité, réalisée par l'architecte américain Richard Neutra originaire d'Autriche, en collaboration avec les Cubains Álvarez et Gutiérrez. **CI-DESSOUS** Les différents espaces de la maison sont savamment séparés par des différences de niveaux du sol et de la hauteur sous plafond, ainsi que par le recours à différents matériaux et textures.

❄ **ABOVE** The dining room, located just off the living room, also enjoys unhampered views of the garden and the swimming pool. **BELOW** A lounge chair, model B306, designed in 1928 by Le Corbusier in one of the corners of the living room, next to the library. ❄ **OBEN** Das Esszimmer liegt im Anschluss an das Wohnzimmer und bietet ebenfalls einen umfassenden Blick auf Garten und Swimmingpool. **UNTEN** Ein Liegestuhl, Modell B306 aus dem Jahr 1928, nach einem Entwurf von Le Corbusier steht in einer Ecke des Wohnzimmers neben dem Bücherregal. ❄ **CI-DESSUS** La salle à manger, située dans le prolongement du séjour, bénéficie elle aussi de belles vues sur le jardin et la piscine. **CI-DESSOUS** Dans un coin du séjour, près de la bibliothèque, une chaise longue, modèle B306, dessinée par Le Corbusier en 1928.

La familia se retrata ✴ La familia se sonríe

Apartamento Fofi-Lan

A Cuban House in the Tradition of Japanese Architecture.

Cuban architect Mario Romañach's interest in integrating contemporary and traditional architecture encouraged him to use elements from the Japanese architectural tradition, particularly "shoin-zukuri," in some of his work. The 1958 Fofi-Lan apartment building is an example of this kind of modernism. Its reinforced concrete structure references a post and lintel skeleton frame, based on the use of the "ken" module – a unit related to the human scale. The ground floor of this building is devoted to parking, so access to the apartments is via a staircase that opens into a small transitional space. It is defined by intricate wooden latticework and clay-tile jalousies that filter sunlight. The living rooms have "tatami"-like floors and shallow display alcoves, or "tokonoma." The almost hermetic main façade with small windows reveals its introverted purpose – to shut out the noise of the street – and alternating forms (which are closets) that protrude out of the façade create a dialogue between order and diversity. Light, shadow, geometry, and detailing contribute to Romañach's reinterpretation of the modern Cuban house while simultaneously instilling a spiritual content into modern architecture.

Der kubanische Architekt Mario Romañach hatte ein Faible dafür, zeitgenössische Elemente in traditionelle Architektur einfließen zu lassen. Es scheint deshalb naheliegend, dass er Teile der alten japanischen Architekturtradition »Shoin-Zukuri« in seine Werke übernahm. Die »Fofi-Lan«-Wohnung von 1958 zeigt, was Romañach unter Moderne verstand. Das verstärkte Betongebäude ist auf dem »ken«-Modul aufgebaut, dessen Gerüst sich an menschlichen Maßen orientiert. Das Erdgeschoss dient als Parkplatz, und über ein Treppenhaus und einen schmalen Durchgangsraum mit aufwändigem Gitterwerk aus Holz und Lehmziegel-Jalousien, gelangt man in die Wohnungen. Die Wohnräume haben »tatami«-ähnliche Böden und schmale »tokonoma«-Alkoven. Die fast hermetisch geschlossene Hauptfassade mit schmalen Fenstern soll den Straßenlärm draußen halten. Einbuchtungen in den Wänden dienen als Schränke und sind von außen zu sehen. Sie erzeugen dadurch einen Dialog zwischen Ordnung und Vielfalt. Romañachs Neuinterpretation des modernen kubanischen Hauses zeigt sich im Spiel von Licht und Schatten und seiner Liebe zur Geometrie und zum Detail. Gleichzeitig verleiht er der modernen Architektur ein Stück Spiritualität.

Cherchant à conjuguer le contemporain et le traditionnel, le Cubain Mario Romañach s'est inspiré de l'architecture japonaise, notamment le «shoin-zukuri». L'appartement Fofi-Lan, datant de 1958, illustre ce modernisme. Sa structure en béton armé repose sur une carcasse en poutres et linteaux, utilisant le module «ken», une unité basée sur l'échelle humaine. Le rez-de-chaussée abrite un parking. On accède aux appartements par un escalier qui débouche sur un petit espace de transition, défini par un fin treillage en bois et des jalousies en tuiles d'argile qui filtrent le soleil. Les séjours ont des sols en «tatami» et des alcôves peu profondes ou «tokonoma». La façade principale quasi hermétique percée de petites fenêtres révèle sa nature introvertie (cherchant à se protéger des bruits de la rue). Les formes saillantes (en fait des placards) créent un dialogue entre l'ordre et la diversité. La lumière, les ombres, la géométrie et les détails contribuent à la réinterprétation que Romañach offre de la maison cubaine tout en instillant un contenu spirituel dans l'architecture moderne.

HELADERÍA
COPPELIA

The Hottest Spot in Town for Cuban Ice Cream.

"Coppelia" is not only the name of a beautiful ballet, it is also a brand of famous, internationally acclaimed Cuban ice cream. It is the only rival in Cuba for the hedonistic trio of cigars, rum and coffee, and its quality has been compared to that of Italian "gelato." "Heladería Coppelia" is a landmark in the heart of La Rampa, in Vedado. Since it was built in 1966, it has been the most popular spot in town, a unique gathering place where youngsters hang out, lovers date, and students and friends meet. It was the backdrop for the first scene of the Oscar-nominated 1995 Cuban film "Fresa y chocolate." Designed by Cuban architect Mario Girona, it was conceived as a huge, lightweight concrete structure surrounded by gardens in the center of a city block. The design consists of two structures connected by a bridge: the secondary one is a service block, and the main one is a circular structure covered by a single slab and crowned with a truncated cone; this ring has a tinted-glass clerestory and anchors the exposed concrete girders that cover six drum-like dining halls subdivided by wood and glass partitions on the upper floor. The whole ambience is open and very Cuban.

Zigarren, Rum und Kaffee – diese Genüsse aus Kuba haben Weltruhm erlangt. Weniger bekannt ist Kuba für sein leckeres Eis, das von Kennern mit dem italienischen »gelato« verglichen wird. »Coppelia« steht nicht nur für das fantastische Ballett, sondern auch für das beste Eis in Kuba. Die »Heladería Coppelia« wurde 1966 eröffnet und liegt auf der La Rampa von Vedado. Sie ist eine Attraktion und einer der beliebtesten Treffpunkte der Jugend, Liebespaare und Studenten. Hier wurde auch die erste Szene des Oscar-nominierten kubanischen Films »Erdbeer und Schokolade« aus dem Jahr 1995 gedreht. Mario Girona, der kubanische Architekt, entwarf das Gebäude. Es ist eine riesige und dennoch leicht wirkende Betonkonstruktion, die aus zwei Gebäuden, die mit einer Brücke miteinander verbunden sind, in einer Gartenanlage besteht. Eines dient als Betriebsgebäude. Das runde Haupthaus ist von einer einzigen Betonplatte abgedeckt, auf der ein abgebrochener Kegel mit Buntglasoberlichter steht. Er verankert die nach außen gestellten Betonträger, die sechs Zylinder zusammenhalten. Die Speisesäle im oberen Stockwerk sind mit Holz- und Glaspaneelen voneinander abgetrennt. All dies wirkt durch und durch kubanisch.

«Coppelia» n'est pas qu'un beau ballet classique, c'est aussi une marque de crèmes glacées cubaines de renommée internationale. D'une qualité comparable aux «gelato» italiens, elles rivalisent avec le trio hédoniste : cigare, rhum et café. Depuis son ouverture en 1966 au cœur de la Rampa, à Vedado, le glacier «Coppelia» est l'établissement le plus populaire de la ville, le rendez-vous des adolescents, des amoureux, des étudiants et des amis. Il a servi de décor à la scène d'ouverture de «Fresa y chocolate», le film cubain nominé aux Oscars en 1995. Conçu par l'architecte Mario Girona, c'est une immense structure en béton léger entourée de jardins occupant tout un pâté de maisons. Deux bâtiments sont reliés par une passerelle, le premier abrite les services, le second, circulaire, est recouvert d'une seule dalle couronnée d'un cône tronqué. Il comporte un étage protégé de vitres teintées. Les piliers en béton cachent six tambours. Les salles de restaurant à l'étage sont divisées par des cloisons en bois et verre, créant une ambiance ouverte et très cubaine.

✳ **ABOVE LEFT** The "Coppelia" ice cream parlor, surrounded by gardens, is located in the middle of a city block right in the heart of Havana. The radial reinforced concrete girders, support by V-shaped columns, converge in the middle of the building. **LEFT** A bridge joins the two volumes of the building, establishing a clear formal, spatial and volumetric separation between the different functional areas. An orthopolygonal staircase leads to the administrative area. **ABOVE** The transparent, open atmosphere in the building encourages communication and impersonal mingling, part of the charm of a place that skillfully assimilates Cuban idiosyncrasies. **FOLLOWING PAGES** The exposed reinforced concrete structure and the solid terrazzo floors, with a design based on freeform curves, encompass a spacious, open, well-ventilated public area. ✳ **OBEN LINKS** Das Eiscafé »Coppelia« liegt umringt von Grünanlagen inmitten eines Blocks im Zentrum Havannas. Die strahlenförmigen Stahlbetonträger lehnen an V-förmigen Stützen und laufen in der Mitte des Gebäudes zusammen. **LINKS** Eine Brücke verbindet die beiden Gebäudeteile und erzielt gleichzeitig eine formale, räumliche und volumetrische Trennung der verschiedenen Funktionsbereiche. Eine rechtwinklig-polygonale Treppe bietet Zugang zur Verwaltung. **OBEN** Das transparente Gefüge des Gebäudes begünstigt die Kommunikation und die menschliche Begegnung und ist mitverantwortlich für den Zauber dieses Treffpunkts, der den kubanischen Charakter einfängt. **FOLGENDE DOPPELSEITE** Die unverhüllte Stahlbetonstruktur und der Terrazzoboden mit seinem wellenförmigen Design bilden einen großen, offenen und gut durchlüfteten Raum. ✳ **PAGE DE GAUCHE, EN HAUT** Le glacier « Coppelia », entouré de jardins, se dresse en plein cœur de la Havane. Les poutres radiales en béton armé, prenant appui sur des colonnes en V, convergent vers le centre du bâtiment. **A GAUCHE** Une passerelle relie les deux volumes du bâtiment, établissant une séparation claire, formelle, spatiale et volumétrique entre les différentes zones fonctionnelles. Un escalier orthopolygonal mène à la partie administrative. **CI-DESSUS** L'atmosphère du bâtiment favorise la communication et les contacts humains, ce qui fait partie du charme de ce lieu typiquement cubain. **DOUBLE PAGE SUIVANTE** La structure en béton armé brut et les sols en granit décorés de motifs aux courbes libres accueillent une vaste salle publique ouverte et bien aérée.

✳ **ROW ABOVE** The reinforced concrete bridge connecting the two volumes is covered by vertical concrete sun breaks whose rhythm reinforces the linear nature of the space. The wooden jalousies and the skylight provide a great deal of color and rhythm to the site. ✳ **OBERE REIHE** Die Stahlbetonbrücke zwischen den beiden Gebäudeteilen wird von vertikalen Betonstreben als Sonnenschutz verschlossen, was den linearen Raumaufbau verstärkt. Die Holzgitter und das Buntglasfenster verleihen dem Bau Farbenpracht und Rhythmus. ✳ **LINIE EN HAUT** La passerelle en béton armé qui relie les deux volumes est fermée par des pare-soleil verticaux en ciment qui accentuent le caractère linéaire de l'espace. Les jalousies en bois et vitraux projettent une belle lumière colorée et rythment l'espace.

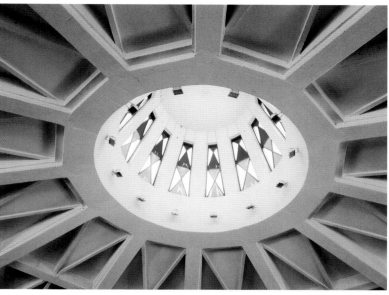

※ **BOTH BELOW** The staircase made of solid terrazzo is the center of the building's spatial composition and joins both floors. On the lower storey, the walls delimiting the service area do not reach the mezzanine in order to ease ventilation. **FOLLOWING DOUBLE PAGE** The spatial fluidity of the interior is ensured by the enormous light on the roof which has no intermediate supports. The interior space of the upper floor is solely delimited by airy partitions. ※ **UNTEN, LINKE UND RECHTE SEITE** Die spiralförmige Terrazzotreppe steht im Mittelpunkt des räumlichen Gebäudegefüges und verknüpft die beiden Stockwerke. Im Erdgeschoss wurden die Mauern im Servicebereich nicht bis zum Zwischenbereich aufgezogen, um die Belüftung zu gewährleisten. **FOLGENDE DOPPELSEITE** Die fließende Struktur des Innenraums wird durch den starken Lichteinfall gewährleistet, welcher auf der Decke ohne Zwischenstützen beruht. Das Innere des Obergeschosses ist nur mit grazilen Raumtrennern unterteilt. ※ **CI-DESSOUS, PAGE A GAUCHE ET PAGE A DROITE** L'escalier en granit se trouve au centre de la composition spatiale du bâtiment. Au rez-de-chaussée, les murs délimitant la partie des services n'atteignent pas la hauteur de l'entresol afin de faciliter la ventilation. **DOUBLE PAGE SUIVANTE** À l'intérieur, la grande quantité de lumière qui filtre sous la coupole surélevée créé une atmosphère fluide. Dans la grande salle à l'étage, seules de légères cloisons délimitent les espaces.

Parque Lenin

One of the Paradigms
of Modern Cuban Architecture.

In the early 1970s, Parque Lenin was planned in an effort to increase the percentage of green land per citizen while protecting the Vento basin, Havana's main source of water. A team of architects led by Antonio Quintana transformed a wasteland into an idyllic forest of bamboos, palms and pines, punctuated with kiosks, cafeterias, restaurants, and even an amphitheater. Cuban architect Joaquín Galván designed one of the paradigms of modern Cuban architecture, "Las Ruinas". An orthogonal white concrete structure wraps around the stone ruins of a 19th century farm, creating a highly original setting for a restaurant. The cantilevered beams stretch into the landscape, framing views of the park and establishing a delightful transition between indoors and out. The free-flowing interior space is formed by changes of floor level and a variety of textures. A staircase bridges the two-storey vestibule with the mezzanine dining area, where one can see a freestanding stained-glass mural by Cuban artist René Portocarrero. This addition of vibrant color adds to the sublime experience of being in "Las Ruinas".

Der Parque Lenin wurde in den frühen 1970ern angelegt, um die Grünfläche in der Stadt zu vergrößern. Gleichzeitig konnte damit die Hauptwasserversorgung Havannas aus dem Vento-Becken geschützt werden. Ein Architektenteam unter der Leitung von Antonio Quintana verwandelte das einstige Ödland in einen idyllischen Wald aus Bambus, Palmen und Pinien mit Kiosken, Cafés, Restaurants und einem Amphitheater. Zu einem Standardwerk der modernen kubanischen Architektur wurde das Restaurant »Las Ruinas«, das der Architekt Joaquín Galván entworfen hatte. Das weiße rechtwinklige Betongebäude wurde um Steinruinen eines Bauernhofes aus dem 19. Jahrhundert angelegt. Ausladene Betonträger erstrecken sich nach außen und rahmen die Sicht auf den Park ein. Dadurch ergibt sich ein harmonischer Übergang zwischen Innen und Außen. Der schwebende Innenraum wird durch Treppen auf ungleichen Ebenen und mannigfaltigen Strukturen bestimmt, und das Treppenhaus verbindet ein zweistöckiges Vestibül, dessen Mezzanin als Essraum dient. Von hier aus sieht man auf ein freistehende Wand aus einem Buntglasfenster, das der kubanische Künstlers René Portocarrero gestaltet hat und dem Besuch von »Las Ruinas« etwas Erhabenes verleiht.

Le Parque Lenin fut planté au début des années 1970 afin d'augmenter le pourcentage d'espaces verts par habitant tout en protégeant le bassin du Vento, principale source d'eau de la Havane. Sous la direction d'Antonio Quintana, une équipe d'architectes a transformé un terrain vague en forêt idyllique de bambous, de palmiers et de pins, parsemée de kiosques, de cafés, de restaurants et même d'un amphithéâtre. «Las Ruinas», un des fleurons de l'architecture moderne cubaine, a été dessinée par le Cubain Joaquín Galván. Cette structure octogonale blanche en béton s'enroule autour des ruines en pierres d'une ferme du 19e siècle, créant un décor très original pour un restaurant. Les poutres en console s'étirent dans le paysage, encadrant des vues du parc et établissant une belle transition entre le dedans et le dehors. À l'intérieur, l'espace ouvert se distingue par ses différents niveaux et une variété de matières. Un escalier relie le haut vestibule à la salle de restaurant en mezzanine. Celle-ci est ornée d'un vitrail sur pied signé de l'artiste cubain René Portocarrero, une touche de couleur qui ajoute encore à la sublime expérience de dîner à «Las Ruias».

❋ **ABOUT LEFT** A melding of new and old. The Cartesian structure of columns and reinforced concrete beams envelops the remains of an old building belonging to a 19th century coffee plantation and creates an exceptional ambiance inside the building. **LEFT** An integration of avant-garde art and architecture. A beautiful, enormous stained glass window with floral motifs by the famous Cuban artist René Portocarrero is located at the entrance to the restaurant on the upper floor. **ABOVE** The main entrance to the restaurant, "Las Ruinas", is made up of a series of terraces and staircases that resolve the different levels of the terrain where the building is located. ❋ **OBEN LINKS** Alt und neu vereint. Die kartesianische Struktur aus Stahlbetonsäulen und -trägern umschließt Reste eines alten Gebäudes, das im 19. Jahrhundert zu einer Kaffeeplantage gehörte. Diese Verbindung erzeugt im Innern des Baus ein einzigartiges Ambiente. **LINKS** Künstlerische Avantgarde verschmilzt mit Architektur. Ein herrliches Buntglasfenster mit Blumenmotiven aus der Hand des berühmten kubanischen Künstlers René Portocarrero schmückt den Eingang des Restaurants im Obergeschoss. **OBEN** Der Haupteingang des Restaurants »Las Ruinas« besteht aus einer Reihe von Terrassen und Treppen, welche die Höhenunterschiede des Geländes überbrücken. ❋ **PAGE DE GAUCHE, EN HAUT** L'intégration du nouveau et de l'ancien. La structure cartésienne avec colonnes et poutres en béton armé entoure les vestiges d'une ancienne plantation de café du 19ᵉ siècle, créant une atmosphère exceptionnelle à l'intérieur de l'édifice. **A GAUCHE** L'avant-garde artistique intégrée dans l'architecture. À l'entrée du restaurant situé à l'étage, un beau vitrail aux motifs floraux, œuvre du célèbre artiste cubain René Portocarrero. **CI-DESSUS** Le bâtiment étant construit sur un terrain pentu, on accède au restaurant « Las Ruinas » par une série de terrasses et d'escaliers.

✳ **FACING PAGE** The trees on the site were left intact and made an integral part of the new building. **ABOVE** The refined interior is the result of a skillful manipulation of the space and the interplay of volume, light and shadow which together with the different levels of Cuban marble floors and the play of different ceiling heights, creates an intriguing atmosphere.
✳ **LINKE SEITE** Die Bäume wurden erhalten und in den Bau integriert. **OBEN** Das elegante Ambiente im Innern ist das Ergebnis einer feinsinnigen Verarbeitung des Raums und der Kombinationen von Volumina, Lichtern und Schatten. So wird zusammen mit den unterschiedlich hohen Böden aus kubanischem Marmor und den verschiedenen Deckenhöhen eine faszinierende Atmosphäre erzeugt. ✳ **PAGE DE GAUCHE** Les arbres du site ont été respectés et inclus dans le nouveau bâtiment. **CI-DESSUS** L'intérieur raffiné est le fruit d'une savante manipulation de l'espace, des volumes, des lumières et des ombres associée aux différents niveaux des sols en marbres cubains et aux jeux des lignes verticales.

CASA ELEJALDE

In the Mode of Yin and Yang.

"If space is halfway between cosmos and chaos, and we human beings are the play of light and shadow traveling in time and occupying a space, then the architect's task is to create spaces for man to dwell." Cuban architects Julio César Pérez and Esteban Martínez made this statement in 2000 in their proposal for a friend's low-budget home in Míramar, an elegant district west of Havana. The design combined a rational approach, based on geometry and form, with a philosophical one involving the notion of voids and solids, expressed in the use of varying ceiling heights. Set back from the street in the middle of a block, and leaving room from adjacent properties to allow for privacy, cross-ventilation, and natural light, the two-storey façade is framed by a lofty portico supported by concrete columns and steel beams that imply urban dignity and a certain monumentality. The entrance leads to a series of rooms defined by changes in the floor levels and materials: a grand two-storey space with a dining room and rock garden is bisected by a metal bridge. The upstairs bedrooms at the back overlook the central core, and a minimalist staircase anchors the bridge, and in doing so becomes a piece of sculpture.

»Die Aufgabe des Architekten ist es, Raum zu bauen, um dem Menschen Schutz zu gewähren« sagten die kubanischen Architekten Julio César Pérez und Esteban Martínez zu einem Freund, als sie ihm im Jahr 2000 einen Entwurf für ein Billighaus im eleganten Viertel Míramar im Westen von Havanna unterbreiteten. Der Entwurf ist genau so rational wie philosophisch. Geometrische Formen treffen auf ein Spiel zwischen Leerflächen und Festkörpern, das durch den Einsatz verschieden hoher Decken entsteht. Das zweistöckige Haus liegt etwas zurückversetzt in einem Straßenblock in einigem Abstand zu den Nachbarhäusern. So kann die Luft zirkulieren, genügend Tageslicht einfallen, und man bleibt ungestört. Rund ums Haus liegt ein luftiger Säulengang, der von Betonpfeilern gestützt und mit Stahlbalken verstärkt wird. Das Haus wirkt dadurch monumental und fast erhaben. Im Innern sind die unterschiedlichen Zimmer durch verschieden hohe Niveaus und jeweils andere Materialien definiert. Eine Metallbrücke unterteilt den großen zweistöckigen Wohnraum und das Esszimmer mit einem Steingarten, ein schlichtes Treppenhaus verankert die Brücke, die damit zur Skulptur wird. Im oberen Stockwerk gehen die Schlafzimmer nach hinten hinaus.

«Si l'espace se situe à mi-chemin entre le cosmos et le chaos et si les êtres humains ne sont que des jeux d'ombre et de lumière voyageant dans le temps et occupant un espace, alors la tâche de l'architecte est de créer des espaces où l'homme peut s'arrêter». Cette déclaration figurait dans le projet des architectes cubains Julio César Pérez et Esteban Martínez auxquels, en 2000, un ami sans beaucoup de moyens avait commandé une maison à Míramar, quartier élégant à l'ouest de la Havane. Leur plan est à la fois rationnel, basé sur la géométrie et la forme, et philosophique, reposant sur les notions du solide et du vide, se traduisant par diverses hauteurs sous plafond. Située en retrait de la rue au milieu d'un pâté de maisons, espacée des voisins pour plus d'intimité, la façade est dominée par un haut portique en colonnes de béton et poutres d'acier dont la distinction urbaine n'est pas dépourvue de monumentalité. L'entrée donne sur une série de pièces définies par des différences de niveau et de matériaux. Un haut espace accueillant la salle à manger et un jardin de pierres est traversé par une passerelle en métal. On y accède par un escalier minimaliste, sculpture à part entière. Les chambres à l'étage, situées à l'arrière de la maison, donnent sur le puits central.

❋ **ABOVE** The core of the home is an atmosphere characterized by great spatial richness, with floor coverings of different materials and textures to distinguish the different functional areas. The color of the steel structure contrasts with the carpentry and the walls. **RIGHT** A minimalist staircase with a steel frame and varnished wood steps links both floors of the house. The columns in the middle frame the walk-in entrance to the house. **FACING PAGE** A steel-framed bridge divides the centrally-located double-height core of the house, where there is a rock garden and the dining room, and which leads to the private bedroom area at the back of the upper storey. ❋ **OBEN** Das Herzstück des Hauses ist das großräumige Erdgeschoss mit Böden aus unterschiedlichen Materialien und Texturen, welche die einzelnen Funktionsbereiche definieren. Die Farbe der Stahlstruktur steht im Kontrast zum Holz und zu den Farben der Wände. **RECHTS** Eine minimalistisch gestaltete Treppe mit gebeizten Holzstufen verbindet die beiden Etagen des Hauses. **RECHTE SEITE** Eine Brücke aus Stahlrahmen unterteilt den doppelstöckigen Raum, der einen Steingarten und das Esszimmer enthält. Diese Brücke führt zum Privatbereich am Ende des Obergeschosses, wo die Schlafzimmer liegen. ❋ **CI-DESSUS** Le cœur de la maison est d'une grande richesse spatiale avec des sols dont les matériaux et textures varient selon les aires fonctionnelles. La couleur de la structure en acier contraste avec celle de la charpente et des murs. **A DROITE** L'escalier minimaliste avec des marches en bois vernis. **PAGE DE DROITE** L'espace central, d'une double hauteur sous plafond, accueille un jardin de pierres et la salle à manger. À l'étage, une passerelle en acier mène aux chambres situées à l'arrière de la maison.

Finca Vigía

Cojímar is a quiet and very picturesque fishermen's town located almost half an hour east of Havana after driving through the bay tunnel. It is world famous because the North American writer Ernest Hemingway had his boat "El Pilar" anchored in Cojímar. His usual daily routine went from writing in the very early the morning – standing in front of his portable Remington typewriter until shortly before noon and then driving to Cojímar where he used to have lunch at "La Terraza" restaurant – the place where several scenes for the film "The Old Man and the Sea", based on the short novel written by Hemingway, and featuring Spencer Tracy, were shot. An extension of the town

Cojímar, ein ruhiges, malerisches Fischerdorf, liegt etwa eine halbe Autostunde östlich von Havanna. Der Weg dorthin führt durch einen Tunnel, der unter der Bucht von Havanna durchgeht. Weltberühmt wurde Cojímar durch den amerikanischen Schriftsteller Ernest Hemingway. Er hatte dort sein Boot »El Pilar« geankert und pflegte einen regelmäßigen Tagesablauf: frühmorgens wachte er auf und machte sich unverzüglich auf seiner tragbaren Remington-Schreibmaschine ans Schreiben. Dann, gegen Mittag, fuhr er nach Cojímar ins »La Terraza«. Das Restaurant diente auch als Kulisse für Szenen des Films »Der alte Mann und das Meer«, der auf der gleichnamigen Hemingway-Kurz-

Cojímar est un paisible village de pêcheurs très pittoresque à environ une demi-heure de voiture à l'est de la Havane après voir franchi le tunnel de la baie. Il est mondialement connu grâce à Ernest Hemingway, qui y ancrait son bateau «El Pilar». L'écrivain américain se mettait généralement à l'écriture de très bonne heure, travaillant debout devant sa Remington portable, puis, peu avant midi, se rendait à Cojímar pour déjeuner au restaurant La Terraza, où furent tournées plusieurs scènes du film inspiré de son court roman «Le Vieil homme et la mer», avec Spencer Tracy dans le rôle principal. Extension du village, le complexe de la Villa Panamericana fut construit en 1991 pour

Casa Fúster

a Mederos

Cojímar etc.

242 Finca Vigía, *San Francisco de Paula*
250 Casa Mederos, *Cojímar*
260 Casa Fúster, *Jaimanitas*

- the Villa Panamericana complex – was built in 1991 o house the athletes who took part in the Pan American Games that were held in Havana that same year. t was inspired by the traditional city, with a median of rees, and a regular grid with blocks containing build-ngs aligned to the sidewalk. Sports facilities were built s well as housing – later given to the workers – with then fashionable postmodern architectural style as was the international trend.

geschichte basiert. Spencer Tracy spielte die Haupt-rolle. Das Dorf vergrößerte sich 1991 mit dem Bau der Anlage »Villa Panamericana«. Sie wurde als Unterkunft für die Athleten gebaut, die an den panamerikani-schen Spielen in Havanna im gleichen Jahr teilnahmen. Wie ein traditionelles Dorf besteht sie aus schach-brettartig angelegten Häuserblocks – durch deren Mitte ein Streifen mit Bäumen führt. Dazu wurden Sportanlagen gebaut. Später übergab man die Unter-künfte der Athleten den Arbeitern. Und Cojímar kann sich mit einem postmodernen Bau schmücken, der hier als Denkmal der Architektur der frühen Neunzi-ger steht.

héberger les athlètes participant aux jeux panaméri-cains qui se tenaient à Cuba cette année là. Il s'inspi-rait de la ville traditionnelle, avec une artère centrale bordée d'arbres et un plan régulier de blocs d'immeu-bles bien alignés. Les installations sportives et les loge-ments (plus tard distribués aux travailleurs) suivaient le style postmoderne alors en vogue un peu partout dans le monde. Les façades sans grand charme pré-sentent des frontons démesurés.

Finca Vigía

Where Hemingway Wrote
"The Old Man and the Sea."

Ernest Hemingway lived in several countries, but Finca Vigía was his only permanent home, the place where he wrote "The Old Man and the Sea," for which he won the Nobel Prize in 1954. He first rented the estate in 1939 from the French owner for $100 per month, but he bought it the following year with royalties from "For Whom the Bell Tolls." The house is on a hill in San Francisco de Paula, a small town about 10 miles from Havana. It is kept exactly as the writer left it, according to an agreement signed in 1962 between his fourth wife Mary Welsh and the Cuban government. It is a white 19th century villa surrounded by gardens with mature trees, a pool, and his fisher boat "El Pilar". Access to the interior is strictly forbidden to visitors, but all the rooms, decorated with sober elegance, can be looked at through the windows. The living room still has Hemingway's armchair by the bar, the library has his hunting trophies and collection of books. The dining room table is set with an extra place setting of silver for an unexpected guest, and the writer's study has his typewriter and glasses ready for their owner to begin work. Even in the bathroom we can detect the presence of the writer: his fluctuating weight is documented in pencil on the wall just next to the scale.

Ernest Hemingway war ständig auf Reisen. Einzig die »Finca Vigía« war sein festes Zuhause. Hier verfasste er den Roman »Der alte Mann und das Meer«, der 1954 mit dem Nobelpreis ausgezeichnet wurde. 1939 mietete er das Haus für 100 Dollar im Monat, und bereits im nächsten Jahr konnte er es mit den Tantiemen für den Roman »Wem die Stunde schlägt« erwerben. Das Haus liegt auf einem Hügel in San Fancisco de Paula, einem kleinen Ort rund 16 Kilometer von Havanna entfernt und, aufgrund einer Vereinbarung von 1962 zwischen seiner vierten Frau Mary Welsh und der kubanischen Regierung, ist es noch genau so, wie es der Schriftsteller verlassen hatte. Das weiße Gebäude steht in einem Garten mit alten Bäumen und Pool, in dem auch sein Fischerboot »El Pilar« steht. Der Eintritt ins Haus ist nicht erlaubt, die schlichten, eleganten Zimmer kann man aber durch die Fenster anschauen. An der Bar steht immer noch sein Polstersessel, im Esszimmer liegt auf dem Tisch ein Gedeck für unerwartete Besucher bereit, und in der Bibliothek stehen Jagdtrophäen. Als ob Hemingway gleich zur Arbeit erscheinen würde, stehen im Studierzimmer Schreibmaschine und Brille bereit. Sogar im Badezimmer ist der Schriftsteller präsent: Hier hat er auf einer Wand sein ständig wechselndes Gewicht verewigt.

Ernest Hemingway vécut dans plusieurs pays mais Finca Vigía fut sa seule résidence permanente, le lieu où il écrivit «Le Vieil homme et la mer» qui lui valut le prix Nobel en 1954. En 1939, il loua le domaine à un Français pour 100 dollars par mois, avant de l'acheter l'année suivante avec les droits d'auteur de «Pour qui sonne le glas». Perchée sur une colline à San Francisco de Paula, une petite ville à environ 16 km de la Havane, la maison a été conservée telle qu'il l'a laissée, conformément à un accord signé en 1962 entre sa quatrième épouse Mary Welsh et le gouvernement cubain. La villa néoclassique blanche du 19e siècle, entourée de grands arbres, possède une piscine et une terrasse sous une pergola fleurie. L'intérieur ne se visite pas mais, par les fenêtres, on peut voir toutes les pièces, décorées avec une élégante sobriété. Le fauteuil d'Hemingway est toujours près du bar dans le salon ; sa bibliothèque est ornée de trophées de chasse et de livres ; dans son bureau, ses lunettes et sa machine à écrire attendent qu'il se mette au travail ; et, dans la salle à manger, on a mis un couvert supplémentaire pour l'invité de dernière minute. La présence du romancier hante même la salle de bains, où son poids fluctuant est écrit au crayon sur le mur près de la balance.

※ **ABOVE AND LEFT** The entrance to the Ernest Hemingway House in "Finca Vigía", on top of a hill in San Francisco de Paula on the outskirts of Havana. The property has been preserved as a museum since 1962. The former car garages were converted into the museum's offices. **ABOVE** The guest bedroom in the garage area. The bedrooms, furnishings, and books are kept intact just as they were when the writer lived in the home. ※ **LINKE SEITE** Der Eingang zum Wohnsitz Ernest Hemingways, der »Finca Vigía«, die auf einem Hügel in San Francisco de Paula, etwas außerhalb von Havanna, liegt. Das Gebäude wird seit 1962 als Museum genutzt. Die einstigen Garagen wurden in Museumsbüros verwandelt. **OBEN** Das Gästezimmer im Garagenbereich. Die Zimmer, Möbel und Bücher sind seit der Zeit, als der Schriftsteller in dem Haus lebte, erhalten geblieben. ※ **PAGE DE GAUCHE** Le porche surélevé de la « Finca Vigía », la maison d'Hemingway bâtie sur une colline à San Francisco de Paula, une banlieue de La Havane. La propriété est un musée depuis 1962. L'ancien garage accueille désormais les bureaux du musée. **CI-DESSUS** Le pavillon des invités, situé près du garage. Les chambres, les meubles et les livres ont été conservés tels qu'à l'époque où l'écrivain vivait ici.

❊ **PREVIOUS DOUBLE PAGE** The austere dining room in "Finca Vigía", with some of writer Ernest Hemingway's hunting trophies on the walls, was always ready to welcome a guest. **ABOVE** The room used by the writer as a library, where the majority of his books were kept. **ABOVE** The third floor of the home that Hemingway's third wife, Mary Welsh, had built. The writer did not work there for long, but he used it to revise some texts and took occasional catnaps on the "chaise longue". ❊ **VORHERGEHENDE DOPPELSEITE** An den Wänden des nüchternen Esszimmers der »Finca Vigía« hängen einige Jagdtrophäen des Schriftstellers Ernest Hemingway. Der Raum war jederzeit für den Empfang von Besuchern hergerichtet. **OBEN** Der Raum, der dem Schriftsteller als Bibliothek diente, enthält die meisten seiner Bücher. **RECHTE SEITE OBEN** Der dritte Stock des Turms, der auf Wunsch von Hemingways vierter Ehefrau

Mary Welsh errichtet wurde. Der Schriftsteller nutzte den Raum nicht oft zum Arbeiten, überarbeitete dort jedoch einige Texte und hielt hin und wieder ein Nickerchen auf der Chaise-longue.   ❋ **DOUBLE PAGE PRÉCÉDENTE** Dans la salle à manger austère, avec, aux murs, quelques-uns des trophées de chasse de l'écrivain, un couvert supplémentaire était toujours mis pour un invité de dernière minute. **PAGE DE GAUCHE** La bibliothèque de l'écrivain, où il conservait la plupart de ses livres. **CI-DESSUS** Le troisième étage de la tour que fit construire Mary Welsh, la quatrième épouse d'Hemingway. L'écrivain n'y travailla pas beaucoup mais l'utilisait pour réviser certains textes et pour faire la sieste dans la chaise longue.

casa Mederos

A House with Naval and Marine References.

Cojímar is a nice, quiet fishing town 30 minutes east of Havana with a colonial fortress built around 1645 by Italian engineer Bautista Antonelli at the mouth of the Cojímar river to protect the bay from pirates. A gazebo with a bronze statue of the giant of American literature, Ernest Hemingway, is across from the fort since the writer used to go for lunch with Gregorio Fuentes, the captain of his boat "El Pilar," at the nearby La Terraza restaurant in the 1950s. A few meters away from the restaurant, on a steep site on the bank of the river, Cuban architect Arquímedes Poveda designed a modern house in 1958 with a complex floor plan resulting from the clever use of the slope and the nautical leanings of the reinforced concrete roofs. This allowed for a dynamic interior space where the street-level entrance forks into two floors connected by a wooden staircase – one located some steps downwards and containing the living room and a pier-like deck, the other a mezzanine for the command-bridge-like dining room that both overlooks the entrance and benefits from an outside view. Naval and marine references are further displayed in the whale-shape dining table, the porthole windows, and the mariner's compass at the entrance.

Cojímar ist ein ruhiges, hübsches Fischerdorf 30 Minuten östlich von Havanna. Seine Festung wurde 1645 vom italienischen Ingenieur Bautista Antonelli an der Mündung des Cojímar-Flusses erstellt, um die Bucht vor den Piraten zu schützen. Auf der anderen Seite der Festung steht ein Pavillon mit einer Bronzestatue von Ernest Hemingway. Der amerikanische Schriftsteller pflegte im nahegelegenen Restaurant »La Terraza« mit dem Kapitän seines Bootes »El Pilar«, Gregorio Fuentes, zu Mittag essen. Ein paar Meter vom Restaurant, direkt am Flussufer, liegt das moderne Haus des kubanischen Architekten Arquímedes Poveda, Baujahr 1958. Der komplexe Grundriss nützt die Hanglage geschickt aus und vermittelt dem Innern des Hauses Dynamik. Der ebenerdige Eingang verzweigt sich im Inneren auf zwei Ebenen, die durch eine Treppe aus Holz miteinander verbunden sind. Auf der ein paar Stufen tiefer gelegenen Ebene befindet sich der Wohnraum und eine Terrasse, die einem Landungssteg nachempfunden ist. Die andere Ebene bildet ein Zwischengeschoss. Dort liegt das Esszimmer wie auf einer Kommandobrücke. Von hier sieht man auf den Eingang und nach draußen. Und überall zieht sich das Seefahrts-Thema durch: der Tisch hat die Form eines Walfischs und die Eingangshalle einen Seefahrerkompass und runde Guckfenster.

Cojímar est un joli et paisible port de pêche à trente minutes à l'est de la Havane, doté d'une forteresse coloniale bâtie vers 1645 par l'ingénieur italien Bautista Antonelli à l'embouchure du fleuve pour protéger la baie des pirates. Juste en face, un kiosque abrite une statue en bronze d'Ernest Hemingway car, dans les années 50, ce géant de la littérature américaine avait l'habitude d'aller déjeuner avec Gregorio Fuentes, le capitaine de son bateau «El Pilar», au restaurant voisin de «La Terraza». Quelques mètres plus loin, sur la berge du fleuve, l'architecte cubain Arquímedes Poveda a conçu en 1958 une maison moderne avec un plan complexe et dynamique qui tire le meilleur profit du terrain escarpé et des appuis nautiques des toits en béton armé. Côté rue, l'entrée donne sur un escalier en bois qui descend vers le séjour et la terrasse embarcadère, ou monte vers une mezzanine accueillant la salle à manger / passerelle de commandement qui jouit d'une belle vue. Les références navales et marines se retrouvent dans la table en forme de baleine, les fenêtres en hublots et le compas de l'entrée.

✴ **ABOVE LEFT** The house's façade faces the main street of the fishing town of Cojímar. **LEFT** An enormous reddish compass motif juts out in relief from the black background of the front door to the Guillermo Mederos house in Cojímar. **ABOVE** The main façade of the house appears to be hermetically sealed, with few openings, since the building is seared by the sun as it faces the west. The surfaces of the blind walls have been treated using rough textures and slight reliefs in order to give them some visual interest. ✴ **OBEN LINKS** Die Fassade des Hauses liegt zur Hauptstraße des Fischerorts Cojímar und zeigt deutlich das Gefälle und die Neigung des Dachs bzw. der Mauern. **LINKS** Eine große rote Windrose schmückt als Relief vor schwarzem Hintergrund die Eingangstür des Hauses von Guillermo Mederos in Cojímar. **OBEN** Die Hauptfassade des Hauses ist geschlossen und besitzt aufgrund der Westausrichtung und der damit verbundenen starken Sonneneinstrahlung nur wenige Lichtöffnungen. Die Oberflächen der Mauern wurden mit faltigen Texturen und kleinen Reliefs versehen, um sie interessanter zu gestalten. ✴ **PAGE DE GAUCHE, EN HAUT** La façade de la maison donne sur la rue principale du village de pêcheurs. Son toit et ses murs ont été conçus de sorte à épouser sa dénivellation. **A GAUCHE** Sur la porte d'entrée, une énorme rose nautique en relief, rouge sur fond noir. **CI-DESSUS** La façade principale de la maison est hermétique, avec peu d'ouvertures afin de la protéger de son exposition à l'ouest, en plein soleil. Les surfaces aveugles sont été enduites de textures rugueuses et de légers reliefs afin de les rendre plus intéressantes.

❋ **FACING PAGE** The entrance is located on a level halfway between the living room and the dining room. Above the entrance is a cabinet with a design inspired by the works of Piet Mondrian. **RIGHT AND BELOW** The living room is located on a level below the entrance in order to take advantage of the proximity of the terrace located on the same level, which looks out over the Cojímar river. From the high ceiling of the house's entrance, one can see its spatial layout, with the mezzanine-type dining room and the living room on a lower level. **FOLLOWING PAGES** The dining room, located on the house's topmost floor, has the most privileged location for enjoying the views of the Cojímar river. The whale-shaped table is yet another allusion to the marine theme. ❋ **LINKE SEITE** Der Eingang befindet sich auf halber Höhe zwischen Wohn- und Esszimmer. Über der Eingangstür ist ein Schrank zu sehen, dessen Türen von Werken Piet Mondrians inspiriert werden. Das Wohnzimmer liegt unterhalb des Eingangs. **RECHTS UND UNTEN** Dank der doppelten Deckenhöhe des Eingangsbereichs kann man die räumliche Aufteilung erkennen, dieser Aufbau verleiht dem Hausinnern sehr viel Dynamik. **FOLGENDE DOPPELSEITE** Das Esszimmer im obersten Geschoss des Hauses besitzt auch die beste Lage, um die Aussicht auf den Cojímar-Fluss zu genießen. Der Tisch in Form eines Wals ist eine weitere Anspielung auf die Meereswelt. ❋ **PAGE DE GAUCHE** L'entrée surplombe le séjour et la salle à manger. Au-dessus de la porte, un placard dont les portes s'inspirent des œuvres de Piet Mondrian. **A DROITE ET CI-DESSOUS** Depuis la haute entrée, on peut apprécier la distribution spatiale très dynamique de la maison, avec sa salle à manger en mezzanine et son séjour en contrebas. **DOUBLE PAGE SUIVANTE** C'est de la salle à manger, située à un niveau supérieur, que l'on a la plus belle vue sur le Cojímar. La table en forme de baleine est une autre référence marine.

※ **ABOVE LFT** The house's current owner, Guillermo Mederos, smoking a cigar on the terrace of his house with the Cojímar river in the background. **LEFT** From the roof over the bedrooms, one can appreciate the volumetric conception of the house, with its different colored walls and the geometrical shapes of the different spaces. **ABOVE** The roof over the bedrooms is used as an open terrace accessible from the house's dining room. ※ **OBEN LINKS** Der gegenwärtige Besitzer des Hauses, Guillermo Mederos, beim Rauchen einer Zigarre auf der Terrasse mit dem Cojímar-Fluss im Hintergrund. **LINKS** Vom Flachdach der Schlafzimmer aus sieht man den Aufbau des Hauses mit den verschiedenfarbigen Mauern und den geometrischen Formen der einzelnen Gebäudeteile. **OBEN** Das Flachdach der Schlafzimmer dient ebenfalls als offene Terrasse, die an das Esszimmer anschließt. ※ **PAGE DE GAUCHE, EN HAUT** Le propriétaire actuel de la maison, Guillermo Mederos, fumant un havane sur sa terrasse, avec le Cojímar en toile de fond. **A GAUCHE** Depuis le toit au-dessus des chambres, on apprécie la conception de la maison, avec ses murs de différentes couleurs et les formes géométriques des divers espaces. **CI-DESSUS** La salle à manger s'ouvre sur le toit au-dessus des chambres, qui forme une terrasse.

Casa Fúster

Ode to Joy.

José Rodríguez Fúster's artistic vision is like the universe: always expanding. It is optimistic and joyful, a lesson about life and the art of Cuba. A painter, sculptor and ceramist indebted to Picasso and Gaudí, he is also a storyteller who moves between fantasy and reality. The vibrant colors and recognizable motifs of his work announce the proximity of his home when you approach his neighborhood in Jaimanitas, west of Havana. The creative spirit of its owner has haunted this house: men, animals, strange creatures, and everyday objects connive to express the artist's vitality in an endless discourse where you cannot discern categories or techniques. Hats, bottles, benches, and tables are incorporated into the decoration. The richness of this world of textures and colors is found in every corner of the house. The swimming pool reflects an octopus gazebo on the upstairs terrace, a bull's figure glares from the roof, and painted faces appear in the carport's tiled columns and trees from the neighbor's yard. The home is an ode to life and joy, where an overflowing creativity and a fine sense of humor salute life the Fúster way.

Die künstlerische Vision des Malers, Bildhauers und Keramikers José Rodríguez Fúster erweitert sich, genau wie das Universum, ständig. Sie ist eine optimistische, lebensfrohe Darstellung des Lebens und der Kunst in Kuba. Fúster, dessen Werke von Picasso und Gaudí beeinflusst sind, ist ein fantastischer Geschichtenerzähler, der sich auf einer dünnen Linie zwischen Fantasie und Realität bewegt. Die für ihn typischen, lebhaften Farben und Motive findet man auch in seinem Haus in Jaimanitas, westlich von Havanna. Der kreative Geist des Besitzers manifestiert sich überall: Bewohner, Haustiere, seltsame Kreaturen und Alltagsobjekte strahlen die Vitalität des Künstlers aus. Hüte, Flaschen, Bänke und Tische sind Teil der Einrichtung, und bis in den hintersten Winkel findet man eine Fülle an Formen und Farben. So spiegelt sich der Tintenfisch-Pavillon auf der Terrasse im oberen Stockwerk im Schwimmbecken. Vom Dach blickt die Figur eines Bullen, und Gesichter gucken aus den mit Kacheln verkleideten Säulen des Parkplatzes und den Bäumen im Garten des Nachbars. Fústers Haus ist eine Hommage an die Lebensfreude. Überall spürt man die überschäumende Kreativität und den feinen Sinn des Hausherrn für Humor.

La vision artistique de José Rodríguez Fúster est comme l'univers : en expansion constante. Optimiste et joyeuse, elle est une leçon de vie et d'art cubain. Peintre, sculpteur, céramiste influencé par Picasso et Gaudí, c'est aussi un conteur qui navigue entre le rêve et la réalité. Dès que l'on pénètre dans son quartier de Jaimanitas, à l'ouest de la Havane, on reconnaît sa maison aux couleurs vives et aux motifs typiques de son œuvre. La créativité du maître des lieux est partout : hommes, animaux, chimères et objets quotidiens s'unissent pour exprimer sa vitalité dans un discours continu où l'on ne discerne plus les genres et les techniques. Chapeaux, bouteilles, bancs et tables sont intégrés dans la décoration. Aucun recoin n'échappe à cette richesse de textures et de couleurs : la piscine reflète la pergola en pieuvre de la terrasse à l'étage, un taureau vous observe depuis le toit et des visages peints apparaissent sur les colonnes carrelées de l'abri pour voiture et les arbres du voisin. Cette demeure est un hymne à la joie de vivre, sa créativité débordante et son humour rendant hommage à la vision du monde selon Fúster.

* **PREVIOUS DOUBLE PAGE** Fúster rejected the typically anonymous prefabricated system of building using concrete panels decorated his surfaces with murals. The exterior walls of the house next door are enlivened with sculptures and ceramic pieces created by the artist. **ABOVE LEFT** At the entrance of the Fúster house, one already discerns the artistic universe of his oeuvre. **LEFT** Fúster has claimed that Picasso is one of his masters as indicated by a table lamp with a bottle-shaped base. **ABOVE** Fúster also feels indebted to Antonio Gaudí. Large ceramic hands rendered in the technique known as "trencadís" emerge from the vault of a gazebo next to a Picasso-like female torso and a figure reminiscent of certain works by Joan Miró.

* **VORHERGEHENDE DOPPELSEITE** Fúster hat mit dem üblicherweise anonymen Bausystem anhand vorgefertigter Betonwände gebrochen und die großen Wände seines Hauses mit Gemälden versehen. Auch den Außenbereich des Nachbarhauses hat er ausgeschmückt. **OBEN LINKS** Schon am Eingang seines Hauses nimmt man das künstlerische Universum Fústers wahr. **LINKS** Fúster hat Picasso als einen Lehrmeister angegeben. Seine Tischlampe mit flaschenförmigem Fuß verdeutlicht den Einfluss Picassos auf den Künstler. **OBEN** Fúster räumt ein, auch in Gaudís Schuld zu stehen. Große Keramikhände sind mit einer als Trencadís-Mosaik bekannten Technik gestaltet und ragen aus der Kuppel eines Pavillons hervor. Im Hintergrund sieht man einen weiblichen Torso in Picasso-Manier und eine Figur, die an Werke von Joan Miró erinnert. * **DOUBLE PAGE PRECEDENTE** Fúster a transformé la structure habituellement anonyme des panneaux préfabriqués en béton en décorant toutes les surfaces de grandes fresques. Il a donné du caractère au jardin de son voisin en le remplissant de sculptures et de figures en céramiques de son cru. **PAGE DE GAUCHE, EN HAUT** Dès le seuil de la maison, on est plongé dans l'univers de l'artiste. **A GAUCHE** Fúster a déclaré que Picasso était l'un de ses maîtres, comme en témoigne cette lampe avec un pied en forme de bouteille. **CI-DESSUS** Fúster s'inspire également d'Antonio Gaudí. De grandes mains, réalisées avec des pièces de céramique cassées, soit la technique du « trencadís », émergent de la voûte d'une gloriette, aux côtés d'une figure féminine à la Picasso et d'une silhouette rappelant des œuvres de Joan Miró.

❋ **PREVIOUS DOUBLE PAGE** A riot of colors and shapes reflects the immense, contagious joie de vivre of the artist, who can leave no surface untouched by his creativity. Multicolored ceramic tiles cover every nook and cranny of his home. **ABOVE** A king wearing his crown decorates one of the walls on the property. **RIGHT** A ceramic tree is used to provide shade over one of the house's open terraces. **FACING PAGE** Different sculptures featuring whimsical shapes populate another terrace of the house of artist José Rodríguez Fuster.

❋ **VORHERGEHENDE DOPPELSEITE** Eine wahre Farben- und Formenpracht spiegelt die ungeheure und ansteckende Lebensfreude des Künstlers, der keine Fläche für Kreationen ungenutzt ließ. Die verschiedenfarbigen Keramikfliesen bedecken jeden Winkel seines Hauses. **OBEN** Ein gekrönter König schmückt eine der Grundstücksmauern. **RECHTS** Ein Keramikbaum spendet einer offenen Terrasse des Hauses Schatten. **RECHTE SEITE** Verschiedene Skulpturen mit verspielten Formen bevölkern die Terrassen des Künstlers José Rodríguez Fúster. ❋ **DOUBLE PAGE PRECEDENTE** Le carnaval de couleurs et de formes reflète l'immense et contagieuse joie de vivre de l'artiste dont la créativité touche les moindres surfaces. Des carreaux en céramique de toutes les couleurs recouvrent chaque recoin de sa maison. **CI-DESSUS, A DROITE ET PAGE DE DROITE** Un roi couronné décore un des murs de la propriété. Sur une terrasse, un arbre en céramique fait office de parasol. Une autre terrasse est peuplée de sculptures aux formes capricieuses.

※ **ABOVE, RIGHT AND FACING PAGE** A fear of plain surfaces. Both the indoor and outdoor spaces in Fúster's work are innovative, bold, and authentic. An enormous sense of carefree ease is present in all the artist's works, in his sense of both color and shape. **FOLLOWING PAGES** In the kitchen decoration, Fúster's hand touches the everyday and transforms it into art.
※ **LINKS OBEN, LINKS UND OBEN** Angst vor der Leere. Das Werk Fústers zeigt sich im Innen- wie im Außenbereich innovativ, verwegen und authentisch. Seine gesamte Kunst ist hinsichtlich der Farben und Formen von großer Lässigkeit geprägt. **FOLGENDE DOPPELSEITE** Bei der Einrichtung der Küche verwandelt Fúster Alltägliches in Kunst. ※ **PAGE DE GAUCHE, EN HAUT A GAUCHE CI-DESSUS** L'horreur du vide. L'intérieur comme l'extérieur de la maison de Fúster est innovateur, audacieux et authentique. L'œuvre de l'artiste est marquée par une grande insouciance ainsi que par son sens de la couleur et des formes. **DOUBLE PAGE SUIVANTE** Jusque dans la cuisine, la main de l'artiste s'empare du quotidien et le transforme en art.

Varadero

276 Hotel Internacional Varadero, *Varadero*

Varadero, located on the northernmost tip of the Hicacos Peninsula in Matanzas province, lies 100 miles east of Havana. Its beaches of fine white sand and swaying palms make Varadero one of the most famous resorts on the island, and one of the finest in the world. With almost 12 miles of limpid warm waters and enchanting natural beauty, it has long been a favorite destination for tourists. Even before the town was laid out in 1883, rustic summer homes were built in Varadero. The first tourism boom took place in the first half of the 20th century when picturesque wooden houses and buildings of local stone, clay tile roofs and ample windows characterized the beach town.

Varadero liegt ganz oben am nördlichsten Punkt von Hicacos, auf einer Halbinsel der Provinz Matanzas, rund 160 Kilometer östlich von Havanna. Die wunderschöne Landschaft, der 20 Kilometer lange feine, weiße Sandstrand, die Palmen, die sich im Wind wiegen, und das klare, warme Wasser machen Varadero zu einem der bekanntesten Ferienorte Kubas und locken seit Jahrzehnten Besucher an. Bereits vor der Gründung des Ortes 1883 wurden hier rustikale Sommerhäuser gebaut. Der Touristenansturm setzte allerdings erst in der ersten Hälfte des 20. Jahrhunderts ein. Malerische Holzhäuser und Häuser aus dem Stein der Gegend mit Lehmziegeldächern und großen Fens-

Varadero, à l'extrême nord de la péninsule d'Hicacos dans la province de Matanzas, se trouve à 160 kilomètres à l'est de la Havane. Son sable blanc et fin, ses palmiers ondoyants, en font la station balnéaire la plus célèbre de l'île et l'une des plus prisées du monde. Avec sa vingtaine de kilomètres de plages bordant une eau limpide et chaude, sa beauté naturelle enchanteresse, c'est depuis longtemps une destination touristique de choix. Même avant la fondation de la ville en 1883, on venait y passer l'été dans des bâtisses rustiques. Le premier essor touristique eut lieu au début du 20ᵉ siècle avec la construction de jolies maisons en bois ou en pierre locale, avec des toits en tuiles et de

Subsequently, strikingly modern buildings were built in the resort town, inspired by traditional Cuban architecture with porches and balconies, galleries, and patios of great charm and simplicity; many fit harmoniously into the magical landscape. Today, unfortunately, only a few wooden homes from the sensitive tourist development from the 1940s and 1950s survive. The avalanche of undistinguished, gigantic hotel architecture has damaged both the fragile ecosystem and the urban fabric. Moreover, the original character of the Blue Beach has been destroyed.

tern prägen das Gesicht des Strandortes. Später kamen schlichte ultra-moderne Häuser mit Veranden, Balkonen, Galerien und Innenhöfen dazu, die sich an der tradtionellen kubanischen Architektur orientieren und meist nahtlos in die zauberhafte Landschaft einfügen. Von den Holzhäusern sind heute nur noch wenige übriggeblieben. Sie und auch der »sanfte Tourismus«, der in den 1940ern und 1950ern prägend war, fielen dem Massentourismus und einer gigantischen, billigen Hotelarchitektur zum Opfer. Das Ortsbild, das fragile Ökosystem und auch der ursprüngliche Charakter des blauen Strandes wurden dadurch zerstört.

grandes fenêtres. Par la suite, la ville a vu fleurir des bâtiments d'une modernité surprenante inspirés par l'architecture traditionnelle cubaine avec porches, balcons, galeries et patios aussi simples que charmants, la plupart se fondant harmonieusement dans le paysage. Malheureusement, il ne subsiste que quelques-unes de ces maisons en bois et des constructions des années 1940 et 1950 qui respectaient le caractère du lieu. L'avalanche de complexes hôteliers gigantesques et laids a endommagé le fragile écosystème et le tissu urbain. En outre, la vraie personnalité de la plage bleue a été dénaturée.

HOTEL
INTERNACIONAL VARADERO

Sin, Sun, Sand, and Sea.

"Hotel Internacional Varadero" opened on Christmas Eve 1950. William Liebow decided to build his own hotel when he was rejected as a guest at the nearby Kawama Hotel for being Jewish. Soon it became the most glamorous destination in the country, attracting American businessmen and the international elite who played in the casino and were entertained in the cabaret. The elongated four-storey building was designed by the Cuban firm of Mira y Rosich, who positioned the low rectangular block parallel to the dune to take advantage of the excellent views of both the wide strip of sand and sea and the gardens. The lobby is decorated with marble statues, chandeliers, and furniture with marine motifs, expressing what was then considered "good taste." Mobster Meyer Lansky praised this casino as one of the most fascinating places in the world, a place where gamblers could feel comfortable in a distinguished atmosphere. And while the casino has vanished – gambling became illegal in 1959 – the magic remains. The allure of the sea, separated from the sky by the thin, deep blue, virtual line of the horizon, attracts visitors to this still charming hotel.

Als der Amerikaner William Liebow im Kawama Hotel in Varadero absteigen wollte, erlebte er eine böse Überraschung. Ihm wurde klar gemacht, Juden seien unerwünscht. Anstatt die Koffer zu packen, ließ er sich in der Nähe ein eigenes Hotel bauen. An Heiligabend 1950 öffnete das »Hotel Internacional Varadero« seine Türen. Bald gehörte das Haus zu den glanzvollsten Reisezielen Kubas, und eine illustre Gästeschar, von amerikanischen Geschäftsleuten bis zur internationalen Elite, vergnügte sich im Kasino und im Kabarett. Der untere, rechteckige Teil des in die Länge gezogenen vierstöckigen Gebäudes des Architekturbüros Mira y Rosich steht parallel zur Düne und gibt so beste Sicht auf den weiten Sandstrand, das Meer und den Garten frei. Die Marmorstatuen, Kronleuchter und Möbel, verziert mit Meeresmotiven, in der Lobby stehen für den »guten Geschmack« der 1950er. Auch Mafia-Legende Meyer Lansky war vom Hotel begeistert und pries das Kasino als einen der »faszinierendsten Orte« der Welt. 1959 wurde das Glücksspiel verboten, und das Kasino gibt es heute nicht mehr. Doch der Duft der eleganten Spielerwelt hängt immer noch in der Luft. Die Gäste haben bereits eine neue Attraktion gefunden: der faszinierende Ausblick auf das Meer mit dem dünnen, dunkelblauen Streifen am Horizont.

L'«Hotel Internacional Varadero» ouvrit ses portes la nuit de Noël 1950. Il fut construit par William Liebow, furieux d'avoir été éconduit de l'hôtel Kawama voisin parce qu'il était juif. Son établissement devint rapidement la destination la plus chic du pays, son casino et son cabaret attirant les hommes d'affaires américains et la jet-set. Le long bâtiment de quatre étages fut dessiné par le cabinet d'architectes cubains Mira y Rosich, qui placèrent le bloc rectangulaire parallèlement à la dune pour jouir de vues imprenables sur la large plage et les jardins. Le hall est orné de statues en marbre, de lustres et de meubles aux motifs marins, expression du «bon goût» d'alors. Le gangster Meyer Lansky déclarait que le casino était l'un des endroits les plus fascinants du monde, un lieu où les joueurs pouvaient se sentir à leur aise dans une ambiance raffinée. Si les croupiers ont disparu (les jeux d'argent furent interdits en 1959), la magie opère toujours. La beauté de la mer, séparée du ciel par la fine ligne bleu nuit de l'horizon, continue d'attirer les visiteurs dans cet hôtel qui n'a rien perdu de son charme.

※ **ABOVE LEFT** The sentry box at the entrance to the hotel premises with its open marquee of jutting reinforced concrete frames views towards the vast entrance gardens. **LEFT** Thanks to the hotel's privileged location, the sea on both sides of the Hicacos peninsula can be made out from the roof of the "Hotel Internacional Varaderos". **ABOVE** An anonymous stone sculpture rests on a carpet made by the large grassy areas in the hotel's gardens. ※ **OBEN LINKS** Die Pförtnerloge am Eingang des Hotelgrundstücks mit dem auskragenden, aus Stahlbeton gefertigten Vordach rahmt die Aussicht auf die weitläufige Grünanlage. **LINKS** Dank der privilegierten Lage kann man von der Dachterrasse des »Hotel Internacional Varaderos« aus das Meer auf beiden Seiten der Hicacos-Halbinsel sehen. **OBEN** Eine anonyme Steinskulptur ruht auf dem großflächigen Grasteppich des Hotelparks. ※ **PAGE DE GAUCHE, EN HAUT** La guérite qui garde l'entrée du parc de l'hôtel, avec son auvent flottant en béton armé. **A GAUCHE** Grâce à son site privilégié, depuis le toit de l'hôtel on voit la mer des deux côtés de la péninsule d'Hicacos. **CI-DESSUS** Une sculpture en pierre d'un artiste anonyme se dresse sur le tapis de verdure que forment les vastes étendues de gazon tout autour de l'hôtel.

✳ **ABOVE LEFT** The four-storey block of rooms at the "Hotel Internacional Varadero" is close to the sand dunes. A thatched umbrella creates a small shaded spot for swimmers. **LEFT** A recessed wall hides the service area from the sight of tourists at the "Hotel Internacional Varadero". **ABOVE** The spacious terrace serves as a pleasant transition between the beach and the hotel building, which boasts magnificent views of the sea. ✳ **OBEN LINKS** Der vierstöckige Gebäudeblock des »Hotel Internacional Varadero« liegt in der Nähe der Düne. Einen Sonnenschirm aus Palmblättern spendet den Badegästen ein wenig Schatten. **LINKS** Eine Mauer verbirgt den Servicebereich vor den Blicken der Gäste. **OBEN** Die geräumige Terrasse des »Hotel Internacional Varadero« bildet einen angenehmen Übergang zwischen dem Strand und dem Hotelbau, von wo aus man einen prächtigen Meerblick genießen kann. ✳ **PAGE DE GAUCHE, EN HAUT** Côté mer, le bâtiment de quatre étages a les pieds dans le sable. Un parasol en paille offre un peu d'ombre aux baigneurs. **A GAUCHE** Un mur en caissons cache la partie des services. **CI-DESSUS** La vaste terrasse, d'où l'on a une superbe vue sur la mer, établit une transition agréable entre la plage et l'hôtel.

❋ **ROW ABOVE** The sea can be seen from the hotel's entrance. The vestibule, open and transparent, is oriented toward the landscape and decorated with classical and marine-themed statues. Inside, the undulating shape of the counter stands out. **ROW BELOW** The bar is located between the vestibule and the restaurant, where a mural alluding to tobacco cultivation by the artist M. Babilonia occupies the wall dividing them. The café is noteworthy for the color of its floors and walls, which contrasts with its furnishings. ❋ **OBERE REIHE** Vom Hotel-eingang aus kann man das Meer sehen. Das offene, transparente Vestibül ist der Landschaft angepasst und mit klassischen Skulpturen und Meeresmotiven eingerichtet. Besonders her-vorzuheben ist die wellenförmig gestaltete Rezeption. **UNTERE REIHE** Die Bar befindet sich zwischen dem Vestibül und dem Restaurant. Diese sind durch eine Mauer getrennt, die ein Wand-

gemälde des Künstlers M. Babilonia mit Anspielung auf den Tabakanbau einnimmt. Das Café besticht durch die Farbenfreude des Bodens und der Wände, die einen Kontrast zum Mobiliar bilden. ✳ **RANGEE DU HAUT** Depuis l'entrée, on a vue sur la mer. Le hall, ouvert et transparent, est orienté vers le paysage et décoré de statues classiques et de motifs marins. À l'intérieur, la réception aux formes marines. **RANGEE DU BAS** Le bar est situé entre le hall et le restaurant, séparé de ce dernier par une peinture murale de l'artiste M. Babilonia décrivant la culture du café. La cafétéria se distingue par les couleurs de son sol et de ses murs qui contrastent avec le mobilier.

❋ **ABOVE** The entrance to the "Universal" restaurant, where the casino used to be back when the hotel opened in 1950. **RIGHT** The shape of a curved reinforced concrete panel jutting out alludes to the sails of a boat and shades the lovely terrace of the "Hotel Internacional Varadero". **FACING PAGE** The sea grapes and coconut trees on the hotel's terrace frame views towards the lovely beach. **FOLLOWING PAGES** A cluster of thatched umbrellas on the fine white sand of the beach across from the "Hotel Internacional" provides shade for swimmers while they read or gaze out to sea. ❋ **OBEN** Der Eingang zum Restaurant »Universal«, wo sich einst bei der Einweihung des Hotels im Jahr 1950 das Kasino befand. **RECHTS** Eine auskragende, gebogene Stahlbetonplatte erinnert mit seiner Form an die Segel eines Boots und bedeckt die wunderschöne Terrasse des »Hotel Internacional Varadero«. **RECHTE SEITE** Die Seetrauben und Kokospalmen auf der Hotelterrasse rahmen die Aussicht auf den herrlichen Strand. **FOLGENDE DOPPELSEITE** Eine Gruppe von Sonnenschirmen aus Palmblättern steht im feinen, weißen Sand des Strands vor dem Hotel und bietet den Strandbesuchern etwa Schatten beim Lesen bzw. beim Blick aufs Meer. ❋ **CI-DESSUS** L'entrée du restaurant « Universal », où se trouvait autrefois le casino quant l'hôtel fut inauguré en 1950. **A DROITE** Une dalle flottante en béton armé renvoie, par ses courbes, aux voiles d'une embarcation et protège la belle terrasse de l'hôtel. **PAGE DE DROITE** Les raisinniers bord-de-mer et les cocotiers encadrent les vues sur la belle plage. **DOUBLE PAGE SUIVANTE** Devant l'hôtel, un groupe de parasols en paille plantés dans le sable blanc et fin offrent de l'ombre aux baigneurs pendant qu'ils lisent ou contemplent la mer.

Santiago de Cuba & Bayamo

290 Casa Diego Velázquez, *Santiago de Cuba*
296 Casa natal Heredia, *Santiago de Cuba*
800 Casa Quesada, *Santiago de Cuba*
808 Casa natal Céspedes, *Bayamo*

Santiago de Cuba lies in the southernmost part of the eastern region of the Cuban archipelago. Founded by Don Diego Velázquez de Cuéllar in 1515, it can be found in the widest section of this elongated island, which is said to resemble a caiman, or tropical alligator. This coastal city became the island's first capital, perhaps because of its strategic location between the mountains of the Sierra Maestra and a bay deep enough for large ships – "conquistadores" departed from the port of Santiago to take gold from Mexico and Peru back to Spain. The city grew according to its needs, its buildings following the steep topography of the terrain, and a picturesque vernacular architecture

Santiago de Cuba wurde 1515 von Don Diego Velázquez de Cuéllar gegründet und liegt am Südende des östlichen Teils der langgezogenen Insel, die in ihrer Form an einen Alligatoren erinnert. Santiago war die erste Hauptstadt Kubas, vermutlich weil der Ort strategisch günstig lag: zwischen den Bergen der Sierra Maestra und einer tiefen Bucht, in der Schiffe der Spanier gut ankern konnten. Vom Hafen liefen die Conquistadores jeweils Richtung Spanien aus – ihre Schiffe vollgeladen mit Gold aus Mexico und Peru. Im Laufe der Zeit vergrößerte sich die Stadt, und die Bauweise passte sich der steilen Topographie und dem Klima der Gegend an. Für den Bau der Häuser

Santiago de Cuba, à l'extrême sud de la partie orientale de l'archipel cubain, a été fondée par Don Diego Velázquez de Cuéllar en 1515. Elle se situe dans la partie la plus large de cette longue île que l'on compare à un caïman. Sans doute du fait de son site stratégique entre les montagnes de la Sierra Maestra et une baie suffisamment profonde pour accueillir de gros navires, elle fut la première capitale de l'île : dans son port, les conquistadors chargeaient l'or mexicain et péruvien qu'ils emportaient en Espagne. La ville se développa en fonction de ses besoins, ses bâtiments épousant le terrain escarpé, et une architecture locale pittoresque émergea des styles coloniaux adaptés au

Casa Diego Velázquez

Casa natal Heredia

Casa Quesada

Casa natal Céspedes

merged from the colonial styles that were adapted to local climatic conditions: elevated porches and protruding windows were common, and most houses were built with local materials. El Cobre, one of Cuba's most sacred churches, was founded in 1599 near the copper mines. There, the shrine of the "Virgen de la Caridad del Cobre", patron saint of Cuba, symbolizes the variety and mixture of races and religions that live in harmony on the island.

wurden ausschließlich Materialien aus der Umgebung verwendet. Dadurch entstand eine malerische Architektur, und die Kolonialhäuser mit erhöhten Veranden und vorstehenden Fenstern haben viel Lokalkolorit. 1599 wurde in der Nähe der Kupferminen von El Cobre, wenige Kilometer von Santiago, eine der bedeutendsten Kirchen Kubas gebaut. In dieser steht der Schrein der Kirche, mit der »Virgen de la Caridad del Cobre«, welche die Schutzpatronin der Insel ist und das harmonische Zusammenleben der verschiedenen Ethnien und Religionen symbolisiert.

climat tropical. Les porches surélevés et les fenêtres saillantes étaient courants et la plupart des maisons étaient bâties avec des matériaux de la région. El Cobre, une des églises les plus sacrées de Cuba, fut érigée en 1599 près des mines de cuivre. Elle abrite la châsse de la Vierge de la Caridad del Cobre, patronne de Cuba, symbole de la variété et du brassage des races et des religions qui cohabitent en harmonie sur l'île.

CASA DIEGO VELÁZQUEZ

The Place were Gold was Processed.

Headed by Don Diego Velázquez de Cuéllar, the "conquistadores" founded seven settlements across the island, after which Velázquez decided to settle in Santiago de Cuba. His own house was the place where gold was processed before being sent on to Spain, and it was built across from the military parade ground, near the bay and the cathedral. The building is exceptional for its well-balanced proportions and intimate scale, its great coherence, and its elegant detailing. The beautiful façades feature sturdy, overhanging balconies and bay windows protected by wooden latticework of Moorish influence that is set against the ornate ashlar masonry of the walls. The courtyard, surrounded by stone arches and wooden columns on the ground floor, and by screened galleries decorated with friezes on the upper floor, is a masterpiece. The interior spaces are warm and welcoming, featuring terracotta tile floors and finely carved trusses with ornate tie beams, collars, and collar plates. These reflect both the "mudéjar" style and the fine craftsmanship of the carpenters. The beauty and charm of the building reveals the passage of time and reminds us of the words written by the poet John Keats: "A thing of beauty is a joy forever."

Die spanischen Conquistadores gründeten auf der Insel Kuba unter der Führung von Don Diego Velázquez de Cuéllar sieben Städte, darunter Santiago. Velázquez machte sie zu seinem Wohnsitz. Sein Haus liegt gegenüber des Exerzierplatzes, ganz in der Nähe der Bucht und der Kathedrale. Unter seinem Dach wurde auch das Gold verarbeitet, das nach Spanien verschifft wurde. Die Residenz Velázquez' ist eines der elegantesten Gebäude Santiagos. Durch seine ausgewogenen Proportionen wirkt es kompakt und besticht durch elegante Details, eine wunderschöne Fassade aus kunstvoll angelegten Quadersteinen, überhängende, doch stabile Balkone und Erkerfenster mit Holzgittern im maurischen Stil. Der Innenhof ist ein wahres Meisterwerk. Er ist umgeben von Torbögen aus Stein und Holzsäulen. Darüber stehen überdachte Galerien mit Friesdekor. Das Innere des Hauses wirkt warm und einladend. Terrakottaböden, feine Schnitzereien, verziertes Gebälk und Rosetten stehen für den sogenannten »Mudéjar«-Stil und zeugen vom kunstvollen Handwerk der damaligen Schreiner. Auch die Zeit konnte der Pracht und dem Charme dieses Hauses nichts anhaben. Die Worte des englischen Dichters John Keats, »Ein schönes Objekt bringt ewige Freude«, passen hier wunderbar.

Don Diego Velázquez de Cuellar ordonna aux conquistadors de créer plusieurs colonies sur l'île, jusqu'à ce qu'il décide de s'établir à Santiago de Cuba. C'est dans sa propre demeure qu'était traité l'or avant d'être acheminé en Espagne. Elle fut bâtie en face du terrain de manœuvres militaires, près de la baie et de la cathédrale. Ses proportions équilibrées, son échelle humaine, sa grande cohérence et l'élégance de ses détails en font un bâtiment exceptionnel. Ses belles façades se distinguent par leurs robustes balcons et des bow-windows protégés de moucharabiehs d'influence mauresque qui contrastent avec les murs en pierre de taille sculptée. La cour, ceinte d'arches en pierre et de colonnes en bois au rez-de-chaussée et de galeries décorées de frises et abritées derrière des paravents à l'étage, est un chef-d'œuvre. Les espaces intérieurs sont chaleureux et accueillants, avec des sols en carreaux de terre cuite et une charpenterie apparente finement sculptée et peinte. La décoration témoigne à la fois du style « mudéjar » et du grand savoir-faire des artisans locaux. La beauté et le charme du bâtiment reflètent le passage du temps et illustrent les paroles du poète anglais John Keats : « La beauté est une joie éternelle. »

※ **PREVIOUS DOUBLE PAGE** In the interior spaces, the magnificent collar-and-beam trusses of the ceilings with exquisitely decorated rods, braces, and open spaces. The atmosphere is exceptional due to the charm conferred through the use of wood and clay. **FACING PAGE** The thick masonry walls of the galleries wending their way around the lovely inner courtyard on the upper storey are richly adorned with friezes that frame the bays on the doors and the Spanish shuttered windows. **ABOVE** One of the rooms on the lower level with its stone slab floor and the wooden ceiling beams. The heavy furniture imported from Spain is of incalculable value due to the quality of its design and manufacture. ※ **VORHERGEHENDE DOPPELSEITE** Im Innern fallen die prächtigen Kehlbalkendecken mit der erlesenen Verzierung ihrer Sparren, Kopfbänder und Füllungen auf. Die Verwendung von Holz und Ton verleiht den einzigartigen Räumlichkeiten ihren Zauber. **LINKE SEITE** Die dicken Ziegelsteinmauern der Gallerien, die den wunderschönen Innenhof im Obergeschoss umgeben, sind reichlich mit Zierleisten dekoriert, welche die spanischen Paneeltüren und -fenster rahmen. **OBEN** Eines der Zimmer im Erdgeschoss mit seinem Steinboden und den hölzernen Deckenbalken. Die schweren Möbel aus Spanien sind aufgrund ihrer Design- und Fertigungsqualität von unschätzbarem Wert. ※ **DOUBLE PAGE PRÉCÉDENTE** À l'intérieur, on est d'abord frappé par les superbes armatures de chevrons et chevilles de la charpente apparente, avec l'exquise décoration de ses entretoises, de ses arbalétriers et de ses entraits. Le mélange du bois et des murs en terre crée une atmosphère envoûtante. **PAGE DE GAUCHE** À l'étage, les épais murs des galeries qui entourent le beau patio sont décorés de frises qui encadrent les chambranles des portes et des fenêtres espagnoles à panneaux. **CI-DESSUS** Une des chambres du rez-de-chaussée, avec un sol en dalles et des poutres apparentes. Les meubles espagnols massifs et précieux sont d'une qualité exceptionnelle.

CASA NATAL HEREDIA

The Home of a Poet and Patriot.

The short life of the poet and patriot José María Heredia – he was only 36 years old when he died – was filled with love, sadness, and suffering. José Martí, the greatest of all Cuban writers and patriots, praised him as the first romantic poet of the Americas, and his talent earned him a place of honor in 19th century poetry. The 18th century house where Heredia was born, located on one of the busiest thoroughfares of Santiago de Cuba, is preserved in its original state. The façade still retains the asymmetric arrangement of the large studded Spanish entry door and three baroque-style windows protected with turned-wood grillwork. The thick walls were built using the peculiar combination of masonry and woven rods, or "cujes," to resist earthquakes. The entrance to the house, via a small external staircase, or "perron," on the sidewalk, leads to the main room. There, a wooden arch with a foliated intrados frames the doorway to a simple but lovely courtyard surrounded by galleries on three of its sides and planted with the palm trees that always seem to be present in Heredia's poems.

Das kurze Leben des Dichters José María Heredia, er starb mit 36 Jahren, war geprägt von Leidenschaft, Liebe und Schmerz. Der bedeutendste Schriftsteller Kubas, José Martí, bezeichnete ihn als ersten romantischen Dichter des amerikanischen Kontinents. Heredias Talent sicherte ihm einen Ehrenplatz in der Dichtkunst des 19. Jahrhunderts. Sein Geburtshaus aus dem 18. Jahrhundert liegt an einer belebten Durchgangsstraße in Santiago de Cuba und ist noch völlig unverändert. In der asymmetrischen Fassade prangen eine schwere spanische Eingangstüre und drei Barockfenster mit gedrechselten Holzgittern. Die dicken Mauern wurden mit Armierungseisen, den »Cujes«, verstärkt, um sie erdbebensicher zu machen. Vom Gehsteig führt eine schmale Treppe, ein »Perron«, zum Eingang. Von da gelangt man direkt in den großen Wohnraum. Ein Torbogen aus Holz und einem Blätterwerkgewölbe führt zu einem schlichten, reizenden Innenhof, der auf drei Seiten von Galerien umgeben ist. Dort stehen auch die Palmen, die Heredia in seinen Gedichten immer wieder erwähnt.

La vie brève du poète et patriote José María Heredia (il est mort à 36 ans) fut remplie d'amour, de tristesse et de souffrance. José Martí, le plus grand des écrivains patriotes de l'île, le loua comme étant le premier romantique des Amériques. Son talent lui valut une place d'honneur dans la poésie du 19ᵉ siècle. La maison où il est né, datant du 18ᵉ siècle, située dans l'une des artères les plus animées de Santiago de Cuba, a été préservée dans son état d'origine. La façade conserve sa disposition asymétrique avec sa grande porte espagnole cloutée et trois fenêtres baroques protégées de barreaux en bois tourné. Ses épais murs sont construits avec une combinaison singulière antisismique de maçonnerie et de «cujes», des tiges de bois tressées. On y accède par un petit escalier extérieur, menant au perron. L'entrée donne directement sur la pièce principale, surmontée d'une charpente apparente en poutres épaisses. Au fond, une arche mixtiligne avec un intrados en rinceaux s'ouvre sur une cour simple mais charmante entourée de galeries sur trois côtés et plantée de ces palmiers omniprésents dans les poèmes d'Heredia.

ABOUT LEFT Bedroom of the poet Heredia with its 19th century gondola-style mahogany bed. **LEFT** The gallery and simple yet beautiful inner courtyard are reached through the mixtilinear wooden arch with its foliated intrados frame. **ABOVE** The baroque lines of the timbered windows in the living room area are protected by turned-wood grillwork. The Imperial-style Cuban furnishings date from the 19th century. The painting in the oval frame was donated by the poet's son on the centenary of his father's birth ※ **OBEN LINKS** Das Schlafzimmer des Dichters mit dem Mahagonibett im Gondelstil des 19. Jahrhunderts. **LINKS** Durch den Holzbogen mit gelappter Innenfläche gelangt man in den schlichten, jedoch schönen Innenhof. **OBEN** Das Wohnzimmer mit seinen durch gedrechselte Stangen geschützten Fenstern, deren barocken Fensterläden und den kubanischen Möbeln im Imperialstil des 19. Jahrhunderts. Das Gemälde mit dem ovalen Rahmen wurde vom Sohn des Dichters anlässlich der Jahrhundertfeier zum Geburtstag seines Vaters gestiftet. ※ **PAGE DE GAUCHE, EN HAUT** La chambre du poète Heredia avec un lit gondole en acajou datant du 19ᵉ siècle. **A GAUCHE** L'arche en bois avec un intrados à lobes donne sur une galerie et un patio aussi joli que simple. **CI-DESSOUS** Le séjour, avec ses fenêtres à panneaux aux lignes baroques protégées par des barreaux en bois tourné et ses meubles cubains de style empire du 19ᵉ siècle. Le portrait dans un cadre ovale fut donné par le fils du poète à l'occasion du centenaire de sa naissance.

casa

QUESADA

In the Style of French Coffee and Sugar Planters.

Étienne Sulpice Hallet, a French architect known for the original, unused designs for the US Capitol building he drafted in 1792, was living in Havana by 1800. He introduced neoclassical architecture to Cuba. In 1828, Antonio María de la Torre built a pavilion – the "Templete," shaped like a classical temple – on the Plaza de Armas, so furthering the influence of neoclassicism in Cuba. At around the same time, French sugar and coffee planters, who had migrated to Cuba after the 1791 Haitian Revolution, brought with them the spirit of enlightenment as well as economic growth. Their cultural imprint can certainly be seen in the Cuban appreciation of French music and painting, but perhaps more so in the practice of coffee-drinking, which became a quintessential Cuban habit. Those who settled in Santiago de Cuba brought these new ideas and practices with them, as well as their fondness for neoclassicism in their homes. Although the traditional arrangement of a house around a central courtyard was retained, the style of interior decoration was updated and the materials they used also changed. In the Quesada house, the arches facing the patio were enclosed with French louvered doors, or "persiennes," while colored glass windows, or "mediopuntos," filtered the sunlight. Terracotta floors were replaced by marble, and friezes were added to the interior paneling.

Der französische Architekt Étienne Sulpice Hallet entwarf 1792 Pläne für das Kapitol in Washington. Sie wurden aber nie umgesetzt. Um 1800 ließ er sich in Havanna nieder und brachte die neoklassizistische Architektur nach Kuba. Die Strömung gewann an Einfluss, als Antonio Maria de la Torre 1828 den Pavillon »Templete« auf der »Plaza de Armas« nach dem Vorbild eines klassischen Tempels baute. Französische Zucker- und Kaffeeplantagenbesitzer, die 1791 vor der Revolution in Haiti nach Kuba flüchteten, brachten gleichzeitig den Geist der Aufklärung ins Land. Ihr Einfluss ist immer noch spürbar: Die Kubaner haben bis heute eine besondere Vorliebe für französische Musik und Malerei. Auch die Kaffeekultur, heute eine typisch kubanische Angelegenheit, wurde von den französischen Einwanderern eingeführt. Die Häuser wurden damals zwar in alter Tradition rund um einen Innenhof gebaut, doch bei der Wahl der Materialen und der Einrichtung ließ man sich von den neuen Ideen inspirieren. So auch die Familie Quesada aus Santiago. In ihrem Haus ließen sie französische Lamellentüren, »Persiennes«, in die Torbögen beim Innenhof einbauen und in die Oberlichter farbiges Glas, »Mediopuntos«, einsetzen. Die Terrakottaböden haben sie durch Marmor ersetzen lassen und die Wandpaneele mit Friesdekor versehen.

Étienne Sulpice Hallet, un architecte français connu pour ses plans non retenus pour le Capitol de Washington en 1792, s'installa à la Havane vers 1800. Il y introduisit l'architecture néoclassique en dessinant le premier cimetière municipal. En 1828, Antonio María de la Torre érigea un pastiche de temple antique, le Templete, sur la Plaza de Armas, renforçant encore l'influence de ce style. Vers la même époque, les planteurs français de tabac et de sucre, émigrés à Cuba après la révolution haïtienne de 1791, apportèrent avec eux, outre la croissance économique, l'esprit des Lumières. Le goût des Cubains pour la musique et la peinture françaises témoigne de leur empreinte sur la culture locale, mais pas autant que la consommation de café, qui intégra rapidement les mœurs cubaines. Ceux qui s'établirent à Santiago de Cuba importèrent leurs nouvelles idées et pratiques, ainsi que leur attachement au néoclassicisme. Tout en conservant la disposition traditionnelle des pièces autour d'un patio central, ils modernisèrent la décoration et les matériaux. Dans la maison de la famille Quesada, des persiennes protègent les arcades du patio, tandis que les arcs en plein cintre sont dotés de vitraux. Sur les sols, les carreaux de terre cuite ont été remplacés par du marbre et les boiseries enrichies de frises.

※ **ABOVE** All the house's spaces are arranged around the inner courtyard, embellished with plants and sculptures following the tradition, including the kitchen, which can be seen in the background. **RIGHT** The bays are closed with French "persiennes," or louvered doors, and the semicircular arches are surmounted by lovely colored glass windows. **FACING PAGE** The flat roofs act as terraces which are used as additional living and lounging areas and serve to enlarge the house on the upper storey. **FOLLOWING DOUBLE PAGE** The pleasing atmosphere in the dining room is bedecked with neoclassical drapery and fine Cuban wooden furniture, this room occupies a key location near the courtyard. The semicircular colored glass windows filter the harsh outdoor light. ※ **OBEN** Um den traditionsgemäß mit Pflanzen und Skulpturen ausgeschmückten Innenhof liegen die Räumlichkeiten des Hauses, einschließlich der Küche hinten im Bild. **RECHTS** Die Lichtöffnungen werden mit Lamellenläden verschlossen, die Rundbögen mit bunten Oberlichtern. **RECHTE SEITE** Die Flachdächer werden genutzt, um Dachterrassen und daher zusätzliche Aufenthalts- und Ruhebereiche einzurichten sowie um das Haus im Obergeschoss auszubauen. **FOLGENDE DOPPELSEITE** Das Esszimmer ist im neoklassizistischen Stil und mit Möbeln aus kubanischem Edelholz eingerichtet und besitzt eine hervorragende Lage direkt neben dem Innenhof. Die Oberlichter aus Buntglas filtern das von außen einfallende Licht. ※ **CI-DESSUS** Toutes les pièces de la maison donnent sur le patio, agrémenté de plantes vertes et de sculptures comme le veut la tradition, y compris la cuisine que l'on aperçoit au fond. **A DROITE** Les portes-fenêtres sont protégées par des persiennes et surmontées d'arcs en plein cintre ornés de beaux vitraux. **PAGE A DROITE** Les toits plats se convertissent en terrasses, aménagées en aires supplémentaires de détente et en extension de l'étage supérieur. **DOUBLE PAGE SUIVANTE** La salle à manger dégage une atmosphère agréable avec ses draperies néoclassiques et ses meubles cubains en bois précieux. Elle occupe une place de choix devant le patio. Les vitraux filtrent la lumière extérieure.

※ **FACING PAGE** The kitchen at the back of the house. **ABOVE** The living room with wooden trussing, from which a crystal lamp is suspended. The English furniture is crafted of rosewood.
※ **LINKE SEITE** Die Küche im hinteren Teil des Hauses. **OBEN** Im Wohnzimmer hängt eine Lampe aus Kristallglas herunter. Die englischen Möbel sind aus Palisanderholz gefertigt.
※ **PAGE DE GAUCHE** La cuisine est généralement placée au fond de la maison. **CI-DESSUS** Le vaste salon, avec son lustre en cristal très raffiné.

casa

natal céspedes

"Viva Cuba Libre."

On 10th October, 1868, Carlos Manuel de Céspedes, a rich and cultivated lawyer, freed the slaves who worked on his farm "La Demajagua". In doing so, he changed Cuba forever. His historic manifesto claimed the first declaration of independence from Spain, and is famous for its powerful statement, "Viva Cuba Libre!" Afterwards, Céspedes set off for the forest and soon took over several cities, including Bayamo, where the Cuban national anthem was sung for the first time by an excited crowd. The "Father of the Homeland" established a temporary government here, but in 1869 it was decided to set it on fire rather than let it be occupied by the Spanish. Céspedes' birthplace, now a museum on the Plaza de Armas, is a two-storey building with a C-shaped plan based around an inner courtyard with galleries. Although the ground-floor was built in the 18th century, the top floor wasn't added until 1833. The façade features regular openings surrounded by flat moldings and a wooden balcony protected by a wrought-iron railing. A lovely wooden staircase with a mahogany banister leads upstairs, where exquisite furniture, elaborate woodwork, and friezes decorate rooms that are linked by a gallery supported by octagonal stanchions.

Der wohlhabende und kultivierte Anwalt Carlos Manuel de Céspedes befreite am 10. Oktober 1868 auf seiner Farm »La Demajagua« seine Sklaven. Es war die erste Manifestation der Unabhängigkeit von Spanien und die Geburtsstunde des berühmten Leitspruchs »Viva Cuba Libre!«. Céspedes versteckte sich dann im Wald, doch bald schon übernahm er das Kommando über mehrere Städte, darunter Bayamo. Hier sang eine begeisterte Menge zum ersten Mal die kubanische Nationalhymne, und hier gründete der »Vater des Heimatlandes« eine provisorische Regierung. 1869 jedoch setzten die Bewohner die Stadt in Brand, damit die Spanier sie nicht besetzen konnten. Das zweistöckige Geburtshaus Céspedes' an der Plaza de Armas liegt in Form eines »C« rund um einen Innenhof mit Gallerien und ist heute ein Museum. Das Erdgeschoss wurde bereits im 18. Jahrhundert gebaut, das obere Stockwerk kam erst 1833 dazu. Die Fassade wird von regelmäßigen Fensteröffnungen durchbrochen und und hat einen Holzbalkon mit schmiedeeisernem Geländer. Das herrliche Treppenhaus mit einem Geländer aus Mahagoni führt in die oberen Räume. Sie sind durch eine Gallerie mit achteckigen Säulen untereinander verbunden und mit auserlesenen Möbeln, kunstvollen Holzarbeiten und Friesdekor stilvoll eingerichtet.

Le 10 octobre 1868, Carlos Manuel de Céspedes, un avocat riche et cultivé, libéra les esclaves qui travaillaient dans sa ferme «La Demajagua», changeant à jamais Cuba. Son manifeste historique, première déclaration d'indépendance vis-à-vis de l'Espagne, est resté célèbre pour son puissant «Viva Cuba libre!». Céspedes ne tarda pas à convertir d'autres villes, dont Bayamo où l'hymne cubain retentit pour la première fois entonné par une foule en liesse. Le «père de la patrie» y établit un gouvernement provisoire mais, en 1869, il préféra incendier la ville plutôt que de la livrer aux Espagnols. Sa maison natale sur la Plaza de Armas, aujourd'hui un musée, est un bâtiment en U construit autour d'une cour intérieure ceinte de galeries. Le rez-de-chaussée date du 18e siècle mais l'étage fut ajouté en 1833. Sa façade présente des ouvertures rectangulaires encadrées de moulures plates et un balcon en bois protégé d'une balustrade en fer forgé. Un bel escalier en bois avec une rampe en acajou mène à l'étage, où les chambres, meublées avec raffinement, décorées de boiseries ouvragées et de frises, communiquent par une galerie soutenue d'étançons octogonaux.

※ **PREVIOUS PAGES** The courtyard in Carlos Manuel de Céspedes's birthplace is narrow and elongated, with an L-shaped gallery running along both stories. * The gallery on the lower floor, supported by square columns with Tuscan capitals, links all the spaces on the lower level and joins the home's two court-yards. **ABOVE** A bust of lawyer Carlos Manuel de Céspedes, "Father of the Homeland" and first president of the Republic-in-Arms. **RIGHT, FACING PAGE AND FOLLOWING DOUBLE PAGE** The house's living room looks out onto the square from its continuous balcony. Rich Victorian rococo-style furnishings dating from the 19th century are combined with the Cuban Medallón-style furnishings from the same period and a variety of porce-lain knick-knacks and fine glassware. ※ **VORHERGEHENDE DOPPELSEITE** Der Innenhof des Geburtshauses von Carlos Manuel de Céspedes ist schmal und länglich und besitzt eine L-förmige Gallerie, die sich über beide Stockwerke erstreckt. * Die Gallerie des Erdgeschosses wird von Säulen mit toskanischen Kapitells getragen und verbindet alle Räume des Erdgeschosses sowie die beiden Höfe des Hauses. **OBEN** Eine Büste des Anwalts Carlos Manuel de Céspedes, des Begründers der kubanischen Nation und ersten Präsidenten der Untergrundbewegung (der so genannten »Republik in Waffen«). **RECHTS, RECHTE SEITE UND FOLGENDE DOPPELSEITE** Das Wohnzimmer des Hauses ist mit seinem durchgehenden Balkon zur Straße hin ausgerichtet. Prächtige viktorianische Möbel im Rokokostil des 19. Jahrhunderts vermischen sich mit den kubanischen Möbeln im Medaillon-Stil derselben Epoche und verschiedenen Schmuckgegenständen aus Porzellan und Glas. **DOUBLE PAGE PRECEDENTE** Long et étroit, le patio est bordé d'une galerie en L sur deux niveaux.* Au rez-de-chaussée, toutes les pièces donnent sur la galerie, soutenue par des colonnes surmontées de chapiteaux toscans. Celle-ci relie également les deux cours intérieures de la maison. **CI-DESSUS** Un buste de maître Carlos Manuel de Céspedes, père de la patrie et premier président de la République en Armes. **A DROITE, PAGE DE DROITE ET DOUBLE PAGE SUIVANTE** Le long balcon du salon domine la Plaza. Le riche mobilier anglais rococo du 19e siècle côtoie des meubles médaillons cubains de la même époque et des objets d'art d'ori-gines diverses en porcelaine et cristal.

※ **PREVIOUS PAGES** A lovely bronze headboard with inlaid mother-of-pearl from the 19th century. * The walls are decorated with brightly colored friezes. **FACING PAGE** An elliptical-shaped rose window made of colored glass illuminates the simple mahogany staircase. **ABOVE** The kitchen, in the back of the house's lower floor, is roomy. The kitchen is tiled and has a hood for eliminating odors. ※ **VORHERGEHENDE DOPPELSEITE** Ein Bronzebett aus dem 19. Jahrhundert mit Perlmuttintarsien im Schlafzimmer. * Die Wände sind mit farbenfrohen Friesen bemalt. **LINKE SEITE** Ein ellipsenförmiges Buntglasfenster spendet der schlichten Mahagonitreppe Licht. **OBEN** Die Küche ist mit Keramikfliesen verkleidet und mit einer Dunstabzugshaube ausgestattet. ※ **DOUBLE PAGE PRECEDENTE** Un lit en bronze 19ᵉ avec des incrustations de nacre. * Dans une des chambres, une suspension ornée de motifs fleuris et des frises polychromes. **PAGE DE GAUCHE** Le vitrail d'un œil-de-bœuf éclaire l'escalier simple en acajou. **CI-DESSUS** Le plan de travail carrelé est surmonté d'une hotte aspirante.

TRiNiDaD

322 Palacio Brunet
334 Palacio Cantero
342 Casa Font
346 Casa del Cocodrilo

Architecture is the best witness of Trinidad's history: churches and palaces dwell in a spider's web of colonial urban fabric, with narrow, winding cobblestone streets reflecting the irregular topography of the terrain, before expanding and breathing out into squares and alleyways. Trinidad's story of sugar barons, whose fortunes made the city shine, is told in its stones, arches and patios: a beautiful story full of love, passion, and legend. The city's splendor was originally a result of the smuggling of European pirates. Later, wealth from the tobacco plantations and the sugar cane industry continued its affluence. Trinidad was officially founded in 1514 by Don Diego

Die Geschichte Trinidads lässt sich am besten durch ihre Architektur erzählen. Wie ein Spinnennetz hat sich die ehemalige Kolonialstadt ausgebreitet, und überall liegen darin Kirchen und Paläste verteilt. Die schmalen Straßen aus Kopfsteinpflaster ziehen sich kreisförmig um die Hügel der Gegend. Die Gassen und Plätze breiten sich von da weiter hinaus. Trinidad ist auch von der Geschichte der Zuckerbarone geprägt, die mit ihrem Vermögen der Stadt Glanz gebracht haben. Es ist eine wunderbare Geschichte voller Leidenschaften und Legenden. Das zeigt sich in den Steinen, Toren und Innenhöfen. Doch es waren Schmuggelpiraten aus Europa, die zuerst Pracht und Ruhm

L'architecture est le meilleur témoin de l'histoire de Trinidad. Ses églises et ses palais se noient dans un dédale d'étroites rues coloniales, sinueuses et pavées, reflétant la typologie irrégulière du terrain. Les barons du sucre dont la fortune a rejailli sur la ville ont laissé leurs empreintes dans ses pierres, ses arches et ses patios : une belle histoire remplie d'amour, de passion et de légende. La ville doit sa première splendeur à la contrebande avec les pirates européens ; plus tard la richesse des plantations de tabac et de canne à sucre a entretenu sa prospérité. Trinidad fut officiellement fondée en 1514 par Don Diego Velázquez de Cuéllar, au centre-sud de l'île, au pied des montagnes

Casa del Cocodrilo

Palacio Cantero

Casa Font

Palacio Brunet

Velázquez de Cuéllar. It lies in the middle of the island along the south coast, in the foothills of the Guamuhaya Mountains, a few miles from the sea port of Casilda. In 1988 Trinidad and the nearby "Valle de los Ingenios" "Valley of the Sugar Mills" were both declared UNESCO World Heritage Sites, encouraging preservation works in the city to continue.

nach Trinidad brachten. Später kam der Reichtum durch die Tabakplantagen und die Zuckerrohrindustrie. Don Diego Velázquez de Cuéllar gründete 1514 die Stadt mitten auf der Insel. Sie liegt am Fuße der Berge von Guamuhaya an der Südküste, ein paar Kilometer vom Hafen von Casilda entfernt. 1988 erklärte die UNESCO Trinidad und das nahegelegene »Valle de los Ingenios« »Tal der Zuckermühlen« zur Weltkulturerbestätte. Grund genug, um die Renovierungsarbeiten weiter voranzutreiben.

du Guamuhaya et à quelques kilomètres du port de Casilda. En 1988, avec la « Valle de los Ingenios » « Vallée des moulins à sucre » voisine, elle fut déclarée patrimoine universel par l'UNESCO, encourageant les travaux de restauration en cours.

PALACIO BRUNET

A Sugar Baron's Palace.

Trinidad's splendor is on full display at the Brunet Palace on Plaza Mayor. One of the best buildings in the city, its impressive and elegant façade is a masterpiece. The deep porch leads to an 18th century arcade. A continuous balcony with an ornate wrought-iron railing were added in the 19th century. It is crowned by wide eaves covered with clay tiles, and a parapet with urns featuring pineapples. The magnificent inner patio echoes the nearby square, only on a more domestic scale. It is one of the most interesting in Cuban architecture since it is surrounded by two different kinds of galleries, one with pitched roofs held by horizontal brackets, or "aleros en tornapunta," the other with flat roofs above arches supported by pillars. It is accessed through a coffered-ceiling vestibule, or "zaguán," that opens directly onto the gallery containing the main staircase. This leads to the upstairs dining room, where the distinctive fanlights filling the round arches are used in the beautiful cupboards as well. The refined interior decoration reveals the sophisticated taste of the owners: Italian marble floors and wall friezes with floral motifs combine with fine wooden ceilings, imported furniture, beautiful crystal chandeliers, and Meissen and Sèvres porcelains to give the palace an exquisite, hedonistic ambience.

Der prachtvolle »Palacio Brunet« an der Plaza Mayor in Trinidad gehört zu den grandiosen Gebäuden der Stadt. Seine elegante Fassade ist ein Meisterwerk. Eine lange Veranda führt in einen Säulengang aus dem 18. Jahrhundert. Später, im 19. Jahrhundert, wurde ein Balkon mit dekorativem schmiedeeisernen Geländer dazugebaut. Darüber befindet sich ein überhängendes Lehmziegeldach, das mit Urnen und Ananasmotiven verziert ist. Der Palacio Brunet ist ein interessantestes Beispiel kubanischer Architektur. Zwei unterschiedliche Galerien säumen den prächtigen Innenhof. Eine der Galerien hat ein hohes Giebeldach, und über der anderen liegt ein flaches Dach auf den von Säulen getragenen Torbögen. In den Patio gelangt man durch ein Vestibül mit Kassettendecke, dem so genannten »Zaguán«. Die im Patio gelegene Haupttreppe führt nach oben ins Esszimmer. In jedem der Torbögen wurden elegante Oberlichter angebracht, die auch in den wunderbaren Geschirrschränken eingesetzt wurden. Das edle Dekor zeugt vom erlesenen Geschmack der Besitzer: italienische Marmorböden, Wandfriese mit floralen Mustern, exquisite Decken aus Holz, importierte Möbel, Kristallleuchter und Porzellan aus Meißen und Sèvres.

C'est avec le palais Brunet de la Plaza Mayor, un des plus beaux de la ville, que la splendeur de Trinidad se révèle au grand jour. Sa façade impressionnante et élégante est un chef-d'œuvre. Son grand porche débouche sur une arcade du 18e siècle. Le balcon panoramique bordé d'une rambarde en fer forgé a été ajouté au 19e. Il est couronné d'un large auvent en tuiles et d'un parapet orné d'urnes en forme d'ananas. Le magnifique patio rappelle la place voisine, à une échelle plus humaine. C'est l'un des plus intéressants de Cuba car il est entouré de deux types de galeries, l'une avec un toit pentu soutenu par des consoles, des « aleros en tornapunta », l'autre avec un toit plat reposant sur des arches soutenues par des colonnes. On y accède par un vestibule avec un plafond à caissons, ou « zaguán », qui donne directement sur la galerie abritant l'escalier. À l'étage, la salle à manger possède des croisées en éventail sous des arcs, une forme reprise pour les belles armoires qui leur font face. Le décor raffiné révèle la sophistication des propriétaires : les sols en marbres italiens, les frises aux motifs floraux, les beaux plafonds en bois, les meubles importés, les lustres en cristal, les porcelaines de Sèvres et de Meissen participent à l'atmosphère exquise et hédoniste du palais.

✳ **ABOVE** The towers of the churches and convents soar above the skyline of Trinidad, basically made up of one- or two-storied houses and buildings. In the background, the San Francisco de Asís monastery, opened on 11 April 1813. **RIGHT** Across from Plaza Mayor, one of the most prized examples of Trinidad architecture is the house of the Sánchez Iznaga family, dating from 1886, currently home to the Architecture Museum. **FACING PAGE** One of the wrought-iron greyhounds that watch over Trinidad's Plaza Mayor, opened on 26 March 1857, with four symmetrical gardens, paved with stone slabs brought over from Bremen, and a marble sculpture of the muse Terpsichore in the middle. ✳ **OBEN** Die Türme der Kirchen und Kloster stechen aus der Stadtsilhouette Trinidads, die hauptsächlich aus ein- bis zweistöckigen Gebäuden besteht, heraus. Im Hintergrund ist das Kloster »San Francisco de Asís« zu sehen, das am 11. April 1813 eingeweiht wurde. **RECHTS** Vor der Plaza Mayor liegt eines der wertvollsten Beispiele für Trinidads Architektur: das Haus der Familie Sánchez Iznaga aus dem Jahr 1886, das gegenwärtig das Architekturmuseum beherbergt. **RECHTE SEITE** Einer der vier schmiedeeisernen Windhunde, welche die am 26. März 1857 eingeweihte Plaza Mayor Trinidads bewachen. Der Platz besteht aus vier symmetrischen Grünanlagen, einem mit Bremer Fliesen angelegten Boden und einer Marmorstatue der Muse Terpsichore in der Mitte. ✳ **CI-DESSUS** Les clochers des églises et des couvents pointent au-dessus de Trinidad dont la plupart des maisons et bâtiments ne dépassent pas plus d'un étage. Au fond, le monastère de Saint François d'Assise, qui a ouvert ses portes le 11 avril 1813. **A DROITE** Devant la Plaza Mayor, un des plus beaux exemples de l'architecture typique de la ville, la maison de la famille Sánchez Iznaga, construite en 1886, aujourd'hui un musée d'architecture. **PAGE DE DROITE** Un des lévriers en bronze qui gardent la Plaza Mayor, inaugurée le 26 mars 1857. Elle possède quatre jardins symétriques, un pavement en dalles de Brême, et, en son centre, une sculpture en marbre représentant la muse Terpsichore.

FACING PAGE The elegant and light-filled dining room with its semicircular arches leading to the inner courtyard. They are closed with fan-shaped slatted windows to help soften the sunlight and allow a breeze to blow through. **RIGHT** The dining room table in the Palacio Brunet. In the background is a French wood and Bohemian crystal cabinet where the dinnerware is kept. **BELOW** The sitting room in the Palacio Brunet is decorated with profusely colored friezes and French pedestal planters. The furniture, made of fine Cuban wood and wickerwork, dates from the 19th century. The green vases are made of Spanish porcelain, while the tobacco spittoons are French. **FOLLOWING PAGES** Friezes featuring floral and geometrical patterns decorate the wainscoting and frame the entrances to the different areas. On the wall above the sofa, an Italian oval-shaped medallion from the 19th century in one of the sitting rooms off the bedroom. * An image of Jesus Christ on the cross next to two Meissen porcelain pieces. **LINKE SEITE** Das elegante und helle Esszimmer mit seinen zum Innenhof reichenden Rundbögen, deren Oberlichter mit fächerförmig angebrachten Lamellen verschlossen sind, um das Sonnenlicht zu filtern und Luft hereinzulassen. **RECHTS** Eine herrliche Lampe aus Bronze und Baccarat-Kristall hängt von der glatten Holzdecke auf den Esszimmertisch des Palacio Brunet herunter. Im Hintergrund sieht man eine französische Vitrine aus Holz und Glas, in der das Geschirr aufbewahrt wird. **UNTEN** Das Vorzimmer des Palacio Brunet ist mit Zierleisten voller Farbenfreude und französischer Sockel-Blumenschalen dekoriert. Die aus kubanischem Edelholz und Rattan gefertigten Möbel stammen aus dem 19. Jahrhundert. Die grünen Vasen bestehen aus spanischem Porzellan, während die Spucknäpfe für Tabak französischen Ursprungs sind. **FOLGENDE DOPPELSEITE** Friese mit Blumenmotiven und geometrischen Figuren schmücken die Sockel und umrahmen die Zugänge zu den verschiedenen Räumen. In einem der an das Schlafzimmer angrenzenden Zimmer hängt über dem Sofa ein ovales italienisches Medaillonbild aus dem 19. Jahrhundert. * Ein Kruzifix und zwei Dekorationsstücke aus Meissner Porzellan. **PAGE DE GAUCHE** Claire et élégante, la salle à manger possède des arcs en plein cintre qui donnent sur le patio et dont la partie supérieure est fermée par des éventails en lattes de bois qui tamisent la lumière solaire tout en laissant circuler la brise. **A DROITE** Un beau lustre en bronze et cristal de Baccarat est suspendu au plafond en bois dans la salle à manger. Au fond, un vaisselier français en bois et cristal de Bohême. **CI-DESSOUS** Le petit salon est décoré de lambris très colorés et de jardinières françaises sur piédestal. Les meubles en bois précieux de Cuba et en osier sont du 19ᵉ siècle. Les vases en porcelaine verte sont espagnols et les crachoirs français. **DOUBLE PAGE SUIVANTE** Des frises aux motifs floraux et géométriques ornent les murs et encadrent les portes des différentes pièces. Au mur d'une des petites salles contiguës à la chambre, au-dessus du canapé, un médaillon italien ovale du 19ᵉ siècle. Un crucifix flanqué de deux vases en porcelaine de Meissen.

✳ **ABOVE LEFT** The kitchen in the Palacio Brunet, located on the upper floor of the house. Over the stove is a veneer of colorful ceramic tiles and a rustic hood to eliminate gas and odors. **LEFT** A green French opaline vase on a wood and marble table in one of the areas off the sitting room and the master bedroom. The rooms are delimited by lovely varnished wooden doors. **ABOVE** The master bedroom of the house, next to the living room. The 19th century wooden bed was imported from the United States. ✳ **OBEN LINKS** Die Küche liegt im Obergeschoss des Palacio Brunet. Über dem mit farbenprächtigen Keramikfliesen verkleideten Herd befindet sich eine rustikale Dunstabzugshaube. **LINKS** Eine Vase aus grünem französischen Opalglas steht auf einem Tisch aus Holz und Marmor in einem der auf das Vorzimmer und das Schlafzimmer des Hausherrn folgenden Raum. Die Räumlichkeiten sind durch gebeizte, hölzerne Paneeltüren voneinander abgetrennt. **OBEN** Das Schlafzimmer des Hausherrn grenzt an das Wohnzimmer. Das Holzbett aus dem 19. Jahrhundert wurde aus den USA importiert. ✳ **PAGE DE GAUCHE, EN HAUT** La cuisine, située à l'étage. Au-dessus des fourneaux, tapissés d'azulejos en céramique très colorés, une hotte rustique. **A GAUCHE** Dans un des espaces contigus au petit salon et à la chambre des maîtres, un vase français en opaline verte sur une table en bois sculpté et marbre. Les belles portes à panneaux sont en bois vernis. **CI-DESSUS** La chambre des maîtres contiguë au salon. Le lit en bois du 19ᵉ siècle a été importé des États-Unis.

PALACIO CANTERO

One of the Most Luxurious Buildings in Cuba.

Colonial domestic architecture peaked in Trinidad in the 19th century during the boom in the region's sugar industry. Several mansions were built using new artistic concepts influenced by European neo-classicism, which told of the city's economic prosperity while staying true to its past. The fabulous Cantero Palace is composed around an exceptional central courtyard surrounded by arcaded galleries reminiscent of religious cloisters. This palace, built in 1812, is located on a prominent corner site near the Plaza Mayor. The high-ceilinged interior spaces display a riot of colors and shapes, and the airy, spacious rooms are decorated with French, Austrian and German porcelains as well as furniture brought from Europe and the United States. The rooms are divided by round arches, or "mediopuntos," that flow into one another and which are highly decorated with murals by Italian architect and painter Daniel Dall'Aglio. The image of a shell, which is also a religious symbol, is shaped into recesses above the doors and windows. The Cantero Palace, one of the most luxurious buildings in Cuba, is also a landmark in the city, as its three-story tower affords a stunning view of Trinidad's historic center, with the foothills of the Sierra de Escambray in the background.

Die Kolonialarchitektur erlebte in Trinidad mit dem Aufschwung der Zuckerindustrie im 19. Jahrhundert ihren Höhepunkt. Beeinflusst vom europäischen Neoklassizismus wurden damals mehrere Herrschaftshäuser gebaut, die den neuen Reichtum genau so repräsentieren wie alte Traditionen. Der »Cantero Palast« in der Nähe der Plaza Mayor steht rund um einen Innenhof mit gedeckten Galerien, wie man sie von Klöstern kennt. Das Innere dieses außergewöhnlichen Palastes aus dem Jahr 1812 überrascht mit einem Feuerwerk an Farben und Formen. Überall findet man Porzellan aus Frankreich, Österreich und Deutschland. Auch die Möbel stammen aus Europa oder den Vereinigten Staaten. Die luftigen Räume sind mit Böden aus Carrara-Marmor ausgelegt und durch Torbögen, den »Mediopuntos«, voneinander abgetrennt. Die opulenten Verzierungen darauf stammen vom italienischen Architekten und Maler Daniel Dall'Aglio. Über den Türen und Fenstern befindet sich ein fächerartiges Muschelmotiv – ein religiöses Symbol. Der »Cantero Palast« gehört zu den elegantesten und luxuriösesten Gebäuden Kubas. Und vom dreistöckigen Turm hat man eine wunderbare Sicht auf den historischen Kern Trinidads und auf die Sierra de Escambray im Hintergrund.

Le style colonial a connu un apogée à Trinidad au 19e siècle avec l'essor de l'industrie sucrière. Plusieurs grandes demeures furent construites selon de nouveaux concepts artistiques inspirés du néoclassicisme européen, reflet de la prospérité économique de la ville sans toutefois renier son passé. Le somptueux palais Cantero est conçu autour d'une magnifique cour ceinte de galeries dont les arches évoquent un cloître. Le bâtiment bâti de plain-pied en 1812 occupe une place de choix près de la Plaza Mayor. Les intérieurs, spacieux et hauts sous plafond, décorés de porcelaines françaises, autrichiennes et allemandes, explosent de couleurs et de formes. Les meubles viennent d'Europe et des États-Unis. Les sols sont en marbre de Carrare. L'enfilade d'arcs en plein cintre, ou « mediopuntos », est ornée de fresques de Daniel Dall'Aglio, un architecte et peintre italien. Un coquillage, symbole religieux, couronne portes et fenêtres. Le palais, un des plus luxueux de Cuba, est un monument de Trinidad. Du haut de sa tour haute de trois étages, on jouit d'une vue exceptionnelle sur le centre historique, avec la Sierra de Escambray se dessinant au loin.

❋ **ABOVE LEFT** The stunning courtyard of the Palacio Cantero surrounded by semicircular arcaded galleries. **LEFT** The side façade looks out onto the Peña alleyway, where a small crafts fair is held in the mornings. **ABOVE** The dining room in one of the galleries surrounding the exceptional courtyard. **FOLLOWING PAGES** Color and classical shapes characterize the profuse decoration in the sitting room, attributable to the academy-influenced taste of Italian architect, painter and stage designer, Daniel Dall'Aglio. * The Palacio Cantero is regarded as one of the most luxurious neoclassical buildings in Cuba. The Guéridon tables are surrounded by 19th century Cuban rocking chairs. ❋ **OBEN LINKS** Blick aus dem Aussichtsturm auf den Innenhof, der von Galerien mit Rundbögen umgeben ist. **LINKS** Die Seitenfassade liegt in der Gasse Callejón de Peña, in der vormittags ein kleiner Kunsthandwerksmarkt stattfindet. **OBEN** Das Esszimmer liegt in einer der Galerien rund um den einzigartigen Innhof. **FOLGENDE DOPPELSEITE** Eine große Farbenpracht und eine Vielzahl klassischer Formen zeichnen die Dekoration des Vorzimmers aus. Diese geht auf den Geschmack des italienischen Architekten, Malers und Bühnenbildners Daniel Dall'Aglio zurück. * Der Palacio Cantero gilt aufgrund seiner beeindruckenden Größe und Einrichtung als einer der prächtigsten neoklassizistischen Bauten Kubas. Die Guéridon-Tische sind umgeben von kubanischen Schaukelstühlen aus dem 19. Jahrhundert. ❋ **PAGE DE GAUCHE, EN HAUT** Le merveilleux patio entouré de galeries sous des arcades en plein cintre, vu depuis la tour mirador du palais. **A GAUCHE** Le palais jouxte le passage de Peña, où se tient le matin un petit marché d'artisanat. **CI-DESSUS** La salle à manger est idéalement placée dans une des galeries qui bordent le superbe patio. **DOUBLE PAGE SUIVANTE** La riche décoration du petit salon, caractérisée par le mélange des couleurs et une débauche de formes classiques, est attribuée à l'architecte, peintre et scénographe italien Daniel Dall'Aglio. * Le palais est considéré comme le bâtiment néoclassique le plus luxueux de Cuba pour son escalier impressionnant et la richesse des matériaux utilisés dans sa décoration. Autour des guéridons, des fauteuils cubains du 19e siècle.

❉ **FACING PAGE** A brass bedstead in a bedroom. **ABOVE** The living room boasts European finery expressing a Cuban adaptation of classical 19th century tastes. ❉ **LINKE SEITE** Ein stilvolles Bronzebett in einem der Schlafzimmer. **OBEN** Der Salon ist europäisch dekoriert und verbindet damit den klassischen Geschmack des 19. Jahrhunderts mit den Gepflogenheiten des Landes. ❉ **PAGE DE GAUCHE** Dans une des chambres, ce lit à la ligne épurée en bronze incrusté de nacre. **CI-DESSUS** Le salon à l'européenne reflète le goût classique du 19e siècle adapté au pays.

Casa Font

The Home of a Renaissance Man.

German astronomer and geographer Alexander von Humboldt is considered the second man to discover Cuba. His influential visit to Havana and Trinidad in 1801 was recorded in his book "Political Essay about the Island of Cuba." In it he not only refers to Trinidad as "a beautiful and romantic region," he also analyzes the sugar cane industry, and criticizes slavery. The Font family house is a single-storey building dating from the first half of the 19th century, located not far from the place where Humboldt was hosted. Its asymmetrical façade features windows protected by iron grill and a wooden door arch flanked by wooden jambs. The interiors still have the Italian marble floors, the characteristic neoclassical moldings, ornate wrought-iron grills, medallion-style furniture and chandeliers. The courtyard even retains the original reservoir for collecting rainwater. The Font House still reflects its cultural background: the piano, the library, and the telescope preserved in the house tell of a cultivated family man, José Antonio Font Herr. Of German and Catalonian descent, this renowned lawyer and photographer made forays into other branches of knowledge such as hypnotism and meteorology, and he brought the first telescope to Trinidad.

Der deutsche Universalgelehrte Alexander von Humboldt entdeckte 1801 Kuba neu und verewigte seine bedeutende Reise nach Havanna und Trinidad in einem politischen Essay über Kuba. Dabei schwärmt er von Trinidad als »schöne und romantische Gegend«, nimmt aber auch die Zuckerrohrindustrie und die Sklaverei kritisch unter die Lupe. Nicht weit von Humboldts ehemaliger Unterkunft liegt die einstöckige Villa der Familie Font aus der ersten Hälfte des 19. Jahrhunderts. Die asymmetrisch gestaltete Fassade besteht aus Fenstern, die durch Eisengitter geschützt werden, und einer Holztüre mit seitlichen Holzpfosten. Die original italienischen Marmorböden, neoklassizistischen Elemente, verschnörkelten schmiedeisernen Gitter, Möbel und Kronleuchter im Medaillon-Stil sind noch genau so wie damals. Auch das Regenwasserreservoir im Innenhof ist noch vorhanden. Die Familie Font hat das Piano, die Bibliothek und das Teleskop des ersten Hausherrn, José Antonio Font Herr, über die Generationen aufbewahrt. Der angesehene Rechtsanwalt und Fotograf, deutscher und katalonischer Herkunft, war ein äußerst kultivierter und vielseitiger Mann. In seiner Freizeit studierte er Meteorologie und sogar Hypnose. Und er war es, der als Erster ein Teleskop nach Trinidad brachte.

On considère l'astronome et géographe allemand Alexander von Humbolt comme le second homme à avoir découvert Cuba. Il a raconté son séjour à la Havane et à Trinidad en 1801 dans son ouvrage «Essai politique sur l'île de Cuba». Il y décrit Trinidad comme «une région belle et romantique», y analyse l'industrie du sucre de canne et critique l'esclavage. La maison de la famille Font est un bâtiment de plain-pied datant du début du 19e siècle, situé non loin de là où Humbolt séjournait. Sa façade asymétrique se distingue par ses fenêtres à croisillons protégées de grilles et sa porte encastrée dans une arche segmentée, encadrée d'un chambranle en bois massif. Les salles possèdent toujours leurs sols d'origine en marbre italien, leurs moulures néoclassiques, leurs grilles ouvragées en fer forgé, leurs meubles médaillons et leurs lustres. Dans la cour, on a même conservé l'ancienne citerne d'eau de pluie. La demeure témoigne d'un riche passé culturel : la famille a préservé le piano, la bibliothèque et le télescope de l'ancêtre José Antonio Font Herr, d'origine allemande et catalane. Cet avocat et photographe de renom s'intéressa à d'autres sphères de la connaissance telles que l'hypnotisme et la météorologie. Il apporta le premier télescope à Trinidad.

※ **FACING PAGE** The original gas lamp is preserved in the living room alongside other decorative objects and furnishings from the 19th century. The Art Nouveau style screened door ensures the privacy of the bedroom just off the living room. **RIGHT** A corner of the home devoted to worshipping the Catholic religious icons. On the wall is a painting of the Virgen de la Caridad del Cobre, patron saint of Cuba, and over the wood and marble console is a sculpture of a crucified Jesus Christ with two French opaline vases. **BELOW** The dining room in the home of José Antonio Font Herr. Placed at an angle is a 19th century game cabinet made of black mahogany. In the background, the doors and windows with French louvered blinds filter the intense light that enters from the inner courtyard. ※ **LINKE SEITE** Die originale Gaslampe ist zusammen mit weiteren Einrichtungsgegenständen und Möbeln aus dem 19. Jahrhundert im Salon des Hauses erhalten geblieben. Der Wandschirm im Jugendstil bietet dem angrenzenden Schlafzimmer die nötige Privatsphäre. **RECHTS** Eine Ecke des Hauses ist der katholischen Ikonographie gewidmet. An der Wand hängt ein Bild der »Virgen de la Caridad del Cobre«, Kubas Schutzpatronin; auf einem Tisch aus Holz und Marmor steht eine Kruzifixskulptur mit zwei Gefäßen aus französischem Opalglas. **UNTEN** Das Esszimmer im Haus von José Antonio Font Herr. In einer Ecke steht ein aus schwarzem Mahagoniholz gefertigter Spieleschrank aus dem 19. Jahrhundert. Die Türen und Fenstern mit Lamellenläden filtern das starke Licht, das aus dem Innenhof hereindringt. ※ **PAGE DE GAUCHE** Le salon conserve son lustre à gaz d'origine ainsi que d'autres objets décoratifs et meubles du 19e siècle. Le paravent Art nouveau protège l'intimité de la chambre à coucher située derrière. **A DROITE** Un recoin de la maison transformé en autel catholique. Au mur, un tableau de la Vierge de la Caridad del Cobre, patronne de Cuba. Sur le plateau en marbre de la console, un crucifix entre deux opalines françaises. **CI-DESSOUS** La salle à manger. Dans un angle, un charmant cabinet en acajou noir du 19e siècle. Au fond, les persiennes des portes-fenêtres filtrent la lumière intense du soleil provenant du patio.

Casa del Cocodrilo

A Stillife of Magic Realism.

Caught in a time warp, Trinidad is a living museum of architecture in a quiet setting. Sometimes, though, it turns into something amazing. The mind-scrambling array of weird objects on view at the Casa del Dominicano is one of the main attractions in town. This late 18th century house has recently been baptized by tourists as the Casa del Cocodrilo because of the huge embalmed crocodile on display there. This object, a present from a hunter friend who lives in the Ciénaga de Zapata, is displayed in the living room alongside a billiard table, religious icons, a collection of mirrors, old clocks, and old furniture. This room is spacious, airy and is separated from the dining room by a unique arch with an ornate intrados. The hilly site called for an elevated verandah, which has slender posts and protective balusters above an external flight of stairs, or "perron," for access. This feature, as well as it unusual façade, represents a fine example of Cuban baroque. The main door has two wickets and ornate panels, while the thickness of the walls allows for extra sitting space at the base of the windows – an ideal place for watching life go by.

Trinidad ist ein lebendes Architekturmuseum, so als wäre hier die Zeit stehengeblieben. Die Stadt ist zwar ruhig, aber immer für eine Überraschung gut. So werden in der »Casa del Dominicano« aus dem 18. Jahrhundert die skurilsten Objekte ausgestellt, die zu Trinidads wichtigsten Attraktionen gehören. Ein riesiges, einbalsamiertes Krokodil verleitete Besucher dazu, dem Haus einen neuen Namen zu geben: »Casa del Cocodrilo«. Es ist das Geschenk eines Jägers aus Ciénaga de Zapata und steht im Wohnzimmer neben einem Billardtisch, Ikonen, einer Spiegelsammlung, alten Uhren und Möbeln. Durch einen außergewöhnlich verzierten mixtilinearen Torbogen wird das Esszimmer vom Wohnzimmer abgetrennt. Eine außenliegende Treppe, der »Perron«, führt auf die Veranda mit Balustraden. Da das Haus an einem Hang liegt, wurde sie auf schmale Pfosten gesetzt und dadurch erhöht. Die vorstehenden Fenstern, die Formdächer und die ungewöhnliche Fassade machen aus dem Haus ein typisches Beispiel für den kubanischen Barock. Die Wände des Haues sind so dick, dass man unten am Festersims durchaus bequem sitzen kann. Der perfekte Ort, um das Leben draußen zu beobachten.

Hors du temps, Trinidad est un musée vivant d'architecture dans un décor paisible, mais elle recèle également des surprises. Le mélange hétéroclite et déconcertant d'objets qu'abrite la Casa del Dominicano est l'une des principales attractions de la ville. Cette demeure de la fin du 18e siècle a été surnommée par les touristes «la maison du crocodile» en raison de l'énorme reptile empaillé qui orne son salon, présent d'un ami chasseur habitant dans la Ciénaga de Zapata. Il côtoie une table de billard, des icônes, une collection de miroirs, des pendules et des meubles anciens. Cette salle spacieuse et claire est séparée de la salle à manger par une étonnante arche mixtiligne à l'intrados richement décoré. Située sur une colline, la maison possède une véranda surélevée ornée de fines colonnes et protégée d'une balustrade dominant un escalier extérieur. Avec sa façade inhabituelle et ses fenêtres saillantes derrière des grilles incurvées et surmontées de toits moulés, elle représente un bel exemple de baroque cubain. L'épaisseur des murs permet de placer des banquettes sous les fenêtres, lieu idéal d'où contempler la vie qui passe au dehors.

※ **ABOVE** A billiard table to entertain tourists. **FACING PAGE** A beautiful arch between the living room and dining room. **FOLLOWING DOUBLE PAGE** The spacious living room boasts an array of furniture. ※ **OBEN** Ein Billardtisch dient den Gästen zum Zeitvertreib. **RECHTE SEITE** Ein herrlicher Bogen trennt Wohn- und Esszimmer. **FOLGENDE DOPPELSEITE** Das große Wohnzimmer enthält Gegenstände verschiedener Stilrichtungen und Epochen. ※ **CI-DESSUS** Une table de billard permet de faire patienter les clients logés dans la maison pendant que l'on prépare le dîner. **PAGE DE DROITE** Un bel arc sépare le salon de la salle à manger. **DOUBLE PAGE SUIVANTE** Dans le grand salon, des meubles de différents styles et époques cohabitent.

Palacio del Valle

Casa de la Teja

From a distance, Cienfuegos's beauty captivates because of its location on the Bay of Jagua; and at close quarters, the order and purity displayed by the urban fabric and neoclassical buildings is equally impressive. The kindness of its inhabitants is renowned, adding to the appeal of the city founded by both Spanish and French settlers. Don Diego Velázquez explored the bay early in the 16th century when he was founding other settlements throughout Cuba. By 1819 Louis de Clouet, a retired lieutenant-colonel from Louisiana, led a group of settlers to Cienfuegos, and soon it became one of the most important cities in the country. Later many Americans followed, mak-

Cienfuegos liegt an der zauberhaften Bucht von Jagua. Die Stadt, die von spanischen und französischen Siedlern gegründet wurde, beeindruckt durch ihre klare Struktur, neoklassizistischen Gebäude und besonders durch die Freundlichkeit ihrer Einwohner. Als Don Diego Velázquez im frühen 16. Jahrhundert die ersten »Villas« auf Kuba gründete, kundschaftete er auch diese Bucht aus. Zu einer bedeutenden Stadt wurde Cienfuegos aber erst, nachdem 1819 der pensionierte Oberstleutnant Louis de Clouet aus Louisiana mit einer Gruppe von Siedlern nach Cienfuegos zog. Später folgten Amerikaner, die hier vor allem Handel trieben und den wirtschaftlichen Aufschwung

De loin, la beauté de Cienfuegos fascine par son site dans la baie de Jagua. De près, l'ordre et la pureté de son urbanisme et de ses bâtiments néoclassiques sont tout aussi impressionnants. La gentillesse de ses habitants est réputée, ajoutant à l'attrait d'une ville fondée par des Espagnols et des Français. Don Diego Velázquez a exploré la baie au début du 16e siècle quand il établissait des colonies dans toute l'île. En 1819, Louis de Clouet, un lieutenant-colonel à la retraite venu de Louisiane, amena ici un groupe de colons et Cienfuegos devint rapidement une des villes les plus importantes de Cuba. Plus tard, de nombreux Américains les y suivirent, faisant fortune dans le com-

Cienfuegos

354 Palacio del Valle
364 Casa de la Teja

ing their fortunes here mostly as merchants. Because of the resulting prosperity, Cienfuegos witnessed the influence of European neoclassicism in the layout of its urban development in the 19th century, with grids of square blocks and parks. This can be seen in the beautiful Plaza de Armas, and the Paseo del Prado – a central boulevard with a landscaped central section that stretches all the way down to the water. In 1889 Tomás Terry financed the building of a splendid theatre, an act of great civic generosity. The historic center of Cienfuegos was declared a UNESCO World Heritage Site in 2005.

brachten. Dank dieser Blüte erreichte auch der Neoklassizismus aus Europa Cienfuegos und beeinflusste die Stadtentwicklung im 19. Jahrhundert maßgeblich. Die schachbrettartige Anordnung der rechteckigen Häuserreihen und die Parkanlagen stammen aus dieser Zeit – genau wie die wunderschöne Plaza de Armas und der Paseo del Prado, der in der Mitte bepflanzte Hauptboulevard, der bis zum Meer hinunter führt. Tomás Terry, ein steinreicher Zuckerbaron, machte 1889 mit dem Bau eines prachtvollen Theaters, das seinen Namen trägt, der Stadt ein großzügiges Geschenk. Und 2005 erklärte die UNESCO das historische Zentrum Cienfuegos zur Weltkulturerbestätte.

merce. Du fait de cette prospérité, au 19e siècle, le développement urbain de Cienfuegos connut l'influence du néoclassicisme européen, avec un plan géométrique alternant les pâtés de maisons et les jardins. En témoignent la belle Plaza de Armas et le Paseo del Prado, un boulevard central fendu en son milieu d'une allée paysagée qui s'étire jusqu'à la mer. En 1889, Tomás Terry, un riche magnat du sucre, finança la construction d'un splendide théâtre, un acte civique d'une grande générosité. En 2005, le centre historique de Cienfuegos a été déclaré patrimoine mondial par l'UNESCO.

PALACIO DEL VALLE

Enchanting with its Beauty and Magic.

The breeze from the sea fills the building, light filters through the stained-glass windows, and shadows seize the loggias, balconies and belvederes of the Palacio del Valle, a neo-Moorish palace on the beautiful bay of Cienfuegos. This magnificent building is like a strange apparition in its extraordinary setting by the sea. A legend is told about the palace. A settler from Granada married an indigenous woman named Anagueia, and they lived on the spot where the palace is now. After the couple exchanged their vows, the man conjured a Moorish castle from his homeland and it appeared before him. Later one of his sons, afraid of the Inquisition, undid the enchantment and made the house vanish, leaving only the foundation that would be used by Acisclo del Valle, a wealthy Spanish trader, to build the palace of his dreams. He hired Italian architect Alfredo Colli to design it, and brought skilled craftsmen from Morocco, as well as marble and ceramic tile from Italy and Spain to create this architectural jewel. Colli drew inspiration from the scale, decoration, and mysterious atmosphere of the Alhambra palace. The legend has passed into the mists of time, but the palace retains the enchantment of this lovely tale.

Im »Palacio del Valle« füllen Meeresbrisen die Räume, Sonnenlicht drängt sich durch Buntglasfenster, Schatten legen sich auf Balkone und Aussichtspunkte. Der herrliche Palast liegt an der schönen Bucht von Cienfuegos und wirkt in seiner maurischen Pracht fast etwas fremd. Die Legende erzählt, ein Siedler aus Granada habe die Einheimische Anagueia geheiratet. Nachdem sich die beiden das Ja-Wort gegeben hatten, machte der Mann an der Stelle, wo der »Palacio del Valle« steht, einen Zauberspruch. Er wünschte sich ein maurisches Schloss, genau so wie er es aus seiner Heimat kannte. Kaum ausgesprochen, erschien der gewünschte Palast vor seinen Augen. Später, erzählt man sich weiter, habe einer seiner Söhne den Zauberspruch wieder aufgelöst, weil er sich vor den Inquisitoren fürchtete. Einzig das Fundament ließ er stehen. Der reiche spanische Händler Acisclo del Valle ließ später darauf den Palast seiner Träume errichten. Er engagierte den italienischen Architekten Alfredo Colli, holte sachkundige Handwerker aus Marokko, ließ Marmor und Keramikfliesen aus Italien und Spanien hierher transportieren. Colli scheute keine Mittel, um ein architektonisches Juwel schaffen. Als Inspirationsquelle und Vorlage diente ihm der legendäre Alhambra-Palast aus Granada.

La brise marine balaye les pièces baignées d'une lumière filtrée par des vitraux; les loggias, balcons et belvédères offrent une ombre fraîche. Le magnifique Palacio del Valle, un palais néo-mauresque dans la belle baie de Cienfuegos, est une étrange apparition dans un décor extraordinaire dominant la mer. Selon une légende, un colon de Grenade épousa une indigène nommée Anagueia; après avoir échangé leurs vœux, l'homme invoqua un château mauresque de sa terre natale qui se matérialisa devant lui. Plus tard, un de ses fils, craignant l'Inquisition, brisa le sortilège et fit disparaître la bâtisse, ne laissant que ses fondations plus tard réutilisées par Acisclo del Valle, un riche commerçant espagnol, qui érigea le palais de ses rêves. Pour créer ce joyau d'architecture, il engagea l'architecte italien Alfredo Colli, fit venir des maîtres artisans du Maroc, des marbres et des carreaux de céramique d'Italie et d'Espagne. Colli s'est inspiré de l'échelle, de la décoration et de l'atmosphère mystérieuse du palais de l'Alhambra. La légende s'est perdue dans la nuit des temps, mais le palais conserve à ce jour l'atmosphère enchanteresse de ce joli conte.

※ **ABOUT LEFT** The main façade of the Palacio del Valle is reminiscent of the Nazaries Palaces in the Alhambra in Granada, Spain. **LEFT** One of the corner towers at the summit of the Palacio del Valle is like a minaret from which the city and sea can be glimpsed. **ABOVE** The interior of the main living room, now converted into a restaurant, adjacent to the entrance hall with its ornate staircase. The repetition of the arches and the geometrical motifs in the wall and ceiling decorations create an optical illusion of multiplied space. **FOLLOWING DOUBLE PAGE** The cozy atmosphere in the living room of the Palacio del Valle, now converted into a restaurant, with its play of light and shadow. The colored windows that enclose the peak of the Moorish arches on one of the side façades add even more color to the multicolored interior. ※ **OBEN LINKS** Die Hauptfassade des »Palacio del Valle« erinnert an die der großen Nasriden-Paläste der Alhambra im spanischen Granada. **LINKS** Einer der Ecktürme, der sich ähnlich einem Minarett auf dem Dach des »Palacio del Valle« erhebt, bietet eine Aussicht über die Stadt und das Meer. **OBEN** Innenansicht des neben der Einganshalle liegenden Hauptsalons mit der Treppe im Hintergrund. Die Wiederholung der Bögen und die geometrischen Dekorationsmotive an Wänden und Decke erzeugen die optische Täuschung eines um ein Vielfaches größeren Raums. **FOLGENDE DOPPELSEITE** Der heute als Restaurant genutzte Salon des »Palacio del Valle« besticht dank des Licht- und Schattenspiels durch ein intimes Ambiente. Die Buntglasfenster in einer der Seitenfassaden runden die Farbenpracht des Raums ab. ※ **PAGE DE GAUCHE, EN HAUT** La façade du Palacio del Valle, évoque les palais nasrides de l'Alhambra à Grenade. **A GAUCHE** Une des tourelles qui se dressent à chaque angle du toit du Palacio del Valle, telles des minarets d'où l'on peut contempler la mer et la ville. **CI-DESSUS** L'intérieur du salon principal contigu au vestibule, avec l'escalier au fond. La répétition des arcs et des motifs géométriques qui ornent les murs crée une illusion d'optique, donnant l'impression que l'espace se multiplie. **DOUBLE PAGE SUIVANTE** L'atmosphère chaleureuse du grand salon du Palacio del Valle, transformé en restaurant, avec ses jeux d'ombres et de lumière. Les vitraux de l'un des côtés de l'édifice ajoutent encore des couleurs à la décoration chamarrée.

※ **PREVIOUS PAGES** Over thirty Moroccans craftsmen created this spectacular building. * An octagonal lamp is in line with the style and decoration of the building. **FACING PAGE** The sumptuous Italian marble staircase was reconstructed seven times in order to satisfy the tastes of the owner. **ABOVE** A whimsical curved arch on the upper floor. ※ **VORHERGEHENDE DOPPELSEITE** Dreißig Marokkaner gestalteten den Palast. * Das Design der achteckigen Lampe bildet Formen des Geländes nach. **LINKE SEITE** Die Treppe aus italienischem Marmor wurde siebenmal umgestaltet. **OBEN** Ein Bogen mit verspielten Linien. ※ **DOUBLE PAGE PRECEDENTE** Des trente artisans marocains ont exécuté la profusion de détails spectaculaires. * Le lustre octogonal du grand salon est conforme au style du palais. **PAGE DE GAUCHE** L'escalier en marbre italien a été reconstruit sept fois. **CI-DESSUS** À l'étage, une embrasure surmontée d'un arc aux courbes capricieuses.

CASA

DE LA TEJA

An Airy House with Colorful Mosaic Floors.

The impressive main square of Cienfuegos is unified by porticoes of the buildings around it, giving an extraordinary coherence to this two-block-long plaza. The famous Teatro Tomás Terry, the San Lorenzo school, and the 19th century Casa Famillia de la Teja are located on the opposite side of the plaza, across from the Catholic church, the Palatino Bar, the Palacio Ferrer, and the imposing town hall. All the buildings share common features such as public porches, high ceilings, tinted "mediopuntos," beautiful wrought-iron grills, and the ubiquitous yet lovely interior courtyards. This house, like the others, is airy and huge, and the spacious rooms with colorful mosaic floors are divided either by wooden paneled doors or by "mamparas," a Cuban screen door that provides both privacy and ventilation. There are fine examples of these in the Casa Familia, which show how the house has evolved over time, and which include some especially beautiful art nouveau examples. Access to the house is via a "zaguán," a traditional Cuban entry hall, and the reception room, living room, and dining room are connected by a patio – this one is profusely planted with fruit trees and climbing plants.

Der beeindruckende Hauptplatz von Cienfuegos ist so lang wie zwei Häuserblocks und wird von den Säulengängen der umliegenden Gebäude kompakt zusammengehalten. Gegenüber liegen das Teatro Tomás Terry, die San-Lorenzo-Schule, und die Casa Familia de la Teja, die im 19. Jahrhundert erbaut wurde. Das Haus steht neben der katholischen Kirche, der Palatino-Bar, dem Palacio Ferrer und dem imposanten Stadthaus. Die Gebäude sehen sich alle ähnlich: sie haben öffentlich zugängliche Terrassen, hohe Decken, bunte »Mediopuntos«, wunderschöne schmiedeeiserne Gitter und die schon fast inflationären, doch immerschönen Innenhöfe. Das Haus der Familie de la Teja ist, genau wie alle anderen, luftig und riesig. Großzügige Zimmer mit farbigen Mosaikböden werden durch »Mamparas«, getäfelte Türen mit Gittern, getrennt. Sie wahren die Privatsphäre, und gleichzeitig kann die Luft zirkulieren. In diesem Haus gibt es einige schöne Beispiele verschiedener Stilrichtungen, die zeigen, wie sich das Haus im Laufe der Zeit verändert hat: Besonders schön sind die Art-Nouveau-»Mamparas«. Ins Innere des Hauses gelangt man über den »Zaguán«, die traditonelle kubanische Eingangshalle. Empfangsraum, Wohn- und Esszimmer sind über den Innenhof mit üppigen Fruchtbäumen und Kletterpflanzen miteinander verbunden.

L'impressionnante grand-place de Cienfuegos, longue de deux pâtés de maisons, puise son extraordinaire cohérence dans les portiques qui la bordent. Le célèbre Teatro Tomás Terry, l'école San Lorenzo, et la Casa Familia de la Teja se situent d'un côté, faisant face à l'église catholique, au bar Palatino, au Palais Ferrer et à l'imposant hôtel de ville. Tous les bâtiments ont en commun des portiques publics, de hauts plafonds, des arcs en plein cintre ornés de vitraux, de belles grilles en fer forgé et les incontournables mais toujours ravissantes cours intérieures. Comme ses voisines, cette maison construite au 19e siècle est claire et spacieuse, avec des sols bigarrés en mosaïque, des portes à panneaux ou des «mamparas», des paravents ajourés qui assurent à la fois l'intimité et la ventilation. On en trouve de beaux exemples ici, notamment dans le style Art nouveau, ce qui prouve que la maison a évolué avec le temps. On entre par un «zaguán», un vestibule traditionnel cubain. La réception, le séjour et la salle à manger communiquent avec le patio, celui-ci étant rempli de végétation, avec des arbres fruitiers et des plantes grimpantes.

❊ **ABOVE LEFT** From the Teja family house one can see the Plaza Mayor of Cienfuegos. In the background are a neoclassical gazebo and the imposing City Hall building. **LEFT** Across from the Teja family home, the portals of the former Casino Español, built in 1894 and currently home to the City Museum. **ABOVE** The home's dining room is reached through the "zaguán", or entry hall. **FOLLOWING PAGES** The family's dinnerware is kept and displayed in a turned-wood and glass shelf. The mirror in back reflects the books on the opposite wall. * A lovely wrought-iron grill surmounts the doorway dividing the entry hall and the living room. * One of the colored glass semicircular windows surmounting the doorway between the dining room and the living room. ❊ **OBEN LINKS** Vom Haus aus überblickt man die Plaza Mayor von Cienfuegos. Im Hintergrund sieht man einen neoklassizistischen Pavillon und das eindrucksvolle Rathausgebäude. **LINKS** Gegenüber dem Haus liegen die Portale des ehemaligen spanischen Kasinos, das 1894 errichtet wurde und gegenwärtig das Gemeindemuseum beherbergt. **OBEN** Der Zugang zum Esszimmer des Hauses erfolgt über den Hausflur. Der Boden besteht aus Mosaiken und ist ringsum mit einem Zierrand versehen. **FOLGENDE DOPPELSEITEN** Das Geschirr der Familie steht in einem Regal aus gedrechseltem Holz und Glas. Die Spiegelwand zeigt die Bücher der gegenüberliegenden Zimmerseite. * Ein herrliches schmiedeeisernes Gitter verschließt die Lichtöffnung zwischen Hausflur und Wohnzimmer. * Eines der Oberlichter krönt den Durchbruch zwischen Ess- und Wohnzimmer. ❊ **PAGE DE GAUCHE, EN HAUT** Depuis la maison on peut voir la Plaza Mayor. Au fond, une gloriette néoclassique et l'imposant hôtel de ville. **A GAUCHE** En face de la maison, les arcades de l'ancien casino espagnol, construit en 1894 et devenu aujourd'hui le musée municipal. **CI-DESSUS** Le vestibule donne directement sur la salle à manger. Les sols en mosaïque sont bordés d'une frise. **DOUBLE PAGE SUIVANTES** La vaisselle de famille est rangée sur des étagères en bois tourné et verre. * Dans le miroir, on voit la bibliothèque contre le mur d'en face. * Une belle grille en fer forgé sépare le vestibule du salon. * Un vitrail en demi-lune coiffe l'ouverture entre le salon et la salle à manger.

Pinar del Río

374 Casa Duporté & Hotel Moka

Cuban tobacco is, of course, the island's most famous export, and Pinar del Río, with its red, fertile soil, is the prime tobacco-growing region in the country. It can be found in the westernmost province of Cuba, two hours west of Havana. Because reefs hindered easy navigation along its shores, the Spanish were unable to settle here early on; however, by 1571 land in this area was distributed among a group of settlers for agricultural use. By 1669 a group of farmers living in this small village began cultivating tobacco, so establishing a tradition that has remained for centuries. Even today the routine from cultivation to harvest is still almost the same. In the summer, oxen

Tabak ist der bekannteste Exportartikel Kubas. Die beste Anbauregion liegt im Westen der Insel in Pinar del Río, einer Gegend mit roter, fruchtbarer Erde, zwei Stunden von Havanna. Die Westküste mit ihren unzähligen Riffen war für die Schiffe der Spanier kaum zugänglich, und die Gegend blieb zu Beginn der Kolonialisierung unbewohnt. 1571 wurde dann Land zur landwirtschaftlichen Nutzung an Siedler verteilt. Fast hundert Jahre später, 1669, fingen die ersten Bauern an, in Pinar del Río Tabak anzubauen, und legten damit den Grundstein für die nun Jahrhunderte alte Tradition. Auch heute wird Tabak, vom Anpflanzen bis zur Ernte, genau wie damals angebaut. Ochsen pflü-

Le tabac est le produit d'exportation le plus célèbre de Cuba et Pinar del Río, avec son sol rouge et fertile, sa première région tabacultrice. La province se trouve à la pointe ouest de l'île, à deux heures de la Havane. Les récifs qui bordent ses côtes rendant la navigation dangereuse, les Espagnols ne s'y installèrent que tardivement. Toutefois, en 1571, les terres furent réparties entre les colons pour être cultivées. En 1669, un groupe de fermiers commença à y planter du tabac, établissant ainsi une tradition qui devait perdurer des siècles. Aujourd'hui encore, la culture et la récolte suivent pratiquement la même routine. L'été, les bœufs labourent le sol pour préparer les semailles ;

plough the soil to prepare it for seeding; a month later, the plants are protected from insects by cheesecloth. Farmers stroll through the fields working the leaves by hand and picking them from bottom to top when they are ready. Wooden carts are used to transport the green leaves to large houses where they hang to dry for about two months until they are a uniformly brown. At this point they are transferred to warehouses for fermentation and classification, before being taken to their final destination: the cigar factories throughout Cuba.

gen im Sommer die Erde und bereiten sie für die Saat vor. Einen Monat später werden die Setzlinge in ein Käsetuch gepackt, um sie vor Insekten zu schützen. Wenn die Blätter reif zur Ernte sind, gehen die Bauern zu Fuß durch die Felder und pflücken sie in Handarbeit von unten nach oben. Die noch grünen Blätter werden danach mit einem Holzwagen in große Häuser transportiert und zum Trocknen aufgehängt. Nach ungefähr zwei Monaten sind sie regelmäßig braun und können zur Fermentation und Klassifizierung in ein Warenlager gebracht werden. Ihre Endstation erreichen die Tabakblätter in den Zigarrenmanufakturen in ganz Kuba.

un mois plus tard, les plantes sont protégées des insectes avec des étamines. Les agriculteurs sillonnent leurs champs en travaillant puis en cueillant les feuilles à la main. Des carrioles en bois transportent le tabac encore vert dans des hangars où il sèche pendant environ deux mois, jusqu'à atteindre une couleur brune uniforme. Il est alors prêt à être transféré dans des entrepôts pour fermenter et être classé, avant d'être acheminé à sa destination finale, les manufactures de cigares réparties dans toute l'île.

CASA DUPORTÉ

& HOTEL MOKA

Environmental Utopia.

For nature lovers Cuba's charms are not to be found in Havana. In 1968, in the province of Pinar del Río, a government reforestation project was founded. Sponsored by the UN Food and Agricultural Organization, it was called Las Terrazas after the terraced hills of the Sierra del Rosario. The goal was to regenerate, through replanting, a large area that had been dilapidated due to deforestation by the coffee industry, and to develop a sustainable rural economy. Cuban architect Mario Girona designed an unusual rural community housing project that was conceived to blend in with the burgeoning landscape. His buildings on stilts around the artifical lake with tiled roofs were developed for a community of "campesinos" so that they too could take advantage of Cuba's free healthcare and education systems. The nearby ruins of the coffee plantations of Buena Vista and Moka were preserved and integrated as part of the conservation effort. The Hotel Moka was built in 1994 to cater to the growing number of eco-tourists to the region. Girona's design for the hotel features a grand, soaring lobby integrating trees, and galleries that provide access to the rooms. This pleasant, bucolic enviroment has attracted Cuban artists such as painters Jorge Duporté and Lester Campa, and the late musician Polo Montañés to live here.

Den Charme Kubas findet man nicht nur in Havanna. Besonders dann nicht, wenn man die Natur liebt. In der Provinz Pinar del Río wurde 1968 das staatliche Aufforstungsprogramm »Las Terrazas« ins Leben gerufen und nach der terrassenförmigen Sierra del Rosario benannt. Das Projekt, das die Zerstörung und Entwaldung durch extensiven Anbau von Kaffee rückgängig machte, wurde von der Ernährungs- und Landwirtschaftsorganisation der Vereinten Nationen unterstützt. Gleichzeitig entwarf der kubanische Architekt Mario Girona eine außergewöhnliche landwirtschaftliche Sozialsiedlung rund um einen künstlichen See, die sich der Landschaft anpasste. Die Gebäude sind auf Pfählen gebaut, mit Ziegeldächern versehen und wurden den »Campesinos« zugeteilt, damit auch sie Kubas kostenloses Gesundheits- und Erziehungswesen nutzen konnten. Um die steigende Anzahl der Öko-Touristen unterbringen zu können, kam 1994 das von Girona designte »Hotel Moka« dazu. Bemerkenswert ist Gironas prächtige, in die Höhe schießende Empfangshalle mit Bäumen und Galerien, über die man in die Zimmer gelangt. Der reizvolle Ort auf dem Land hat auch einige kubanische Künstler angelockt: Die Maler Jorge Duporté und Lester Campa leben hier, früher auch der verstorbene Musiker Polo Montañés.

Pour les amoureux de la nature, les charmes de Cuba ne se trouvent pas à la Havane. En 1968, le gouvernement a lancé un projet de reforestation dans la province de Pinar del Río. Financé par l'organisation des Nations unies pour l'alimentation et l'agriculture, on l'a appelé «Las Terrazas» en raison des versants en paliers de la Sierra del Rosario. L'objectif était de replanter une vaste zone ravagée par la culture du café et de développer une économie rurale durable. L'architecte cubain Mario Girona dessina des HLM originaux qui se fondent dans le nouveau paysage, autour d'un lac artificiel. Les bâtiments sur pilotis, blanchis à la chaux et avec des toits en tuile, furent conçus pour les «campesinos» afin qu'ils puissent, eux aussi, bénéficier de la gratuité des soins médicaux et de l'éducation. Les ruines voisines de la plantation de café Cafetal Buena Vista les ont transformés en complexe touristique doté d'un musée du café et d'un restaurant. L'hôtel Moka a été érigé en 1994 pour accueillir le nombre croissant d'écotouristes. L'œuvre de Girona comporte un hall grandiose planté d'arbres et des galeries qui permettent d'accéder aux appartements. Ce lieu bucolique et agréable a attiré des artistes cubains dont les peintres Jorge Duporté et Lester Campa ainsi que le regretté musicien Polo Montañés.

❋ **ABOVE LEFT** The buildings blend in with the irregular topography of the terrain and stand out from the natural setting with their colorful façades. **LEFT** A climbing plant with white flowers covers the entrance to the house of the painter Jorge Duporté, watched over by royal palms, Cuba's national tree. **ABOVE** A bar on stilts on the banks of the artificial lake at the Las Terrazas community harks back to the aboriginal constructions. ❋ **OBEN LINKS** Die Gebäude passen sich der unebenen Topographie des Geländes an und stechen aufgrund der Farben ihrer Fassaden aus der Naturlandschaft hervor. **LINKS** Eine Kletterpflanze mit weißen Blüten umrankt den Eingangsbereich des Hauses von dem Maler Jorge Duporté, das von Königspalmen, dem Landesbaum Kubas, umgeben ist. **OBEN** Eine Bar ruht auf Pfahlbauten am Ufer des Sees nahe der Siedlung »Las Terrazas« und erinnert an die Bauten der Urein-wohner an den Flüssen. ❋ **PAGE DE GAUCHE, EN HAUT** Les bâtiments épousent la topographie irrégulière du terrain et se détachent dans le paysage par les couleurs de leurs façades. **A GAUCHE** Une plante grimpante aux fleurs blanches envahit l'entrée de la maison Duporté, gardée par des palmiers royaux (roystonea regia), l'arbre national de Cuba. **CI-DESSUS** Un bar sur pilotis au bord du lac rappelle les constructions aborigènes qui bordent les fleuves.

❋ **FACING PAGE** The house of the talented artist Jorge Duporté decorated with his own works and his exquisitely fine taste. The dining room features wickerwork furniture, which is highly appropriate for the Cuban climate. **ABOVE** The renowned painter Jorge Duporté with a group of children from the Las Terrazas community and the replanted forest in the background. ❋ **LINKE SEITE** Das Haus des talentierten Künstlers Jorge Duporté – geschmückt mit seinen eigenen Werken. Das Wohn- und Esszimmer ist mit Rattanmöbeln eingerichtet, die gut für das kubanische Klima geeignet sind. **OBEN** Der berühmte Maler Jorge Duporté steht mit einer Gruppe von Kindern aus der Siedlung »Las Terrazas« vor dem Wald.
❋ **PAGE DE GAUCHE** Les œuvres du talentueux artiste dans sa maison décorée avec un goût exquis. Le séjour/salle à manger est aménagé avec des meubles en osier bien adaptés au climat cubain. **CI-DESSUS** Le célèbre peintre Jorge Duporté avec un groupe d'enfants de la communauté « Las Terrazas » avec la forêt en toile de fond.

✳ **ABOVE LEFT** The walkway galleries of the rooms at the Hotel Moka were separated from the façades in order to leave the existing trees intact and ensure greater privacy for guests. **LEFT** The vernacular employed at the Hotel Moka includes elements from the Cuban architectural tradition, including sloped roofs made of clay tiles, the interplay of different ceiling heights, semicircular arches and wooden balustrades. **ABOVE** The trees on the site are integrated into the hallway space in the Hotel Moka, from which excellent views of the landscape can be relished. The furnishings are simple, comfortable, and functional through the use of light wickerwork furniture. ✳ **OBEN LINKS** Die Galerien, die zu den Zimmern des »Hotel Moka« führen, liegen von der Fassade abgetrennt, um die Bäume zu erhalten und den Gästen eine größere Privatsphäre zu garantieren. **LINKS** Die landestypische Gestaltung des »Hotel Moka« beinhaltet Elemente der traditionellen kubanischen Architektur wie Schrägdächer aus Tonziegeln, unterschiedliche Deckenhöhen, Rundbögen und Holzbalustraden. **OBEN** Die vorhandenen Bäume sind in das Vestibül des »Hotel Moka« integriert, das einen herrlichen Ausblick auf die Landschaft bietet. Das Mobiliar ist schlicht, bequem und funktional und besteht aus Rattanmöbeln. ✳ **PAGE DE GAUCHE, EN HAUT** Les galeries menant aux chambres de l'hôtel Moka s'écartent de la façade pour respecter les arbres existants et préserver l'intimité des hôtes. **A GAUCHE** L'architecture de l'hôtel Moka incorpore des éléments traditionnels cubains tels que les toits inclinés en tuiles, les jeux de niveaux, les arcs en plein cintre et les balustrades en bois. **CI-DESSUS** Les arbres s'intègrent dans le hall de l'hôtel Moka, d'où l'on jouit d'excellentes vues sur le paysage. Le mobilier léger en osier est simple, pratique et fonctionnel.

Campesino Taller Raíces

Yuseli Otaño

Francisco Menéndez

Located in the mountainous region of the Sierra de los Órganos, Viñales is a land of natural wonders, with picturesque valleys and rivers that sometimes disappear into huge caverns. The town of Viñales is a half-hour drive from the city of Pinar del Río, and lies in a major tobacco-growing area. It was founded in 1868, the same year Cuba began a thirty-year struggle for independence from Spain, although cattle had been farmed in this agricultural area from as early as 1605. The houses in this charming colonial town are all situated along its shady main street; their raised porches are reminiscent of Havana's "calzades," but with a primitive rural touch. A landscaped median

Viñales liegt in den Hügeln der Sierra de los Órganos – eine Gegend voller Naturwunder, malerischer Täler und Flüsse, die manchmal plötzlich in riesigen Höhlen verschwinden. Die Stadt mitten in einem Tabakanbaugebiet ist eine halbe Autostunde von Pinar del Río entfernt und wurde 1868, als Kuba seinen 30-jährigen Unabhängigkeitskampf gegen Spanien begann, gegründet. Seit 1605 wird in diesem Landwirtschaftsgebiet Viehzucht betrieben. Die Häuser dieser charmanten Kolonialstadt, alle entlang der schattigen Hauptstraße, haben erhöhte Veranden, die an die »Calzades«, wie man sie in Havanna sieht, erinnern. Hier sind sie allerdings schlicht und bäuerlich. Das um-

Située dans la Sierra de los Órganos, Viñales est une terre de merveilles naturelles avec des vallées pittoresques et des rivières qui disparaissent parfois dans des grottes. La ville de Viñales est à une demi-heure de route de Pinar del Río, au cœur de la région du tabac. Elle fut fondée en 1868, année où Cuba acquit son indépendance après trente ans de lutte contre l'Espagne, même si on y élevait du bétail depuis 1605. Les maisons de cette charmante ville coloniale bordent toutes sa grand-rue ombragée, leurs porches surélevés rappelant les «calzades» de la Havane, en plus primitifs et ruraux. Un rond-point paysagé indique la route de la vallée verdoyante de Viñales, où les levers

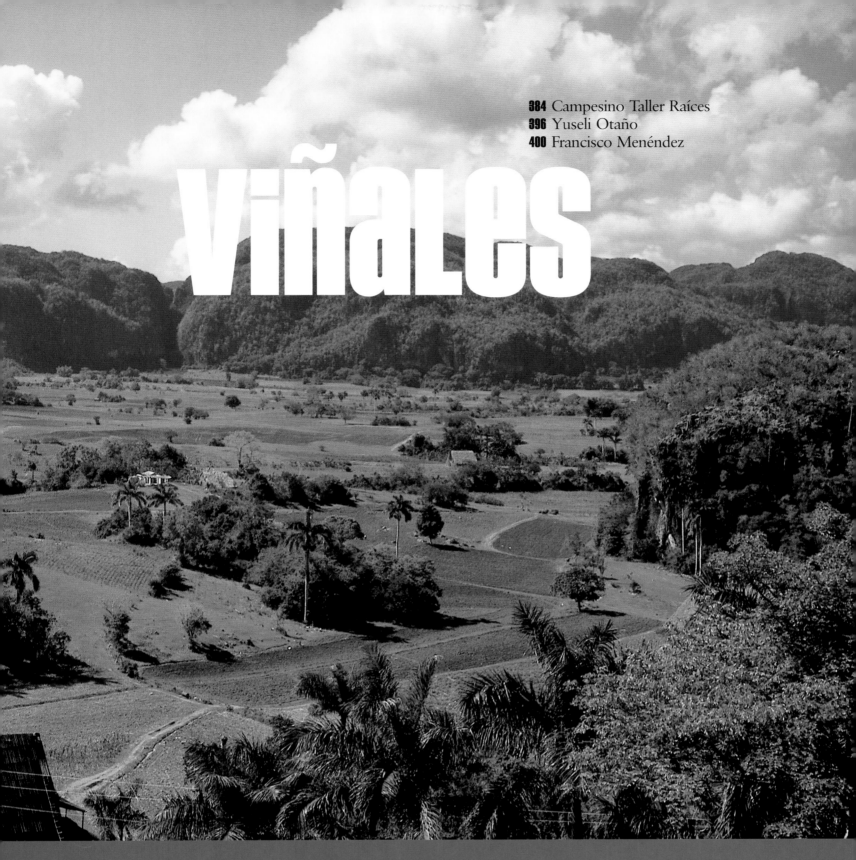

384 Campesino Taller Raíces
396 Yuseli Otaño
400 Francisco Menéndez

Viñales

strip points the way to the green "Valle de Viñales", where sunrises and sunsets are unique because of the gigantic "mogotes" – mountainous hillocks covered in lush tropical vegetation. These geographical anomalies are wonderfully transformed by the changing sunlight and can resemble either strange creatures or the ruins of medieval castles. The best views of this gorgeous valley are from Los Jazmines Hotel, a pink three-storey building with a tiled roof and French louvered windows in each room.

gebende grüne Tal »Valle de Viñales«, ist für seine einzigartigen Sonnenaufgänge und -untergänge bekannt. Die »Mogotes«, bergige Höcker unter tropischer, üppiger Vegetation, sind in diesem Tal eine geografische Besonderheit, und mit wechselndem Sonnenlicht verändern sie sich auf zauberhafte Weise. Dabei entstehen die seltsamsten Gebilde, die manchmal wie Ruinen mittelalterlicher Schlösser aussehen. Die schönste Sicht auf dieses traumhafte Tal hat man vom »Hotel Los Jazmines«, einem dreistöckigen rosa Gebäude mit einem Ziegeldach und französischen Lamellenfenstern.

et couchers de soleil sont rendus uniques par les gigantesques «mogotes», des monticules rocheux couverts d'une végétation luxuriante. La lumière changeante transforme ces curiosités géologiques en créatures étranges ou en ruines de châteaux médiévaux. C'est de l'hôtel Los Jazmines que l'on a les plus belles vues sur cette somptueuse vallée, un bâtiment rose de trois étages avec un toit en tuiles et dont chaque chambre est équipée de portes-fenêtres doublées de persiennes.

Campesino Taller Raíces

A Mystical Revelation.

A stone gate frames the access to the sculpture garden of the "Casa Taller Raíces", the thatched-roof house of Noel Díaz Gala, a religious "campesino" who not only cultivates tobacco in the Viñales Valley but is also a sculptor. One day, before he discovered art, he was carrying home heavy bags of malangas, the edible tubers found in the hills, and stopped for a rest by a dried tree stump. He began to visualize the wood as the face of a man holding both sides of his head as if he were lost in serious thought. At the time he was desperate, praying for a job to help him out of a dire economic situation; this vision made him abandon his load, uproot the trunk, carry it home, and begin carving what he immediately called "Diego, Miraculous Thinker." The face was completed by dusk, but he was frustrated that darkness prevented him from finishing the entire work of art. That night, unable to sleep, he had a vision: an ebony figure told him that God had listened to his prayers and was asking him never to burn another tree trunk again. At dawn he continued to work, and he has not stopped transforming tree stumps into his own beautiful works of naive art ever since.

Am Eingang des Skulpturengartens der »Casa Taller Raíces« im Tal von Viñales steht ein Steintor, das zu einem strohbedeckten Haus führt. Es gehört Noel Díaz Gala, einem Tabakbauern, der auch als Bildhauer tätig ist. Der »Campesino« war lange Zeit so bettelarm, dass er verzweifelt betete, Gott möge ihm aus seiner Misere heraushelfen. Eines Tages schleppte er schwere Säcke mit essbaren Malanga-Knollen, die in den Hügeln wachsen, ins Tal hinunter und machte bei einem Baumstamm halt. Als er das Holz betrachtete, sah er plötzlich das Gesicht eines Mannes, der gedankenversunken den Kopf in die Hände stützte. Ohne zu überlegen, ließ er die Säcke mit den Malangas liegen, grub den Baumstamm aus, trug ihn nach Hause und fing an zu schnitzen. Er nannte sein Werk »Diego, der wundersame Denker«. Bis zur Dämmerung hatte er das Gesicht fertiggeschnitzt, doch wegen der einbrechenden Dunkelheit konnte er sein Werk nicht beenden, was ihn so frustrierte, dass er die ganze Nacht kein Auge zumachen konnte. Dabei erschien ihm eine Figur aus Ebenholz, die ihm sagte, Gott hätte seine Gebete erhört, er möchte ihn aber bitten, nie mehr einen Baumstamm zu verbrennen. Am frühen Morgen arbeitete er sofort weiter und hat nie mehr aufgehört, aus Baumstrünken wunderbare, naive Kunstwerke zu schnitzen.

Un portail en pierre s'ouvre sur le jardin de sculptures de la maison atelier au toit de chaume de Noel Díaz Gala, un «campesino» mystique qui cultive le tabac dans la vallée de Viñales quand il ne crée pas. Un jour, à une époque où il ne savait plus comment joindre les deux bouts, il rapportait chez lui de lourds sacs de «malangas», un légume racine que l'on trouve dans les collines, quand il fit une pause près d'une souche d'arbre mort. Il vit dans l'écorce le visage d'un homme se tenant la tête, comme perdu dans ses pensées. Il abandonna sa charge, déracina la souche, la transporta chez lui et se mit aussitôt à sculpter «Diego, le penseur miraculeux». Le soir venu, il fulmina contre l'obscurité qui l'empêchait d'achever son œuvre presque terminée. Cette nuit-là, incapable de dormir, il eut une vision : un visage d'ébène lui annonça que Dieu avait entendu ses prières et lui demandait de ne plus jamais brûler un tronc d'arbre. À l'aube, il reprit sa tâche et, depuis, il n'a plus cessé de transformer les souches en belles sculptures naïves.

❋ **ABOVE LEFT** The Casa Taller Raíces art workshop. The signs at the entrance are also made with dried wood. **LEFT** The sculpture of the woman appears with her hands covering her face in a gesture denoting shame at her nakedness. **ABOVE** The rustic stone fence separating the Casa Taller Raíces from the road. Behind it is the thatched cabin surrounded by sculptures, with the hillocks in the background. **FOLLOWING DOUBLE PAGE** A farmer plows the land using oxen while smoking a cigar. ❋ **OBEN LINKS** »Casa Taller Raíces«, der »Wurzel-Workshop«. Auch die Beschilderung des Eingangs besteht aus Trockenholz. **LINKS** Die Skulptur zeigt eine Frau, die ihr Gesicht aus Scham über ihre Nacktheit mit den Händen bedeckt. **OBEN** Eine rustikale Steinmauer trennt die »Casa Taller Raíces« von der Straße. Dahinter befindet sich eine von Skulpturen umgebene Hütte mit den Hügeln im Hintergrund. **FOLGENDE DOPPELSEITE** Ein Bauer pflügt den Acker mithilfe von Ochsen und raucht dabei eine Zigarre. ❋ **PAGE DE GAUCHE, EN HAUT** La Casa Taller Raíces. L'enseigne du portail est réalisée elle aussi dans du bois mort. **A GAUCHE** La femme cache son visage dans ses mains, exprimant la honte de sa nudité. **CI-DESSUS** Un muret rustique en pierres sèches sépare la Casa Taller Raíces de la route. Derrière, la hutte au toit en chaume est entourée de sculptures. Au fond, les « mogotes ». **DOUBLE PAGE SUIVANTE** Un paysan aidé de ses bœufs laboure la terre tout en fumant un cigarillo.

✻ **PREVIOUS DOUBLE PAGES** The inside of a wooden tobacco house made of palm tree planks, where the tobacco leaves are hung from wooden lances to dry. **ABOVE LEFT** Master bedroom in the artist's house with a portrait of Jesus Christ above the window. The walls are made of palm tree planks. **LEFT** Interestingly, a structure of wooden logs and planks holds up a hanging ceiling of cement asbestos in the kitchen-dining room. A simple shelf for holding dishes and cups is attached to the walls. **ABOVE** The house has a roof of lances made of wooden logs and thatching with separators made of palm tree plans to delimit each area. The floors are made of polished concrete. **FOLLOWING DOUBLE PAGE** The kitchen, with its rustic table, contains the sink and is used as an auxiliary surface for placing vessels. The nails are used to hang dishes, trays and pitchers. ✻ **VORHERGEHENDE DOPPELSEITEN** Innenansicht eines Tabakschuppens aus Palmholz, wo die Tabakblätter an speziellen Holzstangen aufgehängt trocknen. **OBEN LINKS** Hauptschlafzimmer des Hauses mit einem Portrait Jesu Christi über dem Fenster. Die Wände bestehen aus Palmholz. **LINKS** Erstaunlicherweise trägt ein Fachwerk aus Rundhölzern und Brettern eine Zwischendecke aus Asbestbeton in Küche und Esszimmer. An einer der Wände hängt ein schlichtes Regal, in dem Teller und Gläser aufbewahrt werden. **OBEN** Das Haus besitzt ein Dach aus Rundholzbalken und Palmblättern sowie Trennwände aus Palmholz, welche die einzelnen Räumlichkeiten unterteilen. **FOLGENDE DOPPELSEITE** In der Küche enthält ein grober Arbeitstisch die Spüle und dient zudem als Fläche zum Abstellen des Geschirrs. Teller, Tabletts und Krüge werden einfach an Nägeln aufgehängt. ✻ **DOUBLES PAGES PRECEDENTE** L'intérieur d'une cabane en bois de palmier où l'on fait sécher les feuilles de tabac suspendues à des chevalets. **PAGE DE GAUCHE, EN HAUT** La chambre principale avec une image du Christ au-dessus de la fenêtre. Les murs sont en bois de palmier. **A GAUCHE** Dans la cuisine/salle à manger, une étrange armature en rondins et planches de bois soutient un faux plafond en amiante-ciment. **CI-DESSUS** La maison possède un toit en rondins de bois et en chaume, et des cloisons en planches de palmier qui séparent les différentes pièces. Les sols sont en ciment poli. **DOUBLE PAGE SUIVANTE** Dans la cuisine, une dalle rustique forme un évier et sert de plan supplémentaire où ranger les ustensiles. Des assiettes, des plateaux et des brocs sont accrochés à des clous.

YUSELI otaño

A Peasant's Home.

The first Spanish settlers lived in improvised shacks modeled on "bohíos", the huts of the indigenous people. Small structures made out of tree branches and palm leaves with a few openings for air to circulate, they were low enough to withstand heavy rain and hurricanes. Though somewhat transformed, these huts can still be seen in the countryside and are now considered part of the rural tradition, appreciated for being inexpensive as well as easy to build and maintain. Cuban peasants are attached to the land of their ancestors, and their lifestyles reflect their love of nature. Yuseli's house, tucked away in the "mogotes" of the Viñales valley, closely recalls those early structures in its scale and use of materials. Its wooden walls are whitewashed, and the floors are a shining pavement of polished cement; small windows catch the breeze and light. It is a low house with a corrugated iron roof supported by rough pieces of timber. Set back from the road, it has a narrow porch with only enough room for a few chairs for sitting in the shade and surveying the land in the evening.

Die ersten spanischen Siedler wohnten in improvisierten Baracken, die den Hütten der Einheimischen, den »Bohíos«, nachempfunden wurden. Zweige und Palmenblätter werden dabei zusammengebaut, und ein paar Öffnungen lassen die Luft zirkulieren. Sie sind so niedrig, dass sie auch heftigem Regen und Hurrikanen standhalten können. Solche Häuser findet man in leicht abgeänderter Form noch heute auf dem Land. Sie gehören zur ländlichen Tradition und sind beliebt, da sie einfach und kostengünstig zu bauen und unterhalten sind. Die Kleinbauern in Kuba sind mit dem Land ihrer Vorfahren stark verbunden, und die Liebe zur Natur zeigt sich in ihrem Lebensstil. Das Haus von Yuseli liegt zwischen Mogotes versteckt im Tal von Viñales und erinnert in Größe und Materialwahl an die traditionellen Gebäude. Die Holzwände des niedrigen Hauses mit Wellblechdach sind weiß getüncht und die glänzenden Böden aus poliertem Beton. Durch kleine Fenster wehen Brisen und dringt Sonnenlicht. Das Haus wird von groben Holzbalken gestützt und liegt zurückversetzt zur Straße. Auf der schmalen Veranda haben nur wenige Stühle Platz. Doch wer sich einen ergattert, kann im Schatten seinen Blick über die lauschige Abendlandschaft schweifen lassen.

Les premiers colons espagnols vivaient dans des cabanes de fortune inspirées des «bohios», les huttes indigènes. Ces petites structures construites avec des branchages et des feuilles de palmier possédaient quelques ouvertures pour laisser l'air circuler et étaient assez basses pour survivre aux fortes pluies et aux ouragans. On peut encore en voir dans la campagne, quoique légèrement améliorées. Elles font désormais partie de la tradition rurale, appréciées pour leur coût modique et parce qu'elles sont faciles à bâtir et entretenir. Les paysans cubains sont attachés à la terre de leurs ancêtres et leur mode de vie reflète leur amour de la nature. La maison de Yuseli, nichée dans les «mogotes» de la vallée de Viñales, rappelle ces premières habitations par sa taille et ses matériaux. Basse, avec une toiture de tôle ondulée, soutenue par des poutres grossières, elle a des murs en bois blanchis à la chaux, des sols brillants en ciment poli, de petites fenêtres qui laissent entrer la lumière et l'air. Située en retrait de la route, son porche étroit peut tout juste accueillir quelques chaises pour s'asseoir à l'ombre et regarder le soleil se coucher sur la campagne.

❋ **FACING PAGE** Yuseli Otaño rocks his son in a rocking chair at the doorway of his house, cooled by the same breeze that dries the laundered clothing. **LEFT** The interior design is based on a single motif: the rows of wooden strips blue-painted and attached to the dividing wall. They define each of the spaces within the house. **ABOVE** The open doors ensure that air always circulates through the house. In the middle of the dining room table is a set of ceramic vessels. A lantern hangs from the ceiling to light up the house at night. ❋ **OBEN LINKS** Yuseli Otaño wiegt seinen Sohn in einem Stuhl am Eingangsbereich ihres Hauses, während eine Brise die Wäsche trocknet. **LINKS** Die Inneneinrichtung wird von den blau gestrichenen Holzlatten der Trennwände zwischen den einzelnen Räumlichkeiten des Hauses dominiert. **OBEN** Die offenen Türen sorgen für eine dauerhafte Belüftung des Hauses. In der Mitte des Esszimmertisches steht Keramikgeschirr. Eine Laterne hängt von der Decke herab und sorgt nachts für Licht im Haus. ❋ **PAGE DE GAUCHE, EN HAUT** Assise dans un fauteuil devant sa porte, Yuseli Otaño berce son enfant tandis que la brise sèche le linge. **A GAUCHE** La décoration intérieure est dominée par les lattes en bois peintes en bleu appliquées contre les cloisons qui séparent les différents espaces de la maison. **CI-DESSUS** Les portes ouvertes assurent une ventilation permanente à l'intérieur de la maison. Au centre de la table de la salle à manger, un ensemble de vases en céramique. La nuit, la pièce est éclairée par une lanterne suspendue au plafond.

Francisco MENÉNDEZ

A Tobacco Farmers Home.

Today tobacco is considered a health hazard, but there was once a time when smoking was a more immediate matter of life or death. A Persian sultan ordered that anyone who dared try the so-called "devil grass" should have their ears cut off; a Russian czar punished his subjects by slashing their noses; and Pope Urban VII excommunicated anyone who smoked. The Spanish, however, profited from the European fondness for tobacco, and began cultivating it in the early 17th century in Cuba, after Christopher Columbus's crew discovered its use by the indigenous people. A native plant – "Nicotiana tabacum" – tobacco is cultivated on small farms all over the island. The Vuelta Abajo region, is where the very finest is grown. Francisco Menéndez is a "veguero," a farmer who grows tobacco. His beautiful yet simple home, a "bohío" with white and green wooden walls, thatched roof, and polished cement floor, contrasts with the lush green "mogotes," the red soil, and the gray-blue of the mountains in the background. Though lacking electricity and plumbing, the house's elongated porch simply invites one to sit and enjoy the sunset.

Heute weiß man um die Schädlichkeit von Tabak. Doch es gab Zeiten, in denen Rauchen ganz direkt Einfluss auf Leben und Tod hatte. So ordnete ein persischer Sultan an, jedem, der es wagte, das so genannte »Teufelsgras« auszuprobieren, die Ohren abzuschneiden. Ein russischer Zar bestrafte seine Untertanen mit Abhacken der Nase, und Papst Urban VII. ließ Raucher exkommunizieren. Die Europäer allerdings hatten eine Vorliebe für Tabak, und davon profitierten die Spanier. Im frühen 17. Jahrhundert beobachteten Christoph Kolumbus und seine Leute die Einheimischen beim Rauchen. Daraufhin ließen die Spanier Tabak in Kuba anbauen. Auf der ganzen Insel wird die einheimische Pflanze »Nicotiana tabacum« in kleinen Farmen angepflanzt. In Vuelta Abajo wächst die beste Qualität. Francisco Menéndez ist Tabakbauer, ein »Veguero«. Sein einfaches, jedoch wunderschönes Haus, hat weiße und grüne Holzwände, ein Strohdach und einen polierten Betonboden. Der so genannte »Bohío« steht im Kontrast zu den üppigen, grünen »Mogotes«, der roten Erde und dem Graublau der Berge im Hintergrund. Zwar gibt es hier keine Elektrizität und keine Sanitäranlagen, doch auf der Veranda kann man sich gemütlich niederlassen und sich am Sonnenuntergang erfreuen.

Aujourd'hui, le tabac est considéré comme dangereux pour la santé, mais il fut un temps où fumer était encore plus risqué. Un sultan persan décréta que quiconque oserait goûter à «l'herbe du diable» aurait les oreilles coupées ; un tzar russe punissait ses sujets en leur tranchant le nez ; quant au pape Urbain VII, il excommuniait les fumeurs. Les Espagnols, eux, n'hésitèrent pas à profiter de l'engouement des Européens pour le tabac et commencèrent à le cultiver à Cuba dès le début du 17e siècle, après que les marins de Christophe Colomb eurent découvert que les indigènes en consommaient. Dans toute l'île, de petites exploitations cultivent une souche locale de «nicotiana tabacum». C'est dans la région de la Vuelta Abajo que l'on trouve les meilleurs plants. Francisco Menéndez est un «veguero», un cultivateur de tabac. Sa maison, simple mais belle, est un «bohío» aux murs en bois blancs et verts, avec un toit en chaume, un sol en ciment poli. Elle contraste avec le vert des «mogotes» luxuriants, le rouge de la terre et le gris bleu des montagnes au loin. Il n'y a ni électricité ni plomberie, mais le long porche au toit de zinc est une invitation irrésistible à venir s'asseoir pour admirer le crépuscule.

✳ **ABOVE LEFT** A rustic wooden house where the tobacco leaves are dried and cured for several months after being harvested. **LEFT** The jawbones of a dead pig are used for hanging farming gear and tools. Beside it, an old kitchen pot acts as a planter. **ABOVE** The "campesino" Francisco Menéndez feeding the pig litter on his farm. ✳ **OBEN LINKS** Ein rustikaler Holzschuppen, in dem die Tabakblätter nach der Ernte monatlang getrocknet und aufbereitet werden. **LINKS** Die Kieferknochen eines toten Schweins dienen zum Aufhängen von Ackergeschirr und Werkzeug. Daneben wird ein altes Küchengefäß als Blumentopf genutzt. **OBEN** Der Bauer Francisco Menéndez füttert die Ferkel seines Hofs. ✳ **PAGE DE GAUCHE, EN HAUT** Une grange rustique en bois où le tabac est séché et traité pendant les mois qui suivent sa cueillette. **A GAUCHE** Les os de la mâchoire d'un cochon servent à suspendre des harnais et des outils. À côté, un vieux récipient de cuisine converti en jardinière. **CI-DESSUS** Francisco Menéndez nourrit ses cochons.

❋ **ABOVE LEFT** A rustic ox-drawn cart transports the water receptacles and is placed under the shade of a tree to keep the water cool. **LEFT** An antique iron bed in a corner of one of the bedrooms. **ABOVE** The rudimentary kitchen in the house, with its palm tree plank walls and polished cement floors. **FOLLOWING DOUBLE PAGES** As the family has grown, new auxiliary buildings have arisen alongside the original thatched hut. In the background, one of the lovely hillocks in the valley watches over the house. * The pots and pans hang over an old, primitive coal stove along with other cooking utensils. ❋ **OBEN LINKS** Ein rustikaler Ochsenkarren dient dem Transport von Wasserbehältern und steht im Schatten eines Baums, um das Wasser frisch zu halten. **LINKS** Ein altes Eisenbett in der Eckes eines Schlafzimmers. **OBEN** Die unverzichtbare Küche mit ihren Wänden aus Palmholz und poliertem Betonboden. **FOLGENDE DOPPELSEITEN** Mit dem Wachsen der Familie kamen neue Bauten zu dem ursprünglichen Gebäude aus Palmblättern hinzu. Im Hintergrund wird das Haus durch einen der herrlichen Hügel des Tals geschützt. * Die Töpfe und weitere Küchenutensilien hängen über einem alten, rustikalen Kohleherd. ❋ **PAGE DE GAUCHE, EN HAUT** Un char à bœufs rustique servant à transporter les bidons d'eau est entreposé sous un arbre pour rester au frais. **A GAUCHE** Un vieux lit en fer dans un coin de l'une des chambres. **CI-DESSUS** La cuisine rudimentaire, avec ses parois en planches de palmier et son sol en ciment poli. **DOUBLE PAGES SUIVANTE** À mesure que la famille s'est agrandie, des annexes ont été ajoutées à la cabane originale au toit en chaume. Au fond, un des beaux « mogotes » de la vallée veille sur la maison. * Des casseroles et autres ustensiles de cuisine au-dessus d'une vieille cuisinière à charbon.

❋ **ABOVE** The spaces of the living and dining rooms are physically and visually divided by a shelf where knick-knacks can be displayed. **RIGHT** Wood and wicker chairs, highly appropriate for the Cuban climate, in a corner of the living room with the image of the Virgen de la Caridad del Cobre, patron saint of Cuba, over the divider separating this space from one of the bedrooms. **FACING PAGE** The sewing is done by using an old sewing machine from the U.S. company Singer, which is stowed in one of the bedrooms in the house. **FOLLOWING DOUBLE PAGE** A family scene in the front of an auxiliary building located behind the main house. ❋ **OBEN** Wohn- und Esszimmer sind räumlich und optisch durch ein Regal für Zierrat voneinander getrennt. **RECHTS** Die Stühle aus Holz und Korbgeflecht eignen sich bestens für das kubanische Klima und stehen in einer Ecke des Wohnzimmers. An einer Wand zwischen Wohn- und Schlafzimmer hängt ein Bild der »Virgen de la Caridad del Cobre«, Kubas Schutzpatronin. **RECHTE SEITE** Die Näharbeiten werden mit einer alten, aus Nordamerika stammenden und im Schlafzimmer untergebrachten Nähmaschine der Marke Singer durchgeführt. **FOLGENDE DOPPELSEITE** Familienporträt im vorderen Teil eines Nebengebäudes, das an das Haupthaus angrenzt. ❋ **CI-DESSUS** La salle à manger et le séjour sont séparés physiquement et visuellement par des étagères permettant d'exposer des bibelots. **A DROITE** Des fauteuils en bois et cannage d'osier, bien appropriés au climat cubain, dans un coin du séjour, avec une image de la Vierge de la Caridad del Cobre, patronne de Cuba, sur la cloison d'une des chambres. **PAGE DE DROITE** Dans une des chambres de la maison, la vieille machine à coudre américaine Singer qui sert à effectuer tous les travaux de couture. **DOUBLE PAGE SUIVANTE** Portrait de famille devant un bâtiment annexe derrière la maison principale.

ADDResses

Havana
Museums/interesting places

CASA DE LA OBRA PÍA
Obrapía # 158
La Habana Vieja 10100
fon: +53 7 861 30 97

PALACIO DE LOS CAPITANES GENERALES
Museo de la Ciudad de la Habana
Calle Tacón # 1 between Obispo and O'Reilly
La Habana Vieja 10100
fon: +53 7 861 28 76 or +53 7 863 99 81

HOTEL AMBOS MUNDOS
Hemingways Hotel Room No 511
Calle Obispo # 153 corner Mercaderes
La Habana Vieja 10100
fon: +53 7 860 95 29
fax: +53 7 866 95 32
e-mail: comercial@habaguanexhamundos.co.cu

REAL FÁBRICA DE TABACOS PARTAGÁS
Calle Industria # 520 between Dragones y Barcelona
Centro Habana
fon: +53 7 863 57 66
e-mail: otabaco@catec.co.cu

TEMPLO YORUBA
Calle Concordia # 655 between Oquendo y Soledad
Centro Habana
fon: +53 7 878 36 07

CLUB NÁUTICO
Calle 152 y Mar, Reparto Náutico
Playa
fon: +53 7 208 76 94
fax: +53 7 208 06 84
e-mail: cso.fe@cubacatering.avianet.cu

PARQUE LENIN
Calle 100 and Cortina de la Presa Empedrado # 207
Arroyo Naranjo, Miramar 11300
Ciudad de La Habana
fon: +53 7 44 27 22

Bars/cafés/Restaurants

LA BODEGUITA DEL MEDIO
Calle Empedrado # 207 off Plaza de la Catedral
La Habana Vieja 10100
fon: +53 7 867 13 74/75
e-mail: comercial@bdelm.gca.tur.cu

EL FLORIDITA
Calle Obispo # 557 corner Monserrate
La Habana Vieja 10100
fon: +53 7 867 13 00
e-mail: director@flori.gca.tur.cu

PALADAR LA GUARIDA
(FILM "FRESA Y CHOCOLATE")
Calle Concordia # 418 between Gervasio y Escobar
Centro Habana
Ciudad de La Habana
fon: +53 7 866 67 41
fon: +53 7 863 73 51
e-mail: Enrique@laguarida.com

HELADERÍA COPPELIA
Calle 23 corner Calle L
Plaza de la Revolución
El Vedado 10400
fon: +53 7 202 22 20
e-mail: comercial@coppelia.cu

LAS RUINAS
Calle 100 corner Cortina de la Presa
Empedrado # 207
Parque Lenin
Arroyo Naranjo, Miramar 11300
fon: +53 7 57 82 86

Hotels

AMBOS MUNDOS
Calle Obispo # 152 corner Mercaderes
Habana Vieja, 10100
fon: +53 7 860 95 29
fax: +53 7 866 95 32

HOTEL NACIONAL DE CUBA
Calle 21 y O
Vedado, 10400
fon: +53 7 33 35 64/67 (switch board)
fon: +53 7 55 02 94 (reservation)
fax: +53 7 873 51 71 (reservation)
e-mail: reserva@hotelnacionaldecuba.com
www.hotelnacionaldecuba.com

HOTEL HABANA RIVIERA
Paseo y Malecón
Vedado, 10400
fon: +53 7 33 40 51
fax: +53 7 33 37 39
e-mail: reserva@gcrivie.gca.tur.cu

Cojímar etc.
Museum

CASA MUSEO ERNEST HEMINGWAY
Finca Vigía
km 12,5 Steinhart
San Francisco de Paula 19180
fon: +53 7 91 08 09
e-mail: mushem@cubarte.cult.cu

Bar/café/Restaurant

RESTAURANTE "LA TERRAZA"
Calle Real # 161 corner Candelaria
Cojímar
fon: +53 7 93 92 32
e-mail: Terrazas@cbcan.cyt.cu

Varadero
Hotel

HOTEL INTERNACIONAL VARADERO
Avenida Las Américas
Varadero, 42200
fon: +53 45 66 70 38
fax: +53 45 66 70 45
e-mail: reserva@gcinter.gca.tur.cu
www.grancaribe.cu

Santiago de Cuba & Bayamo
Museum

CASA DIEGO VELÁZQUEZ
(One of the most exceptional buildings on Cuba)
Calle Félix Pena # 612 between Aguilera y Heredia
Santiago de Cuba, 90100
fon: +53 65 26 57

CARLOS MANUEL CÉSPEDES
(Birthplace of Cuban patriot
Carlos Manuel Céspedes)
Calle Maceo # 57
Bayamo 85100
fon: +53 2 342 38 64
e-mail: cespedes@crisol.cult.cu

Trinidad
Interesting Places

PALACIO BRUNET
(One of the most impressive buildings in Cuban architecture)
Calle Fernando Hernández Echemendía # 52
corner Simón Bolívar
Trinidad 62600, Villa Clara

PALACIO CANTERO
(One of the most luxurious buildings in Cuba)
Calle Simón Bolívar # 423
corner Panchito Gómez Toro
Trinidad 62600, Sancti Spiritus

Cienfuegos
Bar/Café/Restaurant

PALACIO DEL VALLE
Calle 37 # 1 Punta Gorda
Cienfuegos
fon: +53 43 251 12 26

Pinar del Rio
Interesting Place

COMMUNIDAD LAS TERRAZAS
Autopista Nacional La Habana–Pinar del Río, km 50
Pinar del Río 22849, Candelaria
fon: +53 77 29 21
fax: +53 33 55 16
www.lasterrazas.cu

Hotel

HOTEL MOKA
Autopista Nacional La Habana–Pinar del Río, km 50
Pinar del Río 22849, Candelaria
fax: +53 8 277 81 26

Viñales
Interesting Place

CASA TALLER RAÍCES
(Art workshop and sculpture garden)
Cooperativa Antonio Maceo, Cuajaní
Pinar del Río 20100, Viñales

Hotel

LOS JAZMINES
Carretera de Viñales, km 25
Pinar del Río 20100, Viñales
fon: +53 8 79 62 05/64 11
www.cuba.tc/PinardelRio/LosJazmines.html

imprint

To stay informed about upcoming TASCHEN titles, please request our magazine at www.taschen.com/magazine or write to TASCHEN, Hohenzollernring 53, D-50672 Cologne, Germany, contact@taschen.com, Fax: +49-221-254919. We will be happy to send you a free copy of our magazine which is filled with information about all of our books.

© 2006 TASCHEN GmbH
Hohenzollernring 53
D-50672 Köln
www.taschen.com

CONCEPT, EDITING AND LAYOUT
Angelika Taschen, Berlin

DESIGN
Sense/Net, Andy Disl and Birgit Reber, Cologne

GENERAL PROJECT MANAGEMENT
Stephanie Bischoff, Cologne

ENGLISH TEXT EDITING
Deborah Irmas, Los Angeles

GERMAN TRANSLATION
Simone Ott Caduff, Pasadena
André Höchemer for LocTeam, S. L., Barcelona

FRENCH TRANSLATION
Philippe Safavi, Paris

ENGLISH TRANSLATION
Mary Black for LocTeam, S.L., Barcelona

LITHOGRAPHY MANAGEMENT
Horst Neuzner, Cologne

ENDPAPERS
From "Album de la Revolución Cubana"
Revista Cinegrafico, S.A.

BACKCOVER
Alberto Korda © VG Bild-Kunst, Bonn, 2006

Printed in China
ISBN 978-3-8228-4597-4

93.—Al aumentar el Ejército Rebelde se sub-
divide en mandos: Columna 1, Fidel; No. 8,
Guevara; Col. "Frank País", Raúl Castro;
Col. 7, Crescencio; Col. 2, Camilo; Col. 3,
Almeida; y la Col. Abel Santamaría.

95.—El segundo encuentro cerca del Río Palma
Mocha. Los rebeldes triunfan. Después, las ba-
tallas de: El Salto; el Uvero; Pino del Agua;
Cieneguilla, etc.

96.—El Com. C
de organizar un
van a llegar re

98.—En una represión sangrienta y cruel, es
asesinado, en Santiago, Frank País, jefe de las
milicias locales, por el feroz Salas Cañizares,
verdugo batistero.

99.—Entierro d
sonas en el ma
tiago. Gran ten